Richard Wagner for the New Millennium

STUDIES IN EUROPEAN CULTURE AND HISTORY

edited by
Eric D. Weitz and Jack Zipes
University of Minnesota

Since the fall of the Berlin Wall and the collapse of communism, the very meaning of Europe has been opened up and is in the process of being redefined. European states and societies are wrestling with the expansion of NATO and the European Union and with new streams of immigration, while a renewed and reinvigorated cultural engagement has emerged between East and West. But the fast-paced transformations of the last fifteen years also have deeper historical roots. The reconfiguring of contemporary Europe is entwined with the cataclysmic events of the twentieth century, two world wars and the Holocaust, and the processes of modernity that, since the eighteenth century, have shaped Europe and its engagement with the rest of the world.

Studies in European Culture and History is dedicated to publishing books that explore major issues in Europe's past and present from a wide variety of disciplinary perspectives. The works in the series are interdisciplinary; they focus on culture and society and deal with significant developments in Western and Eastern Europe from the eighteenth century to the present within a social historical context. With its broad span of topics, geography, and chronology, the series aims to publish the most interesting and innovative work on modern Europe.

Published by Palgrave Macmillan:

Fascism and Neofascism: Critical Writings on the Radical Right in Europe
by Eric Weitz

Fictive Theories: Towards a Deconstructive and Utopian Political Imagination
by Susan McManus

German-Jewish Literature in the Wake of the Holocaust: Grete Weil, Ruth Klüger, and the Politics of Address
by Pascale Bos

Turkish Turn in Contemporary German Literature: Toward a New Critical Grammar of Migration
by Leslie Adelson

Terror and the Sublime in Art and Critical Theory: From Auschwitz to Hiroshima to September 11
by Gene Ray

Transformations of the New Germany
edited by Ruth Starkman

Caught by Politics: Hitler Exiles and American Visual Culture
edited by Sabine Eckmann and Lutz Koepnick

Legacies of Modernism: Art and Politics in Northern Europe, 1890–1950
edited by Patrizia C. McBride, Richard W. McCormick, and Monika Zagar

Police Forces: A Cultural History of an Institution
edited by Klaus Mladek

Richard Wagner for the New Millennium: Essays in Music and Culture
edited by Matthew Bribitzer-Stull, Alex Lubet, and Gottfried Wagner

Richard Wagner for the New Millennium

Essays in Music and Culture

Edited by
Matthew Bribitzer-Stull
Alex Lubet
Gottfried Wagner

palgrave
macmillan

First published in 2007 by
PALGRAVE MACMILLAN™
175 Fifth Avenue, New York, N.Y. 10010 and
Houndmills, Basingstoke, Hampshire, England RG21 6XS.
Companies and representatives throughout the world.

PALGRAVE MACMILLAN is the global academic imprint of the Palgrave Macmillan division of St. Martin's Press, LLC and of Palgrave Macmillan Ltd. Macmillan® is a registered trademark in the United States, United Kingdom and other countries. Palgrave is a registered trademark in the European Union and other countries.

ISBN-13: 9781403973214
ISBN-10: 1403973210

A catalogue record of the book is available from the British Library.

Design by Scribe Inc.

First edition: September 2007

CONTENTS

LIST OF ILLUSTRATIONS

ACKNOWLEDGMENTS

We wish to thank the many people and organizations who made this book possible for their generous gifts of time and resources.

Most of the essays in *Richard Wagner for the New Millennium* were born as papers written for "Lingering Dissonances," an international conference held at the University of Minnesota in 2003. We had many sponsors. They include the Minnesota Opera, members of the Wagner Society of the Upper Midwest, and many units of the University of Minnesota: the Center for Holocaust and Genocide Studies; the Department of German, Scandinavian, and Dutch; the School of Music; the Center for German and European Studies; the Department of Cultural Studies and Comparative Literature; the Center for Jewish Studies; and the Humanities Institute.

Steve Feinstein of the Center for Holocaust and Genocide Studies was absolutely instrumental in conceiving and supporting at every stage the conference that inspired this book. Jeffrey Kimpton of the School of Music (now, the Interlochen Arts Academy) gave us invaluable encouragement. Our School of Music colleagues, David Damschroder and David Walsh, were also extremely helpful.

The success of Lingering Dissonances depended greatly on the industry, multiple talents, and the equanimity of musicology doctoral candidate C. Annett Richter, who also served as our copy editor and occasional translator. Composition doctoral student Seth Mulvihill set the musical and analytical examples. College of Liberal Arts freshman Janessa Macdonald assisted with proofreading and indexing.

Lingering Dissonances was highlighted by an evening concert, which doubtless nourished the intellectual climate for the paper presentations that preceded it that day. The many performers and conductors included Dwight Bigler, Anna Brandsoy, Margo Garrett, Jerry Luckhardt, Brian Rush-Williams, and Wendy Zaro-Mullins. We thank them all.

Finally, we owe a great debt to Leslie Morris, Director extraordinaire of the University of Minnesota's Center for Jewish Studies, who, in addition to providing funding and invaluable advice and moral support, promoted our book idea to our Minnesota colleagues, Eric Weitz and Jack Zipes, editors of the Studies in European Culture and History series, who have shown great vision, moral depth, and courage in endorsing a Wagner book like no other, in which politics and history are for once truly engaged in facing the music.

June 2006

Introduction: Lingering Dissonances in Wagner Scholarship

Matthew Bribitzer-Stull and Alex Lubet

Friederich Nietzsche was correct—Wagner's music is dangerous; and from Wagner's day to the present, anecdotes have accumulated in support of this characterization. Performing Wagner, for instance, led to nineteenth-century singers Alois Ander and Malvina Schnorr losing their voices during rehearsals for *Tristan und Isolde*. The death of tenor Ludwig Schnorr barely three weeks after the premier run of *Tristan*, moreover, served to "confirm" the perils of Wagner's art. Conductors have suffered as well—witness the abuse Daniel Barenboim and Zubin Mehta have endured for performing Wagner in Israel (and the criticism of Israeli institutions for their anti-Wagner resistance). Nor are those who remain off the stage and out of the pit immune; one need only read reactions to Wagner scholars, from Hans von Wolzogen to Deryck Cooke, to witness the viciousness of written excoriations by Wagner's stalwarts, apologists, and critics alike. Most dangerous of all may be listening to Wagner's music: it is natural to hypothesize upon the divergent paths Hitler's career might have followed had he never heard *Rienzi, Meistersinger,* or *Parsifal.* Even the layman is not free from Wagner's dangerous influences; those reading this introduction will, no doubt, sympathize with the hundreds of hours and thousands of dollars Wagner's music demands from those of us who engage it from any perspective.

Wagner's music is dangerous in another regard as well. More than any other composer in the history of Western art music, Wagner demands that we study him from the vantage points of multiple disciplines; his own work engaged not only music but also theater, literature, philosophy, religion, and politics, among others. In today's climate of narrowly defined disciplines, it is dangerous for a lone scholar to attempt research on all these facets of Wagner's life and works because of the level of expertise contemporary scholarship demands. While no volume could hope to address all the ramifications of Wagner's life, music, and prose, *Richard Wagner for the New Millennium* combines, as no previous volume has, articles from Cultural Studies and History with essays in Music Theory and Musicology, representing multiple perspectives on Wagner's music and social impact in a single publication.

A central concern of *Richard Wagner for the New Millennium* is the relationship between Wagner the artist and Wagner the social phenomenon. In particular, many of the essays explore the most difficult yet most crucial issue in Wagner studies: the impact of the composer's problematic worldview and complex personal life on his musical and dramatic creations. A wide variety of positions and perspectives are included, the goal being, as Gottfried Wagner's lead essay so aptly states, to promote much-needed debate on the legacy of this controversial figure. We achieve this in a manner that acknowledges both the artist's vast musical achievements and the troubling uses to which the achievements have often been put, recognizing that Wagner's checkered history as a social force, even decades after his own death, was possible only in the context of a towering musical intellect.

Contributors include many leading authorities on Wagner's life and works: historian Paul Rose, culture theorist Marc Weiner, music theorists Robert Gauldin and Warren Darcy, and musicologist Gottfried Wagner. Equally compelling pieces are offered by scholars whose views are becoming increasingly known: historian Na'ama Sheffi, musicologist Timothy Maloney, music theorists William Marvin and Matthew Bribitzer-Stull, and disability studies specialist Alex Lubet. Representatives from both sides of the "Wagner divide"—the socio-historical and the music analytical—provide a satisfying overview of current trends in Wagner scholarship.

Socio-historical scholars from various disciplines, while taking a variety of stances as regards Wagner's artistic creations, have been principally interested in his political legacy. The primary focus continues to be the impact of Wagner's anti-Semitic and nationalistic polemics seen in the context of the Nazi ascent to power in Germany, World War II, and the Holocaust. Recent work has also focused on Wagner's relationship to women in his music, his writings, and his complex personal life. While the socio-historical element of *Richard Wagner for the New Millennium* emphasizes the Wagner of National Socialism and the Holocaust, women's issues are also contemplated in several essays. Additionally, Wagner's racism is viewed in the broader perspective of the eugenics movement that pervaded the West in the nineteenth and early twentieth centuries.

On the other hand, music theorists and musicologists have generally studied Wagner according to the tradition of their disciplines, focusing primarily on the structure of the music. They have, for the most part, identified in Wagner a musical-dramatic genius and innovator, attributions not generally disputed (with notable exceptions) by his socio-historical critics. Studies concerning Wagner's use of nineteenth-century tonality and the relationships between drama and musical structure continue to uncover landmarks in the history of Western art music. This is also true of the essays in *Richard Wagner for the New Millennium*: the associative use of musical keys, the question of form in Wagner's music dramas, and the issues surrounding their performance comprise angles of inquiry in these articles.

Scholars of Wagner's music typically do not include as a facet of their work the problematization of the social, political, and cultural Wagner. Likewise, socio-historical criticism is rarely, if ever, grounded in enlightening technical analyses of the music. This disciplinary divide thus forms a major component of the "lingering dissonances" in current Wagner scholarship. Acknowledging as valid and essential the approaches of both sides, *Richard Wagner for the New Millennium* refuses to separate "wheat and chaff," or "baby and bathwater." Rather, the two positions and their many nuances can be read here in proximity, an exercise that enriches both. It is most enlightening to read, for example, Robert Gauldin's essay on Wagner's usage of A♭ Major, the key Wagner associated with his love interest, Mathilde Wesendonk, or William Marvin's article on Wagner's relationship to older operatic conventions in light of Gottfried Wagner's rebuke of the composer's relationships with women and his refusal to acknowledge the degree of his dependence on his musical influences. One may also find much to reflect on in comparing pieces from each methodological side that contemplates taxonomic praxis. There is value added to Matthew Bribitzer-Stull's consideration of the importance of attaching names to musical themes in Wagner's *Ring* when read alongside Alex Lubet's examination of the conflation of rhetorics of race and disability in the nineteenth century or Marc Weiner's revelation of the essentialist nature of the contemporary Wagner debate in Germany. Western society's obsessive ambivalence felt toward Wagner is evident from the individual scale, as in Timothy Maloney's discussion of Glenn Gould's relationship to Wagner's music, to the national scale, as Na'ama Sheffi illustrates in elucidating Wagner's emblematic role in Israeli Holocaust discourse. Tensions between the two sides of the "Wagner divide" also remain evident, obvious when one compares, for example, Warren Darcy's fascinating account of the dramatic purposes and music-structural role of C Major in *Meistersinger* with Paul Rose's deconstruction of anti-Semitism in the music and character of meistersinger Sixtus Beckmesser.

Given the unparalleled dichotomy of Wagner's extraordinary musical talent and the magnitude of its sometimes awful resonance in social, political, and cultural spheres, *Richard Wagner for the New Millennium* is an essential tool for understanding the strange symbiosis of art and politics in Western culture through its most controversial composer. These essays, each the creation of a disciplinarily trained scholar, mark but the beginning phase of interdisciplinary Wagner research—an emerging dialogue. Our hope is that their proximity within this volume will prove suggestive for future collaboration and research among scholars from every background and perspective.

KEYNOTE ARTICLE

CHAPTER 1

ON THE NEED TO DEBATE RICHARD
WAGNER IN AN OPEN SOCIETY:
HOW TO CONFRONT WAGNER
TODAY BEYOND GLORIFICATION
AND CONDEMNATION

Gottfried Wagner

This essay is dedicated to Harvey Sachs

Why continue to argue Richard Wagner's legacy at the beginning of the twenty-first century? Why not simply enjoy his music as the apotheosis of the romantic sound ideal of the nineteenth century? Why not just agree with musicologist Donald Grout, a representative of those who glorify Wagner, that "Wagner's particular texture of music is determined in large part by the nature of the melodic lines: long phrased, avoiding periodic points (after *Lohengrin*), so designed that every note tends to move on without ever coming to rest"?[2]

Why not relax and forget all Wagner wrote besides music? Like many of my distinguished colleagues, I do not believe one can explain Wagner exclusively by positivist music analysis. It would falsify both his preeminence in music history and his continuing international impact on culture and politics.

WAGNER'S IMPORTANCE IN OPERA HISTORY

Wagner's importance in opera history is beyond dispute. He is unique for having created, developed, and controlled every single detail of the genre: music, libretto, stage action, sets, and all other aspects of theatre. But he did not limit himself to the creation of the theatrical side of his stage works. He also strongly influenced their realization and their impact on the public. This of course transcended mere theatrical expression.

The uniqueness of Wagner is not a result of his having been ahead of his time as a composer, for example, in his treatment of consonance and dissonance or diatonic and chromatic tonal structure. I agree here with musicologist Arnold Whittall when he writes,

"And yet, although elaborate, psychologically-charged dialogues are at the heart of his musico-dramatic method, Wagner no more escaped associations with older operatic genres (from accompanied recitative to formal aria and ensemble) than he evaded ultimate submission to the authority of resolving dissonances and tonal closure."[3]

The real difference from other composers of his time lies in his militant beliefs in the unique emotional effect of his music on the public and in opera as the quintessential artistic medium. One may describe the function of poetry and music within his *Gesamtkunstwerk* (total work of art) with reference to his key essay, "*Oper und Drama*" (1850–1851). The art of poetry within opera as the epitome of all the arts exists only if it blends perfectly with musical expression, becomes singable, and can be transformed into a motif for opera. The art of music within opera as the epitome of all arts exists only if it serves to realize and express opera's poetic aim.

Figure 1.1: Richard Wagner, 1880 by Joseph Albert[1]

Perhaps, surprisingly to modern readers, Wagner refused to use the term "*Musikdrama*," preferring "drama for the purpose of music,"[4] a designation that has always engendered confusion. It is typical of Wagner that he defined the central issues of his stage works vaguely in order to influence public opinion. By referring to poetry and music as the essential elements of his approach to opera, Wagner indicated his intention to blend these two arts, which he felt had been separate elements in the operas of other composers of his day. In the tradition of Monteverdi, Wagner committed himself to the developing unification of drama and music.

But the blending of poetry and music and the unification of drama and music were not enough for Wagner. He also wished to include the dance—for him, the third original art form—as well as the "fine arts": architecture, sculpture, and painting.[5] Making prominent reference to Greek drama, Wagner used the orchestra to replace the role of the tragic chorus in conveying intricacies of the plot. This replacement not only served the purpose of art for art's sake, but also staked out Wagner's position on the relationship of the art of the classical past to that of contemporaneous romanticism, while articulating his vision of the future of culture after the destruction of the inhuman world of his time by a revolution of mankind. This radical vision of the future history of mankind was the result of Wagner's irrational handling of history with the aim of presenting his work—the integration of poetry and music within opera as the quintessence of the arts—and himself—the personification of this cultural triumphalism—as objective historical consequences.

Wagner intended the artistic integration of all his experiences, experiences both lived and acquired by his voracious reading, which included every facet of the humanities and natural sciences. In his letters and theories, he discussed humanity's most significant authors and their works in so personal a way that for the most part his interpretations had little or nothing to do with the works or the authors themselves. This subjective integration of concrete experiences and reading was followed by a meditative poetic assimilation. In other words, Wagner transformed his first- and second-hand experiences into his poetry to such a degree that the original source was distorted or falsified. Unfortunately, when he referred to these events and sources later, he did not distinguish between his sources and his transformations.

This procedure was a function of Wagner's urgent need to present himself within a direct lineage of humanity's most important authors and their works and then claim, irrationally and egotistically, to be their only valid interpreter. Many examples exist. I shall only mention here Wagner's abuse of Schopenhauer's concept of compassion, which Wagner blended into his *Weltanschauung* (worldview). Little remains here of Schopenhauer himself, and by appropriating his work, Wagner gave himself the image of a serious researcher in another great man's field, thus lending scholarly credibility to his own largely absurd philosophical theories.

Wagner, creator of the greatest imaginable melting pot of disciplines and artistic media, transformed others' material into a monologue that he presented to the world as his own creation. Although he was the most grandiose self-promoter in history, he favored himself as a democrat. Even today, Wagner is represented as such by false democrats throughout the political spectrum. It is interesting to note that in letters and published writings, Wagner used the first person plural when driving home an opinion, self-consciously adopting the royal "we" to refer to Richard Wagner as poet, composer, stage director, theatrical entrepreneur, historian, philosopher, theologian, politician, medical doctor, and natural scientist, among other identities.

WAGNER'S IMPACT ON GERMAN CULTURE AND POLITICS

Among Wagner's contemporaries, *Friedrich Nietzsche* understood best by far the composer's completely irrational artistic attitude. In *Human, All Too Human* (first published 1878), Nietzsche wrote about "the artist's feeling for truth," referring of course to the archetypical Romantic artist, Wagner:

> When it comes to recognizing truths, the artist has a weaker morality than the thinker; on no account does he want his brilliant, profound interpretations of life to be taken from him, and he defends himself against sober, plain methods and results. Ostensibly, he is fighting for a higher dignity and meaning of man; he does not want to give up the most effective presuppositions for his art, that is the fantastic, the mythic, uncertain, extreme, feeling for the symbolic, overestimation of the individual, belief in something miraculous about genius; thus he thinks the continuation of his manner of creating is more than a

scientific dedication to truth in every form, however plain it may appear.[6]

In Wagner's letter, written January 25, 1854, to his friend August Röckel, a confused socialist and Young Hegelian who influenced the composer's philosophy of life, he wrote:

> I only can exist as an artist. Anything else I find disgusting because I am no longer able to cope with life and love, or in case I do, it is only because it is of interest for me as long as it has to do with the arts. . . . I see only that the normal state of my nature as it has developed is exaltation while the common balance is its abnormal state. Indeed, I only feel well when I am "out of myself," because then I am completely with myself.[7]

Figure 1.2: Friedrich Nietzsche in Basel, 1873

One finds this attitude of escape from the real world into the world of the arts in many artists; it is part of the divorce from and repression of failure in real-life relationships. What gives the Wagner case another dimension is Wagner's permanent and incalculable shifting between real life and his fictive world, a state he developed into his sublimation to his own messianic destiny: to save Germany and the rest of the world through his great messages that included the desire to influence and dominate. Through his *Gesamtkunstwerk* and its entire artistic media as *his* genre, Wagner demonstrated his fervent desire to dominate his public, both within and outside the theatre.

Understanding Wagner's vision of himself as mankind's redeemer requires highlighting the emphasis on music within *Gesamtkunstwerk*. Reprising my essential point about "*Oper und Drama*," Wagner regarded the functioning of music within opera as yielding the quintessential art form only when music serves to realize and express opera's poetic aim.

Wagner regarded as music's foremost value its emotional effect on the public. He observed in his time highly developed compositional techniques. He wrote about Beethoven, Weber, Mozart, Liszt, Berlioz, and many others, though always, of course, irrationally. He assimilated their techniques and welded them to parts of his music within the *Gesamtkunstwerk* in the sense noted before. Through a synthesis of musical influences, Wagner radically changed the nature of the opera of his time. His variety of periodic forms is endless. Within them, the continuity and discontinuity of motivic and harmonic procedures constitute the archetypal characteristics of Wagner's compositional style.

Why did Wagner the composer—who advertised himself as a revolutionary innovator—choose to compromise by mixing conventional techniques with his own discoveries? The answer lies in Wagner's overarching concern with music's communicative power through emotion. Such emotional understanding was only to subsequently provoke an intellectual understanding of the drama's temporal unfolding. Simply put, first comes emotion, which then liberates understanding. Wagner was well aware that reaching the traditional opera public and holding its full attention, even subconsciously, required that he carefully balance his sophisticated mixture of proven techniques of earlier composers with his own innovations. Above all, Wagner wanted to control and manipulate the public through a dramaturgical synthesis of poetry, music, and all the other seductive theatrical devices.

Although, as we know, Wagner accomplished this most successfully, there were voices that expressed an anxious awareness of this music theatre of total manipulation and seduction. Among the critics, Nietzsche stands out for having forthrightly rejected Wagner's claim that opera is the epitome of the arts. Even today, his criticism is an important clarifier of the logic behind the necessity to continue to debate Wagner's legacy. The essence of Nietzsche's critique, as expressed in his pamphlet *The Case of Wagner* (first published in 1888), was his warning of the danger connected with Wagner's "corruption of terms."[8] Nietzsche provided a stinging indictment of Wagner and the Wagnerians, while foreshadowing their impact on the culture and politics of the future. For Nietzsche, Wagner and his movement propagated, above all, the presumption of the layman, the art-idiot. That kind now organizes associations, wants its "taste" to prevail, wants to play the judge even in rebus musicis and musicantibus. Secondly: an ever-growing indifference against all severe, noble, conscientious training in the service of art; all this is to be replaced by faith in genius or, to speak plainly, by impudent dilettantism (—the formula for this is to be found in The Meistersinger). Thirdly and worst of all: theatrocracy—the non-sense of a faith in the precedence of the theatre, in the right of the theatre to lord it over the arts, over art. But one should tell the Wag-nerians a hundred times to their faces what the theatre is: always only beneath art, always only something secondary, something made cruder, something twisted tendentiously, mendaciously for the sake of the masses. Wagner, too, did not change anything in this respect: Bayreuth is large-scale opera—and not even good opera. The theatre is a form of popular culture in matters of taste; the theatre is a revolt of the masses, a plebiscite against good taste. This is precisely what is proved by the case of Wagner: he won the crowd; he corrupted taste; he even spoiled our taste for opera![9]

Essential to Nietzsche's criticism of Wagner's "corruption of terms" is his confrontation with such fundamentals as Wagner's ideas on redemption:

Problem Redemption is certainly a venerable problem. There is noth-ing about which Wagner has thought more deeply than redemption: his opera is the opera of redemption. Somebody or other always wants to be redeemed in his work: sometimes a male, sometimes a lit-tle female—this is his problem.—And how richly he varies his leitmo-tif! What rare, what profound dodges! . . . Translated to reality: the danger for artists, for geniuses—and who else is the "Wandering Jew"?—is woman: adoring women confront them with corruption. Hardly any of them have character enough not to be corrupted—or "redeemed"—when they find themselves treated like gods: soon they condescend to the level of the women—Man is a coward, confronted with the Eternal-Feminine—and the females know it. . . . What Goethe might have thought of Wagner? Goethe once asked himself what danger threatened all romantics: the fatality of romanticism. His answer was: "suffocating of the rumination of moral and religious absurdities."[10]

Wagner uses the theme of redemption in most of his operas. However, his definition of redemption in his operas, theoretical works, and letters is often vague and self-contradictory.

Equally important is Nietzsche's discussion of the political after-effects of Wagner's corruption of terms in connection with his attack on Wagner's idea of the theatre as the epitome of the arts:

> Wagner's stage requires one thing only: Teutons! Definition of the Teuton: obedience and long legs. It is full of profound significance that the arrival of Wagner coincides in time with the arrival of the Reich: both events prove the very same thing: obedience and long legs. Never has obedience been better, never has it been more commanding. . . . Wagner understood how to command; in this, too, he was the great teacher. He commanded as the inexorable will to himself, as lifelong self-discipline: Wagner who furnishes perhaps the greatest example of self-violation in the history of art.[11]

Figure 1.3: Kaiser Wilhelm I and his sister, Alexandrie von Mecklenburg-Schwerin in Bad Ems, 1976

Nietzsche was right to warn against Wagner's corruption and confusion of terms and emotions as "impudent dilettantism." Further, he even predicted what Wagner and his movement, in conjunction with the *Bayreuther Festspiele* (Bayreuth Festival), would produce—that it was not by chance that the rise of the First Reich in 1871 and the realization of the first *Bayreuther Festspiele* in 1876 occurred so close together. That Wagner composed his *Kaiser March* in 1871 and premiered it the same year is of course no coincidence: Nietzsche foresaw Wagner's art as part of the propaganda of future German nationalism and militarism, including not only the German disaster intimately associated with the Bayreuth Festival.

The song of the folk at the end of the *Kaiser March* of 1871 expresses clearly Wagner's philosophy of life in Bayreuth:

Figure 1.4: Wagner receives Kaiser Wilhelm I in Die Bombe, Vienna 1876

Volksgesang am Schlusse des Kaisermarsches, 1871
Heil! Heil dem Kaiser!
König Wilhelm!
Aller Deutschen Hort und
    Freiheitswehr!
Höchste der Kronen
Wie ziert dein Haupt sie
    hehr!
Ruhmreich gewonnen,
soll Frieden dir lohnen!
Der neu ergrünten Eiche
    gleich
Erstand durch dich das
    deutsche Reich:
Heil seinen Ahnen,
seinen Fahnen,
die dich führten, die wir trugen,
als mit dir wir Frankreich schlugen!
Feind zum Trutz,
Freund zum Schutz,
    Allem Volk das deutsche Reich zu Heil und Nutz.[12]

Song of the Folk Concluding the Emperor's March, 1871
Hail! All Hail the Kaiser!
King Wilhelm!
Protector of all Germans and defender of their freedom!
Crown exalted above all others,
Ennobled majestically by thy visage!
Freedom won with glory,
May it be thy reward!
Like the fresh green of the young Oak,
    did the German Empire gain life through thee:
Hail to its ancestors,

to its flags
that guided thee, that we bore,
as we, with thee, smote France!
Defy the Foe,
Protect the Friend,
    The German Empire, boon and redemption to all our people.

Nietzsche did not yet foresee the other elements of Wagner's Bayreuth philosophy of life: anti-Semitism and sexism and antifeminism. Distancing himself from Wagner and creating his own frame of reference came only slowly and painfully. It took time for him to detach himself from Wagner's strong influence. It is revealing that Nietzsche, as part of his intellectual emancipation from Wagner, turned down the position of editor in chief of Wagner's Bayreuth propaganda magazine, the *Bayreuther Blätter*.

WAGNER, HIS BAYREUTH ARCHIVES, AND THE *BAYREUTHER BLÄTTER*

Figure 1.5: Front cover, *Bayreuther Blätter*, 1878

Through his Bayreuth philosophy of life, Wagner contributed mightily to the great German disaster that occurred after his death. This impact may be witnessed through a consideration of the Richard Wagner Archives in Bayreuth, as well as the *Bayreuther Blätter* and its most important topics: nationalism, anti-Semitism and racism, and sexism. To objectivize the discussion of these topics, one must ask if Wagner himself tried to provide for the organization of his estate and archives and the future of his festival after his death.

Wagner not only had the intention of safeguarding all his scores, writings, letters, and autobiographical materials; he also dictated and controlled their order and use in accordance with his own Bayreuth philosophy. He did not tolerate any critical collaborators. Wagner could bear only servile yes-men who identified totally with him and were close to him—men like Hans von Wolzogen, lifelong editor of the *Bayreuther Blätter*.

It would be a historical falsification to downplay the impact of the *Bayreuther Blätter* on Germany and even Europe. Wagner scholar Annette Hein rightly emphasizes in her inadequately known but definitive book on the *Bayreuther Blätter* entitled *There is much "Hitler" in Wagner: Racism and Anti-Semitic Ideology of Germanness in the Bayreuther Blätter (1878–1938)*: "[This magazine] is an important journalistic resource of the German empire, the Weimar Republic as well as of the Third Reich."[13]

The *Bayreuther Blätter* contains twenty thousand pages of broadly interdisciplinary cult contributions, edited and published as "the Master" intended. Hein's conclusion regarding the magazine's content—which Wagner himself determined during his lifetime by indicating the "right" direction through his own articles—is essential:

> The analysis of Wagner's articles in the Bayreuther Blätter shows that in this magazine, anti-Semitic and racial thoughts are spread by himself, and have characterized it in this respect. The fact that anti-Semitism, Germanness and nationalistic ideology are also propagated after Wagner's death suggests that . . . no abuse on Wagner's side can be deduced. On the contrary, the ideological orientation is a continuation of the views put forth by Wagner. Yet, not all essays by Wagner in the Bayreuther Blätter deal decidedly with anti-Semitic and racial issues, even though the thematic focus of his longer articles clearly makes them belong to the latter category.[14]

In other words, the *Bayreuther Blätter* is to be understood as the consequent development of Wagner's philosophy of life, which he created only two years after the first *Bayreuther Festspiele*. As early as the late 1840s, Wagner had wanted his own magazine to be a propaganda and publication tool for his writings—to achieve a better understanding of his works and *Weltanschauung*. The *Bayreuther Blätter* survived until 1938—nearly halfway through the Third Reich. Its demise does not mean Wagner's *Weltanschauung* was no longer considered desirable; the opposite is true, as we know from

Figure 1.6: Front cover, "Jewish-ness in Music," 1850

reading Hitler's, Goebel's, and Rosenberg's statements on Wagner.

But there is more. Having renamed the *Bayreuther Festspiele*, with the full support of the Wagner family, *Kriegsfestspiele* (War Festival) at the outbreak of World War Two, the Festival's publications demonstrated the complete unity of the Third Reich with Wagner and his ideas, including the final victory and final solution as part of National Socialist propaganda. *Erlösung* by *Endlösung*—redemption from the Jews included the final solution. Significantly, Wagner wrote his first ideas on his future *Festspiele* in the same year he produced his first public and decisive nationalistic and racial anti-Semitic writings. *Das Judentum in der Musik* (Jewishness in Music) and the first articulation of the Bayreuth Festival concept both appeared in 1850. Both texts posit Aryan-German Bayreuth against Jewish-French Paris, further propounded in Wagner's later writings.

The question of Wagner's culpability in the ideological orientation of the *Bayreuther Blätter* is even today a serious point of contention; nevertheless, Hein and many others confirm his guilt.

The debate becomes even harsher when one considers whether or not Wagner's *Weltanschauung* can be traced in his stage works. One who still presents Wagner as the innocent victim of history is Professor of German Literature Dieter Borchmeyer, known for his affiliation with the Bayreuth Festival. In 1983, Borchmeyer edited Wagner's libretti and writings in connection with the centennial of Wagner's death. He excludes "Das Judentum in der Musik" and some of Wagner's essential and similarly ideologically charged later writings. Even most of the Writings of Regeneration were missing, as Hein rightly noted.[15] Borchmeyer's justification has no basis, in fact:

"The sympathy for so many Jewish artists, the idea of redemption, which also includes the Jews, the lack of anti-Semitic tendencies in his music dramas—all this shows that there was no hatred toward the Jews in the holiest part of his personality as an artist."[16]

Borchmeyer's reaction is interesting when he is confronted with international scholars who do not share his fantasies about Wagner. Borchmeyer decides who is and is not welcome at international Wagner conferences, and who may read their papers without interruption at whitewashing, apologist conferences like *Wagner and the Jews*, which was given at Bayreuth in 1998—all with the wholehearted applause of the financial, political, and cultural circle close to the huge Bayreuth Festival industries. This behavior has, of course, had very negative consequences on open international debate on Wagner.

The list of distinguished Wagner scholars who convincingly prove the opposite of what academics close to Bayreuth say is long and growing. It includes Paul Lawrence Rose and Marc Weiner, both of whom have written standard books on Wagner's anti-Semitism; their new essays can be found in this volume. One might disagree on details, but no one still denies that Wagner, a *Programmusiker*, used his music as a vehicle for his philosophy of life and composed with an ideological purpose.[17]

Connecting music to ideology reveals the realization of Wagner's *Weltanschauung* of "redemption by destruction." Anti-Semitism and racism are central to his *Weltanschauung* in the *Ring of the Nibelungen* and *Parsifal*. Wagner was fully aware of how these works' ideological content is served by music. In his "writings of regeneration," he spoke of his mission to "save the German spirit through his art, when race, mixed with Jewish blood and overpowering Latin influences, will be destroyed."[18]

Here Wagner also declared war against the influence of the Catholic Church—especially the Jesuits—without any serious historical grounding. Finally, in his *Artwork of the Future*, Wagner declared war on the decline of races: "The more unrecognizable the races, the more sunken humanity, the stronger and more clearly the artwork would have to affirm itself."[19]

It is surprising that sexism, the other essential issue in the Wagner debate—in addition to nationalism and anti-Semitism and racism— goes unmentioned by Hein, since "redemption by destruction" is central to a discussion of Wagner's female protagonists.

SEXISM

Wagner's note, written October 23, 1881, in his *"Brown Book"* is revealing with respect to his sexism: "The blood of the more noble male is ruined by that of the less noble female through the mixing of races: the male suffers, character perishes while women win enough in order to be able to take the position of men. . . . For this reason, the female owes redemption: here in the arts—as elsewhere in religion; the untouched Virgin Mary gives birth to the Redeemer."[20]

Obviously, this note refers first to Wagner's racial anti-Semitic polemics and above all to the opera of redemption, *Parsifal*, the climax of Wagner's *Weltanschauung* in his stage works. Most of Wagner's female protagonists end by self-denial, self-destruction, or suicide; they die to save a man. Any examination of Senta, Elisabeth, Elsa, Isolde, Brünnhilde, and Kundry will make clear the absurdity of speaking of equality of the sexes in Wagner's scores, public writings, and letters.

Figure 1.7: The First Kundry in *Parsifal*, Anna Bahr in Bayreuth, 1882

One might object that this is typical of nineteenth-century opera. But why declare a century's madness normal? In today's open society, we can talk about the religious fundamentalist position on women. Why not debate Wagner's ideas? It is the combination of nationalism, anti-Semitism, and sexism as elements of his *Weltanschauung* in his stage works and theories that makes Wagner unique among composers of his time.

None of the deadly sacrifices of Wagner's female characters have a rational or ethical justification. Consider musicologist Eva Rieger's observation in her article, "The Love is the Eternal Feminine Itself—Constructions of the Feminine—the Example of Brünnhilde":

The use of gender-specific metaphors in Richard Wagner's writings, together with his treatment of female roles in his musical works, forms a topic that has barely begun to be explored. Since gender is a basic element of every social relationship, including cultural output, it serves to establish real as well as symbolic order and implicitly demonstrates power relationships within society. This is also valid for Wagner. In his lifetime, the consequences of the French Revolution were still perceptible, and the bourgeoisie was fighting for its own independent culture. The positioning of gender roles also belongs within this framework. Wagner's operas are full of gender constructions that were essential to the establishment of a bourgeois identity. Through his work he built up a stock of visual and aural images that have accu-

Figure 1.8: Dali and the sacrifice of a woman, 1974[21]

*See his autobiography of 1974, How to become Dali in: Christina von Braun, Nicht ich, Logik, Lüge, Libido, Verlag Neue Kritik, Frankfurt 1994, p. 382

mulated in the collective memory and that are localized in certain memories that continue to have an after-effect. Thus, gender roles have a basic importance in the effort to achieve an understanding of the operas. . . . All his life, Richard Wagner sought helpmates who would give him unlimited support. He was convinced that love between two human beings had to strike like a force of nature, and for that reason people were predestined for each other without having a hand in the matter themselves. This message is combined with another: it is a question of survival to be loved—and this is even more important than possessing a woman. Wagner's life-long wish corresponded to the bourgeoisie's attempts to direct woman toward only one man, whom she was to take care of, regenerate, and promote. A woman going off to a male competitor would have been tantamount to dismantling [the first man's] masculinity and was therefore taboo. This conviction is deeply rooted in Wagner's work.[22]

In her review of *The Woman of the Future—Female Figures and Female Voices in Wagner's Vision* (2000), Rieger added that "Wagner's female figures had an ambiguous reception right from the beginning because the composer had to give them erotic sexual passion to underline his favourite thesis that the woman can be ideal only if she is completely under the spell of man in unconditional love. This thesis created contradictory feelings which included enthusiasm and/or repulsion and still today influence discussion of the topic. For Wagner, woman as the Other is by nature inferior to man. The heroic type of man needs woman for the perfection of his own ego."[23]

What are the consequences of Richard Wagner's *Weltanschauung* in the context of his stage works? Again, we refer to Hein: "Wagner himself has contributed decisively through his writings and stage works to the fact that Hitler could find such a profound resonance with his German-nationalistic and anti-Semitic propaganda."[24]

Finally, it is necessary to examine the influence of Wagner's *Weltanschauung* on the twentieth century's two totalitarian systems, communism and fascism. This requires attention to Wagner's social behavior.

WAGNER: THE POWERFUL MAN AND GRUEN'S ANALYSIS

One well-known point of contention, with obvious psychoanalytical ramifications, is the question of Wagner's father. Was he Jewish? Was he Friedrich Wagner or Ludwig Geyer? Wagner is often characterized as a "dwarf" with a big "Jewish nose," growing up as Richard Geyer in the Jewish quarter am Brühl. It is thought that the humiliation Wagner felt led to a conversion from an inferiority complex to egomania, and that this process was fueled by an evil mother. Wagner's social behavior was characterized first by his drive for personal power and then the conservation of that power; this process fueled the stylistic evolution of his stage works.

In *The Madness of Normality*, psychotherapist Arno Gruen describes the social behavior of powerful men who are able to hide themselves behind a mask of kindness. What are their real aims? The following applies to Wagner:

Self pity which is presented as suffering. . . . It is part of the fascist personality, but should not be categorized with only one particular ideology because this type of personality can be found everywhere that power is exercised, and such a person can equally well disguise themselves as a democrat or as a communist. One should not be too concerned with the political orientation of a man but in how honestly he deals with himself as a human being.

The external enemies are continuously increasing in number. They are indicators of the escape from inner phantoms and the attempt to evoke and use the public's latent readiness for hatred that is based on the omnipresence of self betrayal.[25]

Wagner and Totalitarian Systems

Given the history of Wagner in Bayreuth, how could leftists and rightists alike have claimed Wagner for their ideologies both before and after the Third Reich? The path leading from Wagner to Hitler has been well documented but remains a subject of strenuous debate. What has not been thoroughly discussed is leftist Wagner interpretation, normally reduced to *The Perfect Wagnerite*, George Bernard Shaw's amusing interpretation of the *Ring*. Shaw served up many clichés, including Siegfried as a Bakunin figure, a complete historical distortion. We know Wagner hated Marx and Engels, and we know Marx's negative comments on Wagner in Bayreuth.

There was a confused movement in Vienna in the late nineteenth century led by Engelbert Pernertorfer and his friends who were vegetarians and Wagnerians, including Jewish Wagnerians like social democrat Victor Adler and Bernhard Diebold, who at the time of the Weimar Republic tried to defend Wagner against his negative image among communists. Much more important was the pro-Wagner propaganda of Anatoli Lunatcharski, Soviet Minister of Education. In his 1933 article, "Richard Wagner's Path," he depicted Wagner as a "profound thinker" and an "important poet" of socialism who could be used for communist propaganda.[26] Lunatcharski understood perfectly the enormous ideological possibilities of mass demagogy in 1933—as did Hitler, Goebbels, and Rosenberg.

In this connection, one must mention the saints of the New Bayreuth era, Ernst Bloch, Theodor Adorno, and Hans Mayer, who defended the de-ideologized concept of Wagner's grandson, Wieland. Bloch, Adorno, and Mayer were part of the philo-Semitic pose of New Bayreuth after 1945, when an improved cultural image of Germany (and of Bayreuth as an indestructible national myth) was urgently needed. The Marxist Bloch never revised his positive opinion of Stalin, while Wieland, during his lifetime, successfully hid his closeness to "Uncle Wolf," Wolfgang Wagner, as well as his big secret: his time spent in 1944 as supervisor in the exterior concentration camp at Bayreuth, which was affiliated with the Flossenburg concentration camp.[27] These topics were absolutely taboo until the truth was disclosed in May 2002. Little is known of Bloch's furious cancellation of his participation in the festivities for the one hundredth anniversary of the Bayreuth Festival in 1976 because of the 1975 feature film on Winifred Wagner, in which she openly propagandized for Hitler and National Socialism. Discussion of the ideological use of Wagner becomes even more provocative if one examines critically the cooperation of post-Nazi Bayreuth with the East German and Marxist edition of Wagner's letters in Leipzig from 1968 on. This may be looked on, on both sides, as the collapse of any honest academic analysis of the meaning of totalitarian abuse of power.

More unexplored, taboo territory comprises the question of how leftist Wagnerians like Bloch, Adorno, Mayer, Gregor-Dellin, and Jens could have exerted such an enormous influence on Wagner research up to the present day. In Germany, leftist interpretation of Wagner can only be understood as an aftereffect of National Socialism and the situation of the Wagner Festival after Hitler. Anti-Semitism and nationalism were forbidden, and new public relations strategies were needed. The integration of left-wing Jews and prominent non-Jewish voices from the left were the best way of marketing New Bayreuth and covering up the bad image of Wagner left over from the war. A discussion of New Bayreuth and leftist Wagner interpretation could occupy more than one book.

Wagner could be used by both communists and fascists because of the corruption of terms in his works and writings, including especially the antidemocratic, antipluralistic visions from his *Weltanschauung* toward the redemption of mankind. The totalitarian essence of Wagner's work must also be seen in connection with his character per Gruen's analysis of powerful men.

The fundamental issues for future debate on Wagner include corruption of terms, nationalism, anti-Semitism, sexism, the lasting consequences of Wagner's censorship of his archives, his social behavior as a powerful man, and the attractiveness of his work for totalitarian systems. Given the multiplicity and complexity of these issues, one can imagine the difficulties involved in any translation. Let us consider the Italian proverb *traduttore, traditore,* which means that the translator always runs the risk of falsifying, through his own ideas, the original meaning of a text. How can we emerge from this dilemma?

WAGNER RESEARCH

Here are the essential directions for future interdisciplinary and international Wagner research:

- All remaining Wagner documents (many "sensitive" ones were destroyed in order to save the Bayreuth Festival's image and economic interests) should be transferred online with free access.
- Research should be based on criticism of totalitarian ideologies to elucidate the meanings and implications of Wagner's *Gesamtkunstwerk* for international theoretical discussion and for presentation of Wagner's stage works in various media on the basis of new multilingual translations.
- Like the Wagner archives themselves, the results of this debate should be accessible to everyone on a Web site of "alternative Wagner research."
- This instrument of alternative Wagner research should operate outside the sphere of interests of the Bayreuth Festival and its financial, political, and cultural associations due to the festival's past. All Wagner scholars know that the Bayreuth Archives depended on, and in the future will depend on, the festival's "power constellation."
- New translations in transparent prose should be published according to the aforementioned criteria.

In instituting these reforms to the dissemination and investigation of the Wagner legacy, one could finally, someday, go beyond glorification and condemnation and start to debate *all* of Wagner's terms, even allowing for the possibility of historical revisionism. It is basic to an open society to consider the necessity of new paths of inquiry and to facilitate correction of misconceptions. In future

Wagner research, a special priority would be rational discussion of human self-liberation based on knowledge.

In our time—a period of dark irrationalism—those who still believe in the pure aestheticization of Wagner's music will not be interested in clarifying questions such as the manner and degree to which Wagner remains part of an intellectual and moral disaster whose full ramifications have yet to be fully absorbed into the thinking of intellectuals and the public. In spite of the knowledge we have today, they will refuse to contemplate whether German and international culture—including opera as a unique form of art, as Wagner intended the term—might someday recapitulate the intellectual and moral dishonesty of a period blinded by adulation for Wagner and the romantic era. Knowledge of all the facts and their consequences are of critical importance if we are to develop and maintain a sophisticated understanding of the ecology of artistic and political life.

WORKS CITED

Dali, Salvador. "How to Become Dali." *Nicht ich, Logik, Lüge, Libido.* Ed. Christina von Braun. Frankfurt: Verlag Neue Kritik, 1984.

Grout, Donald Jay. *A Short History of Opera.* New York: Columbia University Press, 1965.

Gruen, Arno. *Der Wahnsinn der Normalität.* Munich: Dtv, 1993.

Hamann, Brigitte. *Winifred Wagner oder Hitlers Bayreuth.* Munich: Piper Verlag, 2002.

Hein, Annette. *"Es ist viel 'Hitler' in Wagner": Rassismus und antisemitische Deutschtumsideologie in den "Bayreuther Blättern" (1878–1938).* Tübingen: Max Niemayer Verlag, 1996.

Müller, Ulrich, and Peter Wapnewski, eds. *Richard-Wagner-Handbuch.* Stuttgart: Alfred Kröner, 1986.

Nietzsche, Friedrich. *The Birth of Tragedy and the Case of Wagner.* Trans. Walter Kaufmann. New York: Vintage Books, 1967.

———. *Human, All Too Human.* Trans. Marion Faber and Stephen Lehmann. London: Penguin Classics, 1984.

Rieger, Eva. "Die Liebe ist 'das ewig Weibliche' selbst: Richard Wagners Weiblichkeitskonstruktionen am Beispiel der Brunhilde." In *Der Komponist Richard Wagner im Blick der aktuellen Musikwissenschaft.* Trans. Gottfried Wagner and Harvey Sachs. Ed. Ulrich Konrad and Egon Voss. Wiesbaden: Breitkopf & Härtel, 2003. 151–59.

————. *Minna und Richard Wagner: Stationen einer Liebe*. Düsseldorf: Artemis & Winkler, 2003.

————. *"Das Weib der Zukunft." Frauengestalten und Frauenstimmen bei Richard Wagner*. Susanne Strasser-Vill. Trans. Gottfried Wagner and Harvey. Rev. Ed.

Rose, Paul Lawrence. *Wagner: Race and Revolution*. Boston: Faber and Faber, 1992.

Wagner, Richard. *Das braune Buch: Tagebuchaufzeichnungen, 1865 bis 1882*. Ed. Joachim Bergfeld. Zürich: Atlantis Verlag, 1975.

————. *Sämtliche Briefe*. 14 vols. Leipzig: VEB Deutscher Verlag für Musik, 1986.

————. *Sämtliche Schriften und Dichtungen*. 5th ed. 16 vols. Leipzig: Breitkopf & Härtel, 1911.

Weiner, Marc A. *Richard Wagner and the Anti-Semitic Imagination*. Lincoln: University of Nebraska Press, 1995.

Whitall, Arnold. "Musical Language." *The Wagner Compendium: A Guide to Wagner's Life and Music*. Ed. Barry Millington. London: Thames and Hudson, 1992. 248–61.

NOTES

1 All photographs in this article, save the last, are from the personal archive of Gottfried Wagner.
2. Grout, 411.
3. Whittall, 261.
4. Wagner, "über die Benennung 'Musikdrama,'" Sämtliche Schriften, vol. 9 302–8.
5. Wagner, "Das Kunstwerk der Zukunft," Sämtliche Schriften, vol. 3 42–160.
6. Nietzsche, Human 103–4.
7. Wagner, Sämtliche Briefe, vol. 6 73.
8. Nietzsche, Birth of Tragedy 184.
9. Ibid. 182–83.
10. Ibid. 160–62.
11. Ibid. 80.
12. Wagner, "Gedichte," Sämtliche Schriften, vol. 12, 373.
13. Hein, 1.
14. Ibid. 103–4.
15. Ibid. 111.
16. Ibid. 112.
17. Hein, 112.
18. Ibid.

19. Ibid. 113.
20. Wagner, Das braune Buch 243.
21. Dali, 382.
22. Rieger, "Die Liebe ist 'das ewig Weibliche' selbst"
23. Rieger, "Das Weib der Zukunft," 456–57.
24. Hein, 185.
25. Gruen, 159.
26. Ulrich Müller and Peter Wapnewski, 641.
27. Hamann, 479–84.

PART 1

WAGNER'S MUSIC

C H A P T E R   2

Tracing Mathilde's A♭ Major

Robert Gauldin

One of the perennial questions that continues to fascinate music scholars is the degree of influence that events and personages in composers' lives exert on their artistic output. Oscar Wilde's "The Artist," which concerns a sculptor who melted down his "Sorrow that endureth forever" to provide the metal for his new commission, "the Pleasure that abideth for a moment," suggests that works of art display little, if any, relation to the current physical or emotional state of their creator. Thus, Beethoven's idyllic Second Symphony was contemporary with his agonizing "Heiligenstadt Testament." On the other hand, students of Tchaikovsky have convincingly demonstrated the close ties that, on occasion, link that composer's personal life with his music.

This essay will attempt to forge one such correlation: the association of Mathilde Wesendonck with the key of A♭ major in certain works of Wagner. The celebrated "affair of the heart" between Mathilde and Richard is so familiar and voluminously documented that any further recounting of its circumstances and chronology would prove redundant.[1] No attempt will be made to enter that lion's den of speculation as to the extent of their possible physical intimacy. It will suffice to note that their personal acquaintance and correspondence spanned a remarkable quarter century—from 1852 to about 1877.

On the other hand, some background on Wagner's use of associative tonality is prerequisite to the establishment of our central thesis. The supposed affect of certain keys (or modes) on the listener constitutes a recurring theme in theoretical writings, spanning from Plato's concept of *ethos* to a host of eighteenth-century treatises. Mozart and Beethoven's preferential use of certain keys often reflected commonly held opinions of that period.[2] In addition to the exploitation and recurrence of certain invariant tonal centers in instrumental works and *Lieder*, a topic explored by Patrick McCreless, the dramatic occurrence of associative keys in stage works dates back at least to the Commandant's D minor in *Don Giovanni*.[3] The embryonic existence of this technique in German Romantic opera, as exemplified by Weber, Marschner, and Weigl, could not have gone unnoticed by the young Wagner during his early conducting positions at Würzburg, Magdeburg, and Riga.

The association of specific keys with specific dramatic elements in Wagner's stage works has received increasing scholarly attention in the years following Robert Bailey's seminal 1977 article on the evolution of the *Ring*.[4] Some such relations are common knowledge to the average Wagnerite: thus in the *Ring*, Walhalla = $D^\flat$, Siegmund's Sword = C, and Siegfried's Adventures = F.[5] However, aside from the interrelationships resulting among associative keys in *one* particular music drama, there exists an interesting subset of tonal centers that are linked by more *general* associations—connections that transcend the tonal schemes of individual works. For instance, the foreboding key of F♯ minor forms the basis for Ortrud and Frederick's vindictive plot in *Lohengrin*, Brünnhilde's "Annunciation of Death" to Siegmund in *Walküre*, and Waltraute's warning of impending woe for her sister in Act I of *Götterdämmerung*. In turn, this F♯ functions as the dominant for the equally ominous B minor, which spans Wagner's almost entire output—from the Dutchman through Alberich's Curse, to Klingsor; F♯ (enharmonically, as $G^\flat$) even provides the Watchman's single, unworldly note in *Meistersinger*.

At the opposite end of the affective tonal spectrum, the innocuous C major is continually linked to unspoiled innocence, inherent good, and the *populace*, as exemplified by the Norwegian Sailors in *Holländer*, the King's herald and folk of Brabant in *Lohengrin*, the primal Rhinegold in the *Ring*, the citizenry of Nürnberg in *Meistersinger*, and the Knights of Montsalvant in *Parsifal*. Likewise, E major is frequently linked to feminine sensuality, appearing in the Love Duet of *Holländer*, the whole complex of Venus and sexual desire in *Tannhäuser*, and the mortal womanhood of Brünnhilde in the *Ring* cycle. On occasion, the tonic pitches of these keys may form crucial intervallic relations, such as the pivotal F♯-C tritone in both *Lohengrin* (Ortrud versus the Herald) and the *Ring* (the Curse versus Wotan's plan to redeem the talisman).[6] Although we may never uncover the rationale that led Wagner to these particular associations, some doubtless represent the influence of previous works, a hypothesis pursued by Michael Tusa.[7] For instance, the F♯ minor noted previously could be linked back to the initial gathering of the undead in Marschner's *Vampyr* or the Wolf's Glen scene in Weber's *Freischütz*.[8]

This essay proposes an even more speculative correlation: the possibility that Wagner associated a specific key (A♭ major) with a specific person in his life (Mathilde Wesendonck). A♭ first occurs in this regard as the tonic center of the single-movement piano piece written for Wesendonck in the summer of 1853. Wagner, whose degree of infatuation was probably unbeknown to Mathilde at this time, originally attached a dedicatory quotation from the Norns: "Know you what will follow?" In returning a thank-you note to Minna (Wagner's wife at that time), Mathilde confessed ignorance of its implied meaning. Wagner later gave this work the more familiar title, *Eine Sonate für das Album von Frau M. W.*[9] Robert Gutman suggests that the personages inhabiting the early Acts of *Walküre*, on which Wagner was currently working, may have assumed more personal or real-life connotations (where Siegmund stood in for Richard, Sieglinde for Mathilde, Hunding for Otto, and Fricka for Minna).[10]

But in what contexts had Wagner previously utilized this key in the course of his earlier operas? Although A♭ does not play a significant role in the tonal scheme of *Holländer*, it provides the basis for the Act II Love Duet in *Tannhäuser*. This key choice allowed the composer to set the duet's middle section in the opera's "salvation key" of its dominant relation, E♭ major. During this section, Elizabeth bemoans the knight's extended absence and hints at her hidden desires (denoted by a Neapolitan shift into the "Venus or sensual key" of E major).[11] A♭ resurfaces as one of the four fundamental associative centers in *Lohengrin*.[12] Attached to Elsa and her lingering doubts about Lohengrin's identity, it likewise forms a half step relation to the knight's A major. In fact, in the opening measures of the opera's second scene, Elsa's A♭ minor motif (and its major mode in the succeeding "Dream" sequence) makes a momentary Neapolitan allusion to her approaching champion.[13] Finally, the music of the sirenlike Rhinedaughters in *The Ring's* prologue occurs in the fixed key of A♭ major, either as the subdominant of the Rhine's E♭ (beginning of scene 1), or as the dominant of Walhalla's D♭ (end of scene 4).[14] These three illustrations would seem to indicate that Wagner had already established in his mind certain connections of this key with the fairer sex (Elizabeth, Elsa, and the Rhinedaughters).

The events at the Wesendonck's estate in late 1857, however, precipitated the genesis of the crucial work in our study—an A♭ major setting of the second of five poems which Mathilde had written in the style of the *Tristan* text and sent over to Wagner at his cottage Asyl. Although he confided in Liszt that he was not prone to dabble in "such trifles," Wagner was not above flattering Mathilde by suggesting that "Träume" was the "best thing" he had done up to that time. He even made an orchestral arrangement of the song with which to serenade her while Otto was away. The original version (written on December 4) began with measure sixteen, but in his revision the following day, Wagner borrowed the music from the piano coda to serve as an introduction and appended the first six bars. The initial melodic outline of the enharmonic "Tristan chord" (E♭–F–A♭–C♭) relates this sonority to the key of A♭ (it had already appeared in this form in measures 80–83 of the Prelude to Act I of *Tristan*); in fact, Robert Bailey prefers to view it as a minor triad with an added sixth: A♭–C♭–E♭–F.[15] Yet, it is just possible that the composition of "Träume" may have triggered unconscious recollections from Wagner's earlier *Album Sonate*. A direct comparison of several passages extracted from the song's framing sections, which most closely resemble the harmonic language of *Tristan*, and portions of the *Sonate* displays a striking similarity (Figure 2.1).

Following his hasty retreat from Aysl, Wagner continued to work on Act II of *Tristan*, whose characters were again assuming startling similarities to his own love triangle (Tristan as Richard, Isolde as Mathilde, and King Mark as Otto). Further acknowledging Mathilde's role as his inspirational muse for this music drama, he incorporated a paraphrasing of "Träume" to open "O sink' hernieder, Nacht der Liebe" that initiates the series of love duets in scene 2 of Act II. While the most obvious references are borrowed directly from the song's introduction and postlude, there are more

A.

B.

Figure 2.1: Reductive comparison of similar passages in *Album Sonate* and "Träume"
A. *Sonate* (mm. 23–44) vs. "Träume" (mm. 1–14)
B. *Sonate* (mm. 240–44) vs. "Träume" (mm. 62–64)

subtle parodied relations between the design and tonal structure of the two pieces.[16] Table 2.1 compares the similarities of their overall sectional partitioning.

A♭ major, which had appeared previously in Act I as a mere harmonic component of the "Death" motif, now emerges as the opera's crucial tonal pivot.[17] It initiates a series of significant tonal

**Table 2.1: Structural comparison of *Träume* with *Tristan* Act II
"O sink" love duet**

"*Träume*"	Intro.	(Stanzas 1–3)	E♭ cadence	(Stanzas 4–5)	Vocal closing section	Coda
	mm. 1–16	17–47	48–49	50–60	61–68	68–84
Love duet	Stanza 1	(Stanzas 2–3)		(Stanzas 4–5)		
	mm. 1–21	22–41	42–45	46–85	86–94	94–103

centers by ascending minor thirds that will control the remainder of the music drama's key scheme: $A^\flat$ and B major during the Love Duets in Act II, D minor during Mark's scene in Act II, F minor during the Prelude and most of Act III, leading to the final $A^\flat$ and B major reprise of the Act II Duet in Isolde's Transfiguration. The so-called "Theme in $A^\flat$ major," incorrectly known as the "Porazzi Theme," likewise dates from this period. Appearing in conjunction with a sketch for Act II, it may have been intended to function as the original "O sink'" Love Duet before Wagner decided in favor of his "Träume" parody. The opening melodic line of the succeeding duet, "So stürben wir," also cast in $A^\flat$, may even originate in the beginning gesture of the *Album Sonate* (Figure 2.2A). Just prior to the reprise of this music in Isolde's concluding Transfiguration, the bereaved heroine seems to be searching for the key associated with her one night of stolen love with Tristan. Its initial phrase tentatively recurs first in F, then in $G^\flat$ and G major, before attaining the eventual goal of "Mathilde's $A^\flat$" (Figure 2.2B).

In his revision and expansion of the opening Bacchanal for the 1861 Paris production of *Tannhäuser*, Wagner consciously inserted obvious references to motifs and harmonic progressions drawn from *Tristan*.[18] Prior to the enharmonic "$A^\flat$ form" of the "Tristan chord" that supports an anticipatory statement of Venus's aria (Figure 2.3A), he created a new melodic motif by concluding the original four-note chromatic gesture that opens that opera with a new

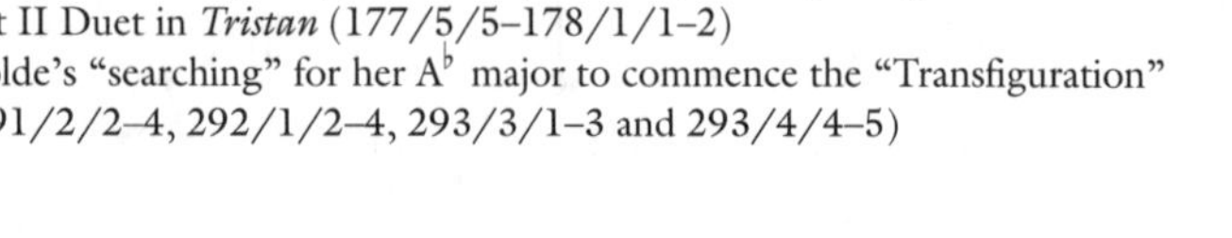

Figure 2.2: The "So stürben wir" gesture
A. Comparison of opening of *Sonate* (mm. 1–2) with opening of "So stürben wir" Act II Duet in *Tristan* (177/5/5–178/1/1–2)
B. Isolde's "searching" for her $A^\flat$ major to commence the "Transfiguration" (291/2/2–4, 292/1/2–4, 293/3/1–3 and 293/4/4–5)

Figure 2.3: Bacchanal revisions in 1861 Paris *Tannhäuser*
A. Venus's aria theme over Tristan chord (Dover: 460, mm. 1–4)
B. Tristan motif (Dover: 436, mm. 3–4)
C. Tristan motif (Dover: 440, mm. 2–3)
D. Tristan motif with "correct harmonies" (Dover: 442, mm. 2–3)

minor-third leap, a contour that would later recur in *Meistersinger*.[19]
The three phrases in Figure 2.3B illustrate how the harmonies gradually evolve into the *bona fide* "Tristan progression."

While Wagner rarely saw the Wesendoncks in the immediate years following his ignoble exit from Asyl, he continued to carry on his correspondence with Mathilde. After the *Tannhäuser* debacle in Paris, he accepted an invitation to meet the couple in November of 1861 for a tour of Venice. Although in his autobiography he cites the affect of Renaissance art on his creative powers as the rationale for returning to *Meistersinger*, a project whose origin dates back to 1845, most scholars consider this but another example of his "constructive memory." John Warrack suggests that "his awareness in Venice that his relationship with Mathilde must be transfigured by renunciation finds an outcome in the renunciation of

Eva by Sachs."[20] In writing to Mathilde about the opera's second prose sketch, Wagner rhapsodized that she must "steel herself against Sachs; you will fall in love with him [he signed many of his letters to her with 'Hans Sachs']. . . . We shall see each other now and then . . . But without any desire! And thus wholly free . . . Ade! *mein Kind!*"[21] The coincidence between the cobbler and the composer's own acceptance of the rejection of the Will in Lucy Beckett's words "turned [into] a powerful sense of identity with both Schopenhauer's moral hero and Sachs, as Wagner struggled with his feelings for Mathilde Wesendonck and managed for once in his life . . . to behave well."[22] One can trace the evolution and intensification of the relationship between Sachs (who represents Richard) and Eva (Mathilde) from *Meistersinger*'s original prose draft to its final text.

In the opera, this is manifested in two scenes that prominently feature Sachs and Eva, both of which open with a change of key into A$^\flat$ major concurrent with her entry. In the F major passage following Sach's monologue in scene 3 of Act II, Wagner first resurrects the extension of the chromatic idea he had borrowed from *Tristan* and exploited in the Paris Venusberg revision (Figure 2.4A). As the music shifts into A$^\flat$, the orchestra develops the primal three-note motif incorporated by Wagner in both *Lohengrin* and *The Ring* cycle to symbolize "Love" (discussed at length by Deryck Cooke [Figure 2.4B]).[23] This in turn reverts to the concluding gesture of the previous theme, which thereafter continues to permeate the remainder of the scene. This last three-tone figure is especially reminiscent of the second chord in the original "Tristan progression," with its characteristic chord degrees $^\sharp\hat{4}$– $\hat{5}$ set against a dominant seventh (Figure 2.4C). After a brief diversion back into F (which incidentally also served as the main area of tonal contrast in "Träume"), the return of A$^\flat$ major leads to the dramatic climax with Eva's inquiry, "Could not a widower go courting?" to which Sachs replies, "*Mein Kind* [the same expression he used in his letters to Mathilde], he is too old for you."

The commencement of scene 4 in Act III with Eva's entry into Sachs's workshop is likewise synchronized with a shift into A$^\flat$ major and a reprise of the fore-mentioned "Love" motif. In this case, however, the key only serves to tonally prepare the third stanza of Walther's "Morning Dream Song" in its fixed center of C major, so

A.

B.

C.

Figure 2.4: A♭ scene between Sachs and Eva in *Meistersinger* Act II, Scene 4
A. Use of Bacchanal/Tristan motif (Schirmer: 218/2/1–2)
B. Use of primal "Love" motif (219/1/3–2/2)
C. Use of last three-note Bacchanal gesture (219/3/1)

that the dramatic climax arrives in the following G major section leading up to the famous *Tristan* quotation. After Eva pours out her admiration and pent-up feelings for Sachs ("O Sachs! My friend! My true hero . . . what would I be without you?"), she confesses to him that now the desire of her heart lies elsewhere in Walther. The accompanying music makes continual reference to materials drawn from *Tristan*, with the melodic gesture cited in Figure 2.5A occurring no less than eight times. Sachs's concluding admonition to the lovers actually quotes the two opening statements from that work (Figure 2.5B). While some scholars have observed the transposition of these progressions from their original implied center of A, they offer few, if any, reasons *why* Wagner lowered them a half step in pitch. But now *we* know better; for this particular tonal shift produces Mathilde's key of A♭ major! Even as Eva christens Walther's new song during the opening strains of the transcendental G♭ major Quintet, its two intertwined motifs suggest a redemptive transformation of the initial anguished gestures in the *Tristan* Prelude (Figure 2.5C).

A.

B.

C.

Figure 2.5: Scene between Sachs and Eva in *Meistersinger* Act III, Scene 4
A. Use of Tristan motif (Schirmer: 450/4/1–2)
B. Transposed quotation from opening of *Tristan* Prelude (452/1/1–4)
C. Opening of G$^\flat$ quintet, echoing motifs that open *Tristan* Prelude (458/4/1–2)

We make the final stop of our survey at *Parsifal*, that most enigmatic of Wagner's music dramas. Although Mathilde and her daughter called on Wagner at the Villa Diana in the Rhineland during June of 1877, their relationship had by this time become purely platonic; for Wagner had shifted his affections to a new muse—Judith Gautier, who was supplying the creative impetus the sixty-four-year-old composer needed to commence his final stage work. As he eagerly plunged with renewed vigor into the compositional sketches for *Parsifal* during the fall of 1877, he wrote to Gautier in French, "I am loved, and I love."

The successful termination of my hypothesis hinges on a plausible explanation as to why Wagner should have tonally framed his final music drama in Mathilde's key of A$^\flat$ major. I do not intend to advance yet one more exegesis on the "true meaning" of this work, since the existing literature, as evidenced by interpretations ranging from Gutman's purging of tainted Jewish blood to the Hutcheons' notion of prostitutes inflected with syphilis, is more than sufficient.[24] My dilemma in this opera centers on an apparent tonal paradox. The key of A$^\flat$ major symbolizes the purity of the Grail and

A.

B.

Figure 2.6: Contradictory associative use of A♭ major in *Parsifal*
A. A♭ "Grail" motif associated with spirituality (Schirmer: 4/4/2–4)
B. A♭ "Flowermaiden" motif associated with sensuality (147/1/1–4)

loyalty of its attendant Knights (Figure 2.6A), an association made overwhelmingly clear in the text and music of Act I. But why are the Flowermaidens in Act II, who obviously personify sexual tempta-tion, also cast in the *same* tonal center (Figure 2.6B)? One might dismiss this "coincidence" by relating the siren-like nature of the Flowermaidens back to Wagner's beloved Rhinedaughters, who also share the same key. Granted, the music of *Parsifal* does exhibit a great deal of self-parody with its many remarkable allusions to specific passages in earlier works. Nevertheless, there may be a deeper rationale that underlies this glib explanation.

The "key" to this quandary may reside in Wagner's program notes for the Prelude, written at King Ludwig's request. Here he specifically entitles two of its principal motifs: the opening A♭ unison theme, "Love" (Figure 2.7A), and the later sequence that initiates the middle section, "Faith" (Figure 2.7B).[25] But the sacrificial "Love" of Christ's blood shed on the cross for the salvation of humanity, as exemplified by the Grail and Knights, cannot equally embody the sensual "Love" of Kundry's Kiss. Perhaps Wagner was intent on exploring and exploiting that single little word's contra-dictory nature. This diametric opposition is most clearly demon-strated in the Greek language, in which spiritual "Love" (that of Christ and the Grail) is represented by the word *agape*, in contrast to physical "Love" (that of sexual desire), represented by the word *eros*. Although in *Parsifal*, both now coexist under the single tonal

A.

B.

Figure 2.7: Wagner's titles for principal motifs in *Parsifal* Prelude
A. "Love" motif (Schirmer: 1/3/2–2/3/1)
B. "Faith" motif (4/4/7–5/5)

umbrella of A♭ major; Wagner carefully distinguishes the "Love" of the Grail from the "Love" of Kundry through his harmonic settings. While the Love of the Grail is supported by essentially diatonic music generated by perfect fifth cycles, the Love of Kundry is characterized by octatonic music generated by minor-third projections.[26]

The chorale-like orientation of the Pilgrim choruses in *Tannhäuser* and Grail passages in *Lohengrin* appears to provide the inspiration for the diatonic music associated with the Eucharist and Knights of Montsalvat. Just as it had previously done in the 1861 Paris revisions of the Venusberg music, the octatonic syntax of *Tristan* appropriately invades the scene between Kundry and Parsifal, commencing with the blatant "A♭ Tristan chord" that marks the exit of the Flowermaidens (Figure 2.8A). In the following exchange there are increasing references to the fixed pitches of this sonority, culminating in the "kiss," which even paraphrases a more extended section of the *Tristan* Prelude (Figure 2.8B).[27] Thus, it would seem that Mathilde's ghost continued to haunt Wagner's libido in the dual personality of her *agape/eros* A♭ major, but perhaps the key of A♭ major is now transferred to the affections of his new muse, Judith Gautier. Suffice it to say, in the final scene where Parsifal in his new guise as priest uncovers the glowing chalice, it is the *spiritual* A♭ diatonicism that triumphs over the *physical* A♭ octatonicism.

In presenting the case for the associative linking in Wagner's mind of Mathilde with the key of A♭ major, the evidence is largely hearsay, based as it is on internal "fingerprints" uncovered in the

A.

B.

Figure 2.8: Use of Tristan harmonies and motifs in Parsifal/Kundry scene (Act II)
A. Enharmonic Tristan chord supporting Parsifal motif (Schirmer: 166/3–4)
B. Paraphrased passage from *Tristan* Prelude at the "kiss" (184/1/5–2/1)

text and music of Wagner's artistic works. Lest we completely condemn such methods, however, one may recall that the identity of Alban Berg's secret mistress, Hanna Fuchs, was discovered on the basis of only four recurring pitch classes in his *Lyric Suite*.[28] If these meanderings have not provided a good detective story, perhaps they will at least pique listeners' curiosity concerning one more intriguing aspect of this most remarkable of nineteenth-century creative artists.

Works Cited

Abbate, Carolyn. "The Parisian 'Venus' and the 'Paris' Tannhäuser." *Journal of the American Musicological Society* 36 (1983): 73–123.

Bailey, Robert, ed. *Richard Wagner: Prelude and Transfiguration from Tristan and Isolde*. New York: W. W. Norton, 1985.

———. "The Structure of the *Ring* and its Evolution." *19th-Century Music* 1.1 (1977/78): 48–61.

Beckett, Lucy. "Sachs and Schopenhauer." *Richard Wagner: Die Meistersinger von Nürnberg*. Ed. John Warrack. New York: Cambridge University Press, 1994. 66–82.

Breig, Werner. "The Musical Works." *Wagner Handbook*. Ed. Ulrich Müller, Peter Wapnewski, and John Deathridge. Cambridge, MA: Harvard University Press, 1992. 397–482.

Bribitzer-Stull, Matthew. "The A♭–C–E Complex: The Origin and Function of Chromatic Major Third Collections in Nineteenth-Century Music." *Music Theory Spectrum* 28.2 (2006): 167–90.

Chafe, Eric. *The Tragic and the Ecstatic: The Musical Revolution of Wagner's* Tristan and Isolde. New York: Oxford University Press, 2005.

Cooke, Deryck. "Wagner's Musical Language." *The Wagner Companion.* Ed. Peter Burbidge and Richard Sutton. London: Faber and Faber, 1979. 225–68.

Darcy, Warren. *Wagner's* Das Rheingold. New York: Oxford University Press, 1993.

———. "'*Die Zeit ist da*'": Rotational Form and Hexatonic Magic in Act II Scene II of *Parsifal*." Paper Presented at the Society for Music Theory National Convention. Columbus, Ohio. Nov. 2002.

Ditzler, Kirk. "Influences of Heinrich Marschner's *Der Vampyr* on Richard Wagner's *Der fliegende Holländer.*" *The Opera Journal* 29.2 (1996): 2–13.

Gauldin, Robert. "The C/F$^\sharp$ Complex in *Der Ring des Nibelungen.*" Paper Presented at the American Musicological Society/Society for Music Theory National Convention. Philadelphia. Nov. 1984.

———. "Wagner's Parody Technique: *Träume* and the *Tristan* Love Duet." *Music Theory Spectrum* 1 (1979): 35–42.

Golther, Wolfgang, ed. *Richard Wagner an Mathilde Wesendonck: Tagebuchblätter und Briefe, 1853–1871.* Berlin: A. Dunker, 1911.

Gutman, Robert. *Richard Wagner: The Man, His Mind, and His Music.* 2nd ed. Lincoln: University of Nebraska, 1996.

Hermann, Richard. Unpublished Analysis of Richard Wagner's *Eine Sonate für das Album von Frau M. W.* 1988.

Hutcheon, Linda, and Michael Hutcheon. *Opera: Desire, Disease, Death.* Lincoln: University of Nebraska Press, 1996.

Knapp, Julius. *The Women in Wagner's Life.* Trans. Hannah Waller. New York: A. Knopf, 1931.

McCreless, Patrick. "Schenker and Chromatic Tonicization: A Reappraisal." *Schenker Studies.* Ed. Hedi Siegel. New York: Cambridge University Press, 1990. 125–45.

Newcomb, Anthony. "The Birth of Music out of the Spirit of Drama: An Essay in Wagnerian Formal Analysis." *19th-Century Music* 5.1 (1981/82): 38–66.

Newman, Ernest. *The Wagner Operas.* New York: A. Knopf, 1949.

Newman, William. *The Sonata since Beethoven.* New York: W. W. Norton, 1972.

Perle, George. "The Secret Program of the *Lyric Suite.*" *The International Alban Berg Society Newsletter* 5 (1977): 4–12.

Rothstein, William. *Phrase Rhythm in Tonal Music.* New York: Schirmer Books, 1989.

Staehlin, Martin. "Von den *Wesendonck-Liedern* zum *Tristan*." *Zu Richard Wagner: Acht Bonner Beiträge im Jubiläumsjahr 1983*. Studium Universale Band 5. Ed. Helmut Loos and Günther Massenkeil. Bonn: Bouvier Verlag Herbert Grundmann, 1984. 45–73.

Tusa, Michael. "Richard Wagner and Weber's *Euryanthe*." *19th-Century Music* 9.3 (1985/86): 206–21.

Wagner, Cosima. *Cosima Wagner's Diaries*. Ed. Martin Gregor-Dellin and Dietrich Mack. Trans. Geoffrey Skelton. New York: Harcourt Brace Jovanovich, 1978–80.

Warrack, John, ed. *Richard Wagner: Die Meistersinger von Nürnberg*. New York: Cambridge University Press, 1994.

Warrack, John. "The Sources and Genesis of the Text." *Richard Wagner: Die Meistersinger von Nürnberg*. Cambridge Opera Handbooks. Ed. John Warrack. New York: Cambridge University Press, 1994. 11.

NOTES

1. In addition to the standard biographies, a good account of their relationship may be found in Knapp.
2. See Bribitzer-Stull, 167–90 for a study of the history of and tonal contexts for the keys of A♭, C, and E in classic and romantic music.
3. McCreless, 125–45.
4. Bailey, "Structure of the *Ring*," 48–61.
5. For instance, see the list in Darcy, *Wagner's* Das Rheingold, 218.
6. Gauldin, "The C/F$^\sharp$ Complex."
7. Tusa, 206–21.
8. Ditzler, 2–13.
9. In addition to Rothstein, 294–97, other commentary may be found in William Newman, 378–88, and in Hermann.
10. Gutman, 166.
11. The A♭-major Act II Love Duet in *Tannhäuser* occurs between 105/2/4 and 122/1/5 of the G. Schirmer piano-vocal score. The shift to E♭ from E major takes place between 110/1/3 and 110/5/1. Score references are given in the format page number/system/measure.
12. The Grail/Lohengrin = A major, Elsa and her doubt = A♭ minor/major, Ortrud and her plot = F$^\sharp$ minor, and the King's Herald = C major.
13. Consult 21/1/1–29/2/1 of the Schirmer vocal score of *Lohengrin*. The Neapolitan shift occurs at 21/2/3–3/2 and later at 23/2/1–3.
14. See 5/4/1–6/1/4 (A♭ as IV/E♭) and 216/2/1–218/1/2 (A♭ as V/D♭) in the Schirmer vocal score of *Das Rheingold*.

15. Bailey, *Richard Wagner,* 122–24.
16. Gauldin, "Wagner's Parody Technique" 35–42 traces the close relationship between these two works. Additional commentary may be found in Staehlin, 45–61, and Newcomb, 38–66.
17. Cosima Wagner, v. 2, 206. Cited in Chafe 302, n. 2.
18. These revisions are discussed in Abbate, 73–123.
19. These observations are made by Breig, 426–27.
20. Warrack, "Sources and Genesis," 11.
21. "Gegen Sachs halten Sie Ihr Herz fest: in den werden Sie sich verlieben! . . . Aber auch sehen wollen wir uns dann und wann. . . . Dann ohne allen Wunsch! Somit auch gänzlich frei! . . . Ade! mein Kind!" As quoted in Golther, 293–94. Trans. Lucy Beckett.
22. Beckett, 73.
23. Cooke, 225–68.
24. See the chapter on "*Parsifal* and Polemics" in Gutman, 389–420, and the chapter on *Parsifal* in Hutcheon.
25. A translation of Wagner's program notes for the *Parsifal* Prelude appears in Hutcheon, 61–93 appears in Ernest Newman, 667–68. It is my belief that the "Love" motif may originate from the Centurion's A$^\flat$ passage near the end of Bach's *St. Matthew Passion*, while the "Faith" motif displays strong ties to the opening minor-third ascent in Isolde's "Transfiguration," employing the same pitches.
26. Darcy, *"Die Zeit ist da"*.
27. The harmonic progression that occurs at Kundry's demise (Schirmer vocal score 276/2/2–3/2 or D$^\flat$ major to A minor to D$^\flat$ major) is especially remarkable. A minor is the only major or minor triad that will produce a hexatonic collection with D$^\flat$ major (C, D$^\flat$, E, F, A$^\flat$, A), thereby evoking one final allusion to the power that Klingsor once exerted over Kundry.
28. Perle, 4–12.

CHAPTER 3

GLENN GOULD AND RICHARD WAGNER

Timothy Maloney

The name Glenn Gould typically evokes images of an iconoclastic pianist with rumpled, ill-fitting clothing, ungroomed hair, undisciplined stage mannerisms, and uncanny technique, performing divinely inspired interpretations of contrapuntal music by J. S. Bach. Gould's name is sometimes also linked to the keyboard music of other "formalist" composers such as Beethoven, Brahms, Hindemith, and Schoenberg. But what connections could there possibly be between Gould and Wagner, a composer from the nineteenth century (already a major drawback for Gould) who wrote large-scale musico-dramatic works (a further obstacle for the pianist, who loathed Italian opera)?

Actually, in a 1974 *Rolling Stone* interview, Gould described himself as "hopelessly addicted" to Wagner.[1] He admitted to sitting down at the piano by himself or in the company of friends and playing long sections of Wagner and Strauss operas. In a letter to his parents while on tour in Vienna in 1957, he reported "stay[ing] up till 11:30 specially to sing *Die Meistersinger* as [his train] went through Nürnberg".[2] On another occasion he claimed to have been moved to tears listening to *Tristan* as a fifteen-year-old,[3] and this possibly apocryphal tale was later given credence in one of François Girard's *Thirty-two Short Films about Glenn Gould*.[4]

As evidence of his "addiction," Gould recorded some of his piano reductions for an all-Wagner disc in 1973, and in 1982, a little over two months before his untimely death from a stroke at age fifty, he conducted a chamber orchestra (in which I had the pleasure of performing) to record the original version of one of the works from the disc. Both the 1973 vinyl disc[5] and the 1991 reissue of the compact disc,[6] which includes the later orchestral track, received mixed reviews. This chapter examines Gould's transcriptions and performances of Wagner, as both pianist and conductor, in the context of that divergent critical reception.

As background to our discussion, there follows a brief sequence of Gould's thoughts on nineteenth-century music and Wagner, assembled from multiple sources:

[W]hat I play for the public and what I play for myself have always been two quite different things.[7]

There is . . . a concept of me as someone who likes nothing between Bach and Schoenberg except for a few stopovers along the way. This is totally wrong. I am immensely influenced by late-Romantic music and always have been.[8]

I do find it very difficult to muster any enthusiasm for the early Romantics.[9]

I have a century-long blind spot approximately demarcated by *The Art of the Fugue* on one side and *Tristan* on the other—everything in between is at best an occasion for admiration rather than love.[10]

I think the piano is a contrapuntal instrument and only becomes interesting when it is treated in a manner in which the vertical and horizontal dimensions are mated. This does not happen in most of the material written for it in the first half of the nineteenth century.[11]

The trouble is that the late nineteenth century is badly represented on the piano.[12]

[T]hose composers [from that era] who could have written with a tremendous . . . intermingling of harmonic and thematic [elements] just basically chose not to write for the piano at all.[13]

This is the great pity—this gap in the piano repertoire. It was an orchestral period, and the piano was little more than a backup, a poor man's orchestra, a substitute, "first draft" kind of instrument.[14]

[W]hen I was about sixteen, I . . . became extremely interested in the literature of the late nineteenth century, the orchestral literature [of] Strauss, Mahler, Bruckner and Wagner, and I began making for myself, for fun, piano transcriptions of things like the Schoenberg chamber symphonies and of Wagner [operas].[15]

I suppose that of those composers who represent the later manifestations of romanticism[,] the one who means the most to me is Wagner.[16]

I've always sort of sat down at night and played Wagner for myself, because I'm a total Wagnerite—hopelessly addicted to the later things especially.[17]

Gould's piano transcriptions of Wagner and other music have been described by some members of the small circle of colleagues who had the rare privilege of hearing them. John Roberts, the former Head of Radio Music for the Canadian Broadcasting Corporation (CBC), recalls, "[H]e had an . . . astounding ability to make transcriptions of orchestral works and operas from memory, while seated at the piano."[18] Roberts witnessed "sessions at the piano that lasted until 3 a.m. [during] which Gould seemed to transcribe the most complex orchestral [compositions] as he went along," without reference to any musical scores.[19] Roberts continues:

From hearing him first-hand, I know he had a total recall of such works as *Pelleas und Melisande* by Schoenberg, the *Passacaglia* by Webern, and the late works of Richard Strauss, as well as much of the standard repertoire. As far as operas were concerned, he ventured from *Elektra* and *Capriccio* by Strauss to cherished operas by Wagner, including *Tristan and Isolde*.[20]

He . . . had whole opera scores in the back of his head. Once he started Wagner's *Tristan*...Glenn would be lost in another world, often oblivious to the presence of anyone else.[21]

However, only a few transcriptions were ever turned into actual piano scores.[22]

In his response to a 1975 fan letter, Gould explained why he did not like Liszt's transcriptions of Wagner's music:

I elected to [prepare my own transcriptions] largely because I felt that the great majority of the Liszt transcriptions either dealt with early operatic excerpts or, in the case of the more mature works, with example[s] which . . . do not really lend themselves to keyboard adaptation—the Liebestod, for example. [I]n my opinion, the works of Wagner which lend themselves most readily to the keyboard are those which least depend upon orchestral colour and/or [are those] in which the structural contours can be delineated abstractly as counterpoint.

For that reason, I selected the "Meistersinger Overture," the
"Siegfried Idyll" and . . . "Dawn and Siegfried's Rhine Journey" [for
my recording].[23]

This citation illustrates the depth of Gould's predilection for poly-
phonic music and of his preoccupation with musical structure.
Regarding the former, he preferred contrapuntal elaboration to dramatic or rhetorical effects even with Wagner, and for him this bias
constituted a strong argument against using Liszt's arrangements.
His keen interest in the architecture of the works he performed will
be discussed later in the chapter.

For Gould there were additional reasons to avoid Liszt's arrangements of Wagner:

> The Liszt transcriptions . . . whether of Beethoven or Wagner, tend
> to be relentlessly faithful, in that if the orchestral texture is thick,
> Liszt will reproduce that thickness on the piano, and of course a
> thickness on the piano doesn't sound good. . . . If the drum roll goes
> on for sixteen bars, there will be a tremolando of sixteen bars in the
> lowest octaves of the keyboard, which is impossible pianistically.[24]

> I tried to avoid what Liszt does . . . I preferred to go, if not all the way,
> then a long way towards a realization rather than a transcription.[25]

By "realization," Gould meant an adaptation for keyboard, though
not a paraphrase or fantasy as Liszt and others did for various Italian
and French operas. Gould spoke of "rebuild[ing] the piece for
piano" while accurately representing the music's structure, insisting
that "[t]here are no cuts, no additions" to the score.[26] He also used
the term "de-orchestrations" to describe his transcriptions, which
clearly succeed as idiomatic piano music while Liszt's literal transcriptions do not.[27]

In the liner notes to Gould's 1973 Wagner LP, which consist of a
transcribed interview from CBC Radio in which Gould discusses
his transcriptions (this was not reproduced in Sony's CD reissue),
he elucidates:

> I decided to pretend Wagner had an acute pianistic sense—which,
> insofar as we can judge from the accompaniments to the
> "Wesendonck" songs—the only relatively "mature" piano writing he
> got involved with—he didn't. But I decided to pretend that he had
> the keyboard flair to match his orchestral flair . . . and I deliberately
> dispensed with all textual scruples and tried to imagine what might

Figure 3.1: Wagner's score to *Siegfried Idyll,* pp. 1–2[28]

have been if someone with both orchestral and pianistic flair—
Scriabin, let's say—had had a hand in it.[29]

As a "pragmatic solution" to the piano's inability to sustain long
chords or to increase the volume of a note once it had been struck,
Gould spoke of "horizontaliz[ing] the sound through arpeggiated
chords and similar devices."[30] He "stagger[ed] incoming motives . . .
to preserve a realistic sense of time and movement" on the keyboard, and "activate[d] inner voices, mak[ing] them imitative,
whenever possible, of Wagner's motivic conceits."[31] And Gould
went one step further:

For example, Wagner frequently sits for six bars or more [in the
Siegfried Idyll] on an E-major chord, and there's simply no way
of doing that on the piano without losing all sense of momen-
tum. Now, Liszt usually falls back on a tremolando, which is

Figure 3.1 (continued)

just so turn-of-the-century I can't stand it. So what I did—
and if you think my Mozart sonatas upset people, wait till the
Wagnerians get hold of this—what I did was to invent whole
other voices that aren't anywhere in the score, except that they
are convincingly Wagnerian.[32]

If we compare the opening of Gould's transcription of *Siegfried
Idyll* (see Figure 3.2) with Wagner's orchestral score (see Figure
3.1), we first notice minor liberties Gould took with the bass line
(entering after the downbeat in mm. 4, 6, 10ff). The first example
of more extensive departures from Wagner's musical text occurs in
m. 18 of Gould's manuscript (p. 1, last system, last bar), where the
alto and tenor voices are more animated than in the orchestral

Figure 3.2: Reproduction of the holograph manuscript of the second draft of Glenn Gould's piano arrangement of *Siegfried Idyll*, pp. 1–2[34]
Note: The numerical annotations (e.g., "2–1," "2–2") and brackets inserted between the staff systems refer to the recorded "takes" and "inserts" Gould chose for the final tape montage of his recording.

score. In mm. 21–24 (p. 2, first and second systems), Gould "activated" a static F♯ minor chord by "invent[ing] a dialogue between two offstage horns, one in the tenor and one in the alto, that try to mimic each other . . . and they go on like this between themselves, and . . . forgive me for saying so, but it's gorgeous!"[33]

Despite his acumen as both pianist and arranger, there were sections of these works that posed distinct challenges. For instance, he had found the "glorious counterpoint" of the first seven minutes of the Prelude to Act I of *Die Meistersinger* "an absolute joy to play," as "a sort of party piece," for many years, but the last three minutes were more problematical because Wagner "condenses all previous motives into a kind of *Kunst der Fuge*-like congestion that is, literally, impossible to render on the keyboard [with two hands]."[35]

Figure 3.2 (continued)

Since Gould had never "bother[ed] to concoct an 'official' transcription," he was always forced to leave out some lines when playing it "live."[36] For the recording, he resorted to another strategy: "In order to accommodate the extraordinarily dense polyphony in the '*Meistersinger Vorspiel*' . . . [I] wrote the last three minutes or thereabouts as though for a piano primo–piano secundo duet . . . and simply over-tracked the material when recording. Consequently, the transcription, strictly speaking, would not be reproducible—except, of course, by two pianists."[37]

Figure 3.3: Reproduction of the holograph manuscript of the second draft of Gould's piano reduction of the Prelude to *Die Meistersinger*, pp. 12–13*[38]
*This figure shows the addition of the *secundo* part in mm. 123 and 125 (first page, above the final measure of each of systems 3 and 4) as the *Im mässigen Hauptzeitmass* section begins, and the continuation of full primo and secundo parts (marked "P" and "S") from m. 128 (second page, systems 2–3 and 4–5).

There are also portions of his arrangement of "Siegfried's Rhine Journey" from the Prelude to *Götterdämmerung* that required a three-handed approach.

Apart from the issues of technological wizardry in the recording studio and textual liberties in Gould's transcriptions of Wagner's music, Gould's performances of it are noteworthy for their own departures from the composer's directions. As he did with all the

Figure 3.3 (continued)

music he played, Gould worked out the interpretive details in his mind. The manuscripts of his Wagner arrangements contain none of the composer's tempo, dynamic, articulation, or phrasing indications, nor does Gould add any fingering annotations. As can be seen in Figures 3.2, 3.3, and 3.4, the only markings in any of his piano scores relate strictly to the process of recording, not to musical interpretation. Still, regarding Gould's failure to transcribe any of Wagner's directions into his piano reductions, it is also possible that he had little or no intention of following them.

Gould plays much of the Prelude to *Die Meistersinger*, for instance, below the *forte* and *fortissimo* levels stipulated by Wagner.

Figure 3.4: Reproduction of the holograph manuscript of page 17A from the second draft of Gould's piano reduction of "Siegfried's Rhine Journey" in the Prelude to *Götterdämmerung*

Note: This figure shows the added *secundo* part (see treble staves marked "S") beginning at m. 720.

In addition, he uses a rather flexible approach to tempo, despite the work's overall marchlike character, and employs his trademark *détaché* articulation even where Wagner did not indicate *staccato*. Much of the time, he seems to be disregarding the typical festive approach to the piece in favor of a more restrained reading that allows him to emphasize the abundant glories of Wagner's busy part-writing by sculpting individual contrapuntal lines with differentiated articulations and dynamics. Such control of fine detail is more

difficult when playing at louder dynamic levels, though Gould suc-
ceeds handily in the overdubbed sections.

Gouldophiles have long been aware that Gould tended to give
quicker, more perfunctory readings of works for which he had little
affection, while lingering more purposefully over those works he
greatly enjoyed. His rendition of *Siegfried Idyll* on the piano is a
prime example of the latter. The year the Wagner LP was issued,
Gould explained in a letter to a record company executive in New
York: "I'm rather pleased with the results of the Wagner transcription disc . . . (I must warn you that the italics re my interpretation of
the "Siegfried Idyll" are very much on "Idyll" and not on
"Siegfried"—i.e. it is probably the most stately rendition since
Knappertsbusch; I've always felt that the piece has an indigenous
languor which the "ruhig bewegt," or whatever, in the score does
not adequately delineate.)."[40]

The Knappertsbusch disc to which Gould refers is a 1955 recording of the Vienna Philharmonic, which lasts just under nineteen
minutes;[41] Gould's timing for his piano rendition of the work is
"stately" indeed, taking over four and a half minutes longer
(23:31). Concerning the reception accorded Gould's piano transcription and his self-described "Germanic" reading of the work, the
critic Joseph Horowitz marveled at the "sublime translucence" and
the "wealth of living, breathing nuance" in Gould's performance,[42]
while William Youngren praised Gould's "extraordinarily sensitive
phrasing" in this "dreamy meditation," found one passage "inde-
scribably moving," and pronounced the end result "fabulous."[43]
But Arnold Whittall regretted Gould's intermittent "Brucknerian
solemnity" and suggested, "had the composer wanted the music to
be played as slowly as this, he probably would have written *Sehr
ruhig*, not *Ruhig bewegt* at the beginning."[44]

Youngren also applauded Gould's other Wagner renditions on
the piano, calling the Prelude to *Die Meistersinger* "a perfectly satisfying performance" and noting the "joy, majesty and sweep" of
the *Götterdämmerung* excerpts. He praised "the textural and
dynamic variety with which [Gould] renders the whole elaborately
contrapuntal fabric—which he has, to be sure, made even more contrapuntal than Wagner left it. It is always moving, always interesting,
always shapely." His one *caveat* focused on "Gould's added lines,
punctuations, tremolos and the like, sometimes . . . subverting the

melody and confusing the sense of progression, but this happens relatively seldom."[45]

Meanwhile, Carl Bauman was completely won over: "I bought the LP to scoff and almost immediately became captivated by what Gould did to and with the music. He somehow manages to go to the heart of the music and make one hear it anew."[46] But Horowitz felt that Gould's "unconventional performances" were "an acquired taste,"[47] and Whittall contrasted Gould's "lumpy presentation of the Prize Song theme" in *Die Meistersinger* with "a mesmerizing multitrack apotheosis," and a "grotesque parody of Wagner's magical Dawn" with an "overwhelming Rhine Journey."[48] Gould himself admitted to some "reservations . . . pertain[ing] to the long-sustained 'Dawn' sequence," presumably concerning the effectiveness of his adaptation of such atmospheric orchestral music to the piano.[49]

Gould's tempos for *Die Meistersinger* and "Siegfried's Rhine Journey," which he called "almost alarmingly conventional," do not seem to have caused the critics any particular unhappiness.[50] The conductor Roger Norrington claims that Wagner conducted the Prelude to *Die Meistersinger* in "a few seconds over eight minutes," but few recordings, if any, come close to that.[51] Norrington, with the London Classical Players, was the quickest at almost eight and a half minutes, and Geoffrey Tate, conducting the Bavarian Radio Orchestra, was the slowest at just over ten and a half. Gould's sits comfortably in between at nine minutes, thirty-five seconds, very close to timings posted by Karajan conducting the Dresden State Opera Orchestra (9:23), Szell and the Cleveland Orchestra (9:31), and Solti with the Chicago Symphony Orchestra (9:41).

Gould's timing for the "Dawn" and "Siegfried's Rhine Journey" sequence is not directly comparable to those of other discs, as his adaptation for piano conforms to neither of the versions used in concert performances by orchestras. In fact, his arrangement of these sections of *Götterdämmerung* merits a brief comment here, as it illustrates the musical genius behind the enigmatic public *persona*. The Prelude to *Götterdämmerung* poses a problem for concert performance because its almost nine hundred bars incorporate both a vocal trio and a duo surrounded by purely instrumental sections. To condense the material for orchestral performances without singers, the two existing arrangements (neither of which is by Wagner) cut and paste portions of the original score with less than ideal results.

Not surprisingly, Gould's condensed version is thoughtfully conceived and based on a thorough understanding of the opera: for example, he begins with an F$^\sharp$ timpani roll (m. 292 of Wagner's score), the tonality used to signify darkness in this opera. The transition from darkness to dawn's light (F$^\sharp$ to F) is thus clearly embedded in the tonal structure of Gould's arrangement—a seemingly obvious choice, yet not that of the other arrangers.[52]

The 1982 chamber orchestra performance of *Siegfried Idyll*, conducted by Gould, is even more "stately" than his 1973 piano recording of the same work, lasting about one minute longer (24:28). The timings of a number of recordings of the work are in the seventeen- to nineteen-minute range, including Klemperer and the Philharmonic Orchestra (17:41), Knappertsbusch and the Vienna Philharmonic (18:52, as mentioned earlier), and Haenchen and the CPE Bach Chamber Orchestra (19:30). At the quick end of the spectrum are discs by Paray and Detroit, and Ormandy and Philadelphia (both just over fifteen minutes), while Toscanini with both the NBC Symphony and the New York Philharmonic orchestras, Rudolph with the Columbia Symphony Orchestra, and Norrington with the London Classical Players all last a little over sixteen minutes. The slower readings include Tilson Thomas and the Boston Symphony Orchestra (21:01), cited by Youngren as a "fine" performance, and Rögner with the Berlin Radio Orchestra (22:21).[53]

Gould's biographer, Peter Ostwald, heard Gould's chamber orchestra reading of *Siegfried Idyll* as "an elegant, slow-paced performance that emphasized the contrapuntal structure of Wagner's composition,"[54] while the Pulitzer Prize–winning music critic Tim Page called it "a reading of melting and surpassing tenderness."[55] But the composer-conductor Gunther Schuller excoriated it as "the most inept, amateurish, wrong-headed rendition of a major classic ever put to vinyl."[56] Regrettably, Schuller offers no explanation for his dismissive comments, which are contained in a monograph arguing strict adherence to the letter of the musical score, but (tellingly?) they are part of a broader rant against "instant" conducting careers by "little qualified" instrumentalists and singers.

Schuller evidently accepted at face value Sony's claim that its CD showcased Gould's "conducting debut," since he characterized the recording as "perhaps the saddest manifestation of this trend" (toward "instant" careers).[57] While it was the first time Gould's conducting was made available on a commercial disc, he had previously conducted in concert, both from the podium and (more often) the piano, and had been heard and seen as an orchestra conductor in Canada on CBC radio and television as early as the 1950s.[58] In other words, the *Siegfried Idyll* project was far from what most people would consider a true conducting debut, and Benjamin Folkman's notes in the CD booklet make that clear by alluding to "early attempts at conducting" that Gould had not continued.[59]

Sony's hyperbole about Gould's so-called debut is understandable as a marketing tool, but one might expect more thorough research from an experienced scholar like Schuller before he delivers such provocative remarks. Quite apart from his opinion of the performance, his indictment of "instant" careers quickly loses credibility when the case for the prosecution turns out to be mistaken. That being so, one wonders how much the misperception may have colored Schuller's thinking about the performance itself.

As to the reactions of other critics, if the tempo of Gould's piano rendition of *Siegfried Idyll* was problematical for some, the pace of his conducted version of the work and its perceived effect on the overall performance drew particular condemnation every bit as damning as Schuller's more generalized scorn. William Youngren described it as "a 45-rpm record being played at 33," and suggested hearing it once and "never listen[ing] to it again."[60] It seems curious that the speed of this performance could be so wrong compared to Gould's piano rendition of the same work, the "dreamy meditation" Youngren had considered "fabulous." But Youngren saw no redeeming qualities at all in the orchestral performance, characterizing it variously as "excruciating . . . grotesque . . . agonizing . . . a nightmare [and] execrable."[61]

Youngren also found the playing "flat, pedestrian, undistinguished,"[62] and Joseph Horowitz essentially agreed: "Not once do the players sound spontaneous or self-willed. No conductor on records . . . has so evoked an ensemble of marionette instrumentalists."[63] But Carl Bauman's reaction was similar to Ostwald's and Page's, though he felt that Gould's orchestral interpretation was "perhaps overly emotional in its tenderness."[64] It is difficult to reconcile such diametrically opposed opinions about the same recording.

Finally, Youngren thought the audio quality strange, complaining that the "players sound airlessly separated from one another, each sealed in his (or her) own isolation booth."[65] Horowitz observed other unwanted elements in the recording: "Gould weights the lines to stress and enforce Wagner's polyphony. He discourages string vibrato to impose a cooling sheen. Some may find this Wagner style hypnotic and otherworldly. I find it Martian. Even the trills are microscopically scrutinized."[66]

Such notions as restricted vibrato, "cooling sheen," isolation booths, and so on do not reflect the reality of that recording. For example, vibrato is clearly audible in all instruments but the horns. As opposed to "airless" separation and isolation booths, the musicians actually sat relatively close together in three narrowly separated rows. There were no acoustical baffles or other sound-deadening furnishings anywhere in the room, which was quite "live,"[67] and only five microphones were used to record the entire group. The microphones were positioned to capture Gould's usual tight audio perspective, which is audible throughout much of the recording, though there is a strange overlay of artificial "reverb" at the end that presumably was added in the editing stage, maybe even after Gould's death, as it seems incompatible with his oft-expressed disdain for the "cathedral-like sound" favored by other artists of his generation.[68]

Regarding consciously "weighted lines," the opposite was the case. I must agree with Horowitz that the audio pick-up of the ensemble is uneven: certain instruments tend to dominate the foreground, and the winds overwhelm the strings at the climax. But this was not by design. On the contrary, Gould seemed unaware of the problem. He had the chance to fix it at an extra recording session called to clean up particular spots five weeks after the original sessions. While it is possible that five microphones were either too few for a group of that size and makeup or were not ideally placed, the fact that balance is imperfect in the final product must be blamed on Gould's relative inexperience at conducting and recording a chamber orchestra. Apropos of the balance issue, Gunther Schuller notes in his book, "the seven kinds of ear [needed by the compleat conductor] . . . are for (1) harmony; (2) pitch and intonation; (3) dynamics; (4) timbre; (5) rhythm and articulation; (6) balance and orchestrational aspects; and (7) line and continuity."[69] Judging by my experience with Glenn Gould and our Wagner recording, the sixth type was not one of his strengths.

Lastly, despite such Gouldian touches as the slow tempo, measured trills, and *secco* horn staccatos, Gould was no puppeteer then or on any other occasions when he conducted; it was simply not his style. As a conductor, he was much more a collaborator than a dictator, though he obviously had a concept of the music he was trying to translate into sound. For me, that recording reflects a higher degree of personal initiative and, for that matter, artistry by the musicians than can be heard on several other recordings of *Siegfried Idyll*. Carl Bauman seemed to recognize that when he wrote, "the Toronto players g[a]ve him their all."[70]

Considering the evident shock caused by Gould's tempo, one cannot help wondering if Schuller, Youngren, and Horowitz simply wrote off the performance without giving due consideration to its merits. Gould had warned the ensemble before our recording sessions that our rendition would be slower than any other rendition then on disc, and he fulfilled his promise. As he had written in 1973, he simply felt more "indigenous languor" in it than perhaps even Wagner had, and, like it or not, he was remarkably consistent in his approach to the work as pianist and, almost a decade later, as conductor. Gould once suggested that "[t]he performer has to have faith that he is doing . . . the right thing, that he may be finding interpretive possibilities not wholly realized even by the composer."[71] His "tender," "meditative" approach to this work bears out that contention.

It should be remembered that none of Wagner's scores after *Tannhäuser* (premiered in 1845) contain metronome markings. When considering Gould's recording of, say, the first movement of Beethoven's "Hammerklavier" Sonata, which he plays at about $\downarrow$ = 88 as compared to the composer's suggested speed of $\downarrow$ = 138, critics have a factual basis for complaint (though the accuracy of Beethoven's metronome has been questioned by some experts). With respect to Gould's tempos for *Siegfried Idyll*, since Wagner did not designate a particular metronome speed, giving only rather conflicting verbal directions (*Ruhig bewegt*: literally, "calm" and "agitated," meaning perhaps something like *Adagio ma non troppo*), there is no specific benchmark for Gould to have contravened, as the seven-minute (or almost fifty percent) differential between Paray's and Rögner's recordings clearly shows.

Critics, musicians, and concertgoers have long debated the relative merits of slower tempos taken by various Germanic conductors
(e.g., Furtwängler, Karajan) *versus* the quicker speeds of some Italian and French maestros (e.g., Toscanini, Monteux) in performances of the standard orchestral repertoire. In Wagner's essay, "On
Conducting," which (ironically) is largely devoted to a discussion of
appropriate tempos, the composer himself intriguingly suggests that
"the pure adagio . . . cannot be taken too slow[ly]."[72] Does
Siegfried Idyll qualify as a "pure adagio," and, if so, is Gould's
"dreamy meditation" on it not the ideal approach, leaving
Ormandy's and Rudolph's and other romps through it in the
"grotesque" category? As Gould pointed out, it is an idyll, after all,
that uses a cradlesong as one of its themes, a work that he felt was
"as lyrical as a Chopin nocturne."[73]

I find Gould's reasoning persuasive but lacking clear direction
from the composer or evidence of a tradition or even a consensus
among conductors about the work's tempo (none of which could
be considered definitive, in any case). The questions posed above
are ultimately unresolvable, hinging completely on current tastes
and personal preferences. While Joseph Horowitz chose Toscanini's
"surpassingly beautiful" 1936 recording with the New York Philharmonic (which lasts 16:08) as the *ne plus ultra* of *Siegfried Idyll*
recordings,[74] I find all the under twenty-minute renditions too
quick for my taste. The performance of the work given at the *Lingering Dissonances: Richard Wagner 2003* conference, in which I
participated as First Clarinetist (reprising the role I played in
Gould's ensemble just over twenty years earlier), took almost
twenty–and–a-half minutes, and our dress rehearsal run-through
was a little slower, lasting just under twenty-one minutes. In my
estimation, there could have been greater breadth to our playing of
at least some sections of the work, which would have brought us
closer to Gould's timing without any danger of approaching "nightmare" territory, wherever that may be.

The reaction to this recording is reminiscent of the uproar that
followed Gould's 1962 performance of the Brahms D-minor Piano
Concerto with the New York Philharmonic. Gould's conception of
that work was so divergent from Leonard Bernstein's (i.e., his preferred tempos were, no surprise, much slower) that the conductor

issued a verbal disclaimer from the stage before the first perform-ance. While Harold Schonberg's review in the next day's *New York Times* was one of the crueler *ad hominem* attacks Gould ever received, other newspaper critics took strong exception to Bern-stein's remarks even while criticizing Gould's interpretation. The performance was recorded for radio broadcast, and the tape sur-vived to be remastered and issued as a compact disc by Sony in 1998.[75] The conductor's controversial comments to the audience are included on the CD.

Gould's unusual approach to the Brahms concerto was predi-cated on a single set of tempo relationships that he felt would more properly reflect the motivic affinities among thematic groups in the work. His application of the concept entailed a dramatic broadening of the opening theme of the first movement, which had major conse-quences for the timing of the entire movement. Far from being capricious, Gould merely wanted to perform the work in a more holistic manner than was usually the case (or at least less dualistic, as between "masculine" and "feminine" theme groups or solo *versus* orchestral episodes). Evidence of a continuing preoccupation with strict tempo relationships can be found throughout his discography thereafter: two examples are his 1966 recording of Beethoven's "Emperor" Concerto with Leopold Stokowski and his 1981 rerecord-ing of Bach's Goldberg Variations, but there are numerous others.

Coincidentally, since the 1960s several scholars have explored the principle of a continuous background pulse—essentially the Renais-sance *tactus* revisited—permeating the music of Brahms. For instance, David Epstein suggests that while "Brahms left us no writ-ten tract on the matter . . . [m]otive and tempo are inextricably bound in [his] scores." However, "[t]he signals are not always obvi-ous [so they] can easily be missed and the proportions lost."[76] Epstein and others have convincingly shown that tempo relation-ships based on simple mathematical ratios (e.g., 2:1, 3:2, 4:3) are implicit across the themes and sections of large- and small-scale works by Brahms.[77] Two of the compositions Epstein cites as extended examples of this phenomenon are Brahms's First Sym-phony and the D-minor Piano Concerto.

It seems likely that Gould arrived independently at his concept of strict tempo relationships in the piano concerto since most of the

Brahms-related publishing on this subject took place after 1962, and Epstein's only since 1979. Was it because Gould's tempos in the Brahms concerto were so much slower than previous performances of the work, or because it was Gould who proposed them that made it so tempting for Bernstein and others to dismiss them out of hand? As the critic Carl Bauman reminds us, "His sometimes perverse imagination and individuality [what Gould himself referred to as the "quirk quotient"[78]] could be both inspiring and maddening."[79] But the fact that music scholars suggest the existence of implied proportional relationships in Brahms (though not specifically about Gould's 1962 application of the principle) is a convincing argument that Gould's attempt was as well-founded as it was bold, and deserving of greater equanimity than it received from Bernstein and the critics.

Bernstein later compounded his original breach of etiquette by insisting in print that "the first movement alone took about as much time as it should take to play the whole concerto."[80] Though it may have seemed that way to him, the CD tells a different story. At fifty-three and a third minutes, the Gould-Bernstein reading of the Brahms concerto is undeniably slow, but the first movement of the performance lasts just under twenty-six minutes while even Vladimir Horowitz required close to forty-one minutes to speed through all three movements with Bruno Walter and the Concertgebouw Orchestra in 1936, the quickest recording of the work I have found. Between those two extremes lie various other recordings, most in the forty-four to forty-seven-minute range: for example, Serkin-Ormandy-Philadelphia (44:23), Fleisher-Szell-Cleveland (46:07), Solomon-Kubelik-Philharmonia (47:31).

But there are slower performances on disc. Rubinstein made three recordings of the work, two of which fell into the mid-forty minute range; but the third, reportedly his favorite, performed with Mehta and the Israel Philharmonic in 1976, lasts just under fifty minutes and leans decidedly toward Gould's understated approach in its broad lines and attention to inner detail. A 1972 Gilels recording with Jochum and the Berlin Philharmonic, cited repeatedly by record reviewers in *Gramophone* and *Fanfare* when considering newer recordings of the work, takes over fifty-one minutes. But most intriguing of all is a disc by none other than Bernstein, with Krystian Zimerman and the Vienna Philharmonic: it actually takes almost a minute longer than Gould's (54:13) and includes no disavowal by the conductor. Interestingly, it was recorded in 1984, only one year after Bernstein published the disparaging remark quoted in the paragraph immediately above. One wonders what Gould might have said about the performance.

By the above Gould-Brahms digression, I do not mean to suggest that the pianist's slow renditions of *Siegfried Idyll* were also based on inferred tempo relationships in Wagner. The point of both that discussion and the earlier one on Gould's *Götterdämmerung* adaptation was to illustrate his remarkable awareness of musical architecture and to underline the fundamental importance of structural considerations to his interpretations. His approach to music, even operatic music, was intellectual, not emotional, and he always had irrefutable logic behind his interpretive decisions.

In many ways Glenn Gould was a pioneer: breathing new life into Bach's keyboard music decades before the period-instrument movement that brought baroque music into fashion in the late twentieth century; completely bypassing the core, romantic piano literature in favor of more cerebral eighteenth- and twentieth-century material; and gambling on a strictly media-based career (via recordings, radio, television, and film) following his "retirement" from the concert stage in 1964 at age thirty-one. His interpretations of most repertoire were as boldly conceived and executed as his sparkling performances of Bach, though clearly not always as well received. Nevertheless, as with his expansive treatment of the Brahms concerto, other pianists subsequently either took their cue from him in a variety of ways or arrived independently at conceptions remarkably similar to those Gould had already explored.

Supporters of the status quo were quick to criticize him, and, as we saw above, some did so quite harshly. It must be admitted that his reasoning was too far "ahead of the curve" for some audiences, but others were more receptive to, and even laudatory of, his experiments. His recording of Beethoven's "Appassionata" Sonata, for example, was almost universally condemned, and Gould himself later referred to it as "the most perverse in history."[81] Yet Allen Hughes, writing in the *New York Times*, found it "the most extraordinary and, in a way, refreshing item of Beethoveniana to be issued in the 200th anniversary year of the composer's birth."[82]

Although I performed in Gould's ensemble—or perhaps *because* I performed in it—it took me some time to see beyond the minor defects in the individual and ensemble playing on the disc and, truth be told, the slow tempos and certain interpretive details, too. But in the years since its release, I have grown to appreciate it much more despite the fact that I do not agree with Gould in every respect. I see his efforts on that disc as a direct and heartfelt tribute to a composer whose music he had loved and played from the time he was a teenager. He was simply giving musical voice to that love in the manner he felt best served the music itself.

The common elements in his solo and ensemble performances of Wagner are a deep respect for, and a focus on, the music, not on himself. One could argue that Liszt's approach still showcased Liszt, the virtuoso heroically reproducing all the elements of Wagner's orchestral scores with just ten fingers. But by Gould's choice of Wagner's repertoire to transcribe and record, and by the drier, more analytical, and (indeed) slower manner in which he performed and conducted some of it, Gould directs the listener's attention inward toward the craft of Wagner's compositions. In their sacrifice of virtuosic display and ego to the service of the music, these performances represent a seriousness (dare one suggest, a purity?) of purpose that merits reconsideration by the naysayers—even as I changed my mind about the *Siegfried Idyll* recording and Leonard Bernstein apparently revised his thinking about the Brahms concerto.

During his career, Gould was sometimes accused of wanton disregard for composers and pianistic tradition. His recordings of certain Mozart and Beethoven sonatas (e.g., K. 331 and the "Appassionata") have often been cited as blatant examples of his willfulness and lack of respect. As we saw earlier, Gould himself admitted that some of his efforts were less than successful. I can only argue that his Wagner recordings represent a humbler, less combative Gould. Had he lived longer, his plan to embark on a new career as a conductor (strictly in the recording studio, of course) would undoubtedly have had its successes and failures, but, above all, he would have engaged many listeners through his unusual premises and fresh interpretations. Critics might not all have agreed with him, but people would have definitely paid attention and ideally, as Carl Bauman suggested, would have heard the music anew. In the final analysis, isn't that what all musicians hope to achieve?

WORKS CITED

Bauman, Carl. "Wagner: *Siegfried Idyll*; Wagner, arr. Gould: *Meistersinger* Overture; Dawn and Siegfried's Rhine Journey from *Götterdämmerung*; *Siegfried Idyll*." *American Record Guide* 54.5 (1991): 146.

Bazzana, Kevin. *Glenn Gould: The Performer in the Work.* Oxford: Oxford University Press, 1997.

———. *Wondrous Strange: The Life and Art of Glenn Gould.* Toronto: McClelland and Stewart, 2003.

Bernstein, Leonard. "The Truth about a Legend." *Glenn Gould by Himself and his Friends.* Ed. John McGreevy. Toronto: Doubleday Canada Ltd., 1983. 17–22.

Cott, Jonathan, ed. *Conversations with Glenn Gould.* Boston: Little, Brown, 1984.

Epstein, David. "Brahms and the Mechanisms of Motion." *Brahms Studies: Analytical and Historical Perspectives.* Ed. George S. Bozarth. Oxford: Clarendon, 1990. 191–226.

Folkman, Benjamin. "Liner Notes to *Glenn Gould Conducts and Plays Wagner*." Compact disc. Sony SK 46279. Austria, 1990.

Forte, Allen. "The Structural Origin of Exact *Tempi* in the Brahms-Haydn Variations." *The Music Review* 18 (1957): 138–49.

Friedrich, Otto. *Glenn Gould: A Life and Variations.* New York: Random House, 1989.

The Glenn Gould Collection, vol. 1. "Prologue." Videocassette. Sony SHV 48402, 1992.

Glenn Gould Conducts and Plays Wagner. Compact Disc. Sony SK 46279, 1973, 1990.

Glenn Gould Papers. Library and Archives Canada: Music Section. File No. 1979–20, 27, 3.

———. Library and Archives Canada: Music Section. File No. 1979–20, 27, 11.

———. Library and Archives Canada: Music Section. File No. 1979–20, 27, 28.

Glenn Gould Plays Wagner. Columbia Masterworks LP M 32351.

Glenn Gould and Leonard Bernstein. Brahms Piano Concerto No. 1. Compact disc. Sony SK 60675, 1988.

Gould, Glenn. "Interview with Ken Haslam." Originally broadcast on CBC Radio, February 1973. Transcribed in insert to Columbia masterworks LP M32351.

Horowitz, Joseph. *The Post-Classical Predicament: Essays on Music and Society.* Boston: Northeastern University Press, 1995.

Hughes, Allen. "Gould's No-Nonsense Beethoven." *New York Times* June 21, 1970.

Jost, Peter, ed. *Richard Wagner. Sämtliche Werke. Band 18/III: Orchesterwerke. Siegfried Idyll,* WWV 103. Mainz: Schott Musik International, 1995.

Knappertsbusch, Hans, cond. *Symphony No. 4 in E-flat Major, by Anton Bruckner.* Vienna Philharmonic Orchestra. Wagner *Siegfried Idyll.* London LP LL 1250, 1955.

Norrington, Roger. CD booklet to *Roger Norrington: Wagner.* EMI 724355547927. London, 1995.

Ostwald, Peter. *Glenn Gould: The Ecstasy and Tragedy of Genius.* New York: Norton, 1997.

Page, Tim, ed. *The Glenn Gould Reader.* New York: Knopf, 1984.

———. *Tim Page on Music: Views and Reviews.* Portland, OR: Amadeus, 2002.

Roberts, John P. L., ed. *The Art of Glenn Gould: Reflections of a Musical Genius.* Toronto: Malcolm Lester Books, 1999.

Roberts, John P. L, and Ghyslaine Guertin, eds. *Glenn Gould: Selected Letters.* Toronto: Oxford University Press, 1992.

Roger Norrington: Orchestral Works. EMI Compact Disc 7243 5 55479 2 7, 1995.

Schuller, Gunther. *The Compleat Conductor.* New York: Oxford University Press, 1997.

Thirty-two Short Films about Glenn Gould. Videocassette. Columbia Tristar Home Video 74359, 2000.

Wagner, Richard. *On Conducting (über das Dirigiren): A Treatise on Style in the Execution of Classical Music.* London: W. Reeves, 1919.

Wagner, Richard. *Siegfried Idyll,* WWV 103. In *Richard Wigner's Sämtliche Werke,* Band 18, III, orchesterwerke. Mainz: B. Schott's Söne, 1995.

Wagner, Richard. "Über das Dirigiren." In Gesammelte Schriften and Dichtungen, Achter Band. Herausg von Wolfgang Golther. Berlin. Deutches Verlagshaw Bong and Company, 1919.

Whittall, Arnold. "Wagner. *Siegfried Idyll.* Piano Transcriptions (Gould)." *Gramophone: Review of New Classical Recordings* 68 (1991): 1873.

Youngren, William. "Wagner: *Siegfried Idyll. Die Meistersinger:* Prelude. *Götterdämmerung:* Dawn and Siegfried's Rhine Journey. *Siegfried Idyll." Fanfare: The Magazine for Serious Record Collectors* 15.1 (1991): 388–90.

NOTES

1. Cott, 65.
2. Roberts and Guertin, 7.
3. Page, *Glenn Gould Reader,* 76.
4. *Thirty-two Short Films about Glenn Gould.*
5. *Glenn Gould Plays Wagner.*
6. *Glenn Gould Conducts and Plays Wagner.*
7. Roberts, 67.
8. Roberts, 191.
9. Cott, 66.
10. Page, *Glenn Gould Reader,* 37.
11. Ibid., 453.
12. Roberts, 191.
13. Page, *Glenn Gould Reader,* 453.
14. Ibid., 454.
15. Roberts, 67–68.
16. Roberts and Guertin, 137.
17. Cott, 65.
18. Roberts, 16.
19. Friedrich, 17.
20. Roberts, 301.
21. Friedrich, 18.
22. Roberts,16.
23. Roberts and Guertin, 220.
24. Cott, 68.
25. Ibid., 67.
26. Gould, "Interview."
27. Bazzana, *Glen Gould,* 141.
28. Richard Wagner *Siegfried Idyll,* 93–94.
29. Gould, "Interview," 2.
30. Cott, 69.
31. Gould, "Interview," 1–2.
32. Cott, 69.
33. Ibid., 70.
34. Glenn Gould Papers, File number 1979-20, 27, 3: 1, 2. Reproduced with the permission of the Estate of Glenn Gould.
35. Gould, "Interview," 2.
36. Ibid.
37. Friedrich, 253.
38. Glenn Gould Papers, File number 1979-20, 27, 8: 12, 13. Reproduced with the permission of the Estate of Glenn Gould.

39. Glenn Gould Papers, File number 1979-20, 27, 11: 17A. Reproduced with the permission of the Estate of Glenn Gould.
40. Roberts and Guertin, 202.
41. *Knappertsbusch.*
42. Horowitz, 136.
43. Youngren, 388.
44. Whittall.
45. Ibid. 388–90.
46. Bauman, 146.
47. Horowitz, 136.
48. Whittall.
49. Roberts and Guertin, 220.
50. Ibid., 202.
51. Norrington, According to Norrington, the Wagner quote supposedly comes from the composer's essay, *On Conducting.* I can find no such statement in Edward Dannreuther's English translation, though Wagner does mention having conducted his overture to *Tannhäuser* at Dresden in twelve minutes.
52. Youngren, 389–90, elucidates on this point in his review.
53. Ibid. 388.
54. Ostwald, 323.
55. Page, *Tim Page on Music* 71.
56. Schuller, 6, footnote.
57. The cover of the CD booklet to *Glenn Gould Conducts and Plays Wagner* reads: "Glenn Gould Conducts Wagner's Siegfried Idyll; Gould's Conducting Debut and Final Recording."
58. See *Glenn Gould Collection* in which the twenty-four-year-old Gould conducts Maureen Forrester and a Toronto orchestra in a performance of the "Urlicht" movement from Mahler's *Symphony No. 2,* from CBC Television, 1957.
59. Folkman.
60. Youngren, 388.
61. Ibid. 388, 390.
62. Ibid. 388.
63. Horowitz, 136.
64. Bauman, 146.
65. Youngren, 388.
66. Horowitz, 136.
67. Rather than an acoustically "dry" recording studio, Gould chose a "heritage" building in which to record his chamber orchestra. Built in the 1850s in the historic St. Lawrence Market district of Toronto, St. Lawrence Hall served in the nineteenth century as a hub of political

meetings (e.g., the anti-slavery movement, reform of the Canadian federation) and popular entertainment (e.g., Jenny Lind performed there in 1851). The room in which we recorded *Siegfried Idyll* was built of plaster and hardwood.

68. Page, 333. The brief application of reverb in this recording should not be confused with the experiments in "acoustic choreography" Gould undertook earlier while recording solo piano music by Bizet, Sibelius, and Scriabin. On those occasions, he used multi-track audio tape to record several "ranks" of microphones deliberately placed at varying distances from the piano, "fading" or "zooming" between different audio perspectives for the final mix based on structural and other considerations of the music he was playing. Reverb is employed only at the end of the *Siegfried Idyll* recording, which otherwise maintains a very close-in audio perspective, and all five microphones were positioned very near the musicians.

69. Schuller, 17–18.
70. Bauman, 146.
71. Roberts, 194.
72. Wagner, *On Conducting*. The original German is: "In einem gewissen zarten Sinne kann man vom reinen Adagio sagen, dass es nicht langsam genug genommen werden kann." Richard Wagner, "Über das Dirigiren," 285.
73. Gould, "Interview," 1.
74. Horowitz, 138.
75. *Gould and Bernstein*.
76. Epstein, 225, 218, 211 (citations respectively).
77. For example, see Forte, 138–49.
78. Page, 78.
79. Bauman, 146.
80. Bernstein, 18.
81. Cited in Bazzana, *Wondrous Strange* draft copy, part 4, 156.
82. Hughes.

CHAPTER 4

SUBVERTING THE CONVENTIONS OF
NUMBER OPERA FROM WITHIN:
HIERARCHICAL AND ASSOCIATIONAL
USES OF TONALITY IN ACT I OF *DER*
FLIEGENDE HOLLÄNDER

William Marvin

When we go to a symphony orchestra concert, we are regularly presented with program headings such as "Symphony No. 33 in B♭
Major." We know that this means that some, but not all, of the separate movements we will hear are in that key. We are probably also
aware that the music will move to other keys within those B♭ major
movements, but that those other keys are somehow subordinate to
B♭, which will act as the point of departure and return, a conceptual
home base for the movement. My point of departure for this chapter asks similar questions about opera: Can we conceptualize operas
as being in keys? Or more specifically, do eighteenth- and nineteenth-
century operas contain musical analogues to movements in symphonic works?

To map eighteenth- and nineteenth-century procedures onto
each other in such an inquiry would be as inappropriate for opera as
it would be for instrumental music. That there are clear differences
between Mozart's and Wagner's uses of tonality is intuitively obvious to all listeners, as it is that Wagner's own uses of tonality differ
among each of his thirteen complete operas and music dramas.

Here I would like to examine some of the assumptions that underlie the description of tonality and form in *Der fliegende Holländer* (1843). This examination is part of a larger research project in which I am searching for better definitions of tonal and formal syntax in nineteenth-century opera generally.

It is extremely difficult for us to hear *Der fliegende Holländer* with the ears of an 1843 audience. Aside from the obvious problem of pretending we have heard none of the music written in the last 160 years, we are confronted with Wagner's own revisions of this work. Admittedly, they are nowhere near as extensive as his wholesale rewriting of entire scenes in *Tannhäuser*, but they do include several major changes in orchestration, the addition of the "transfiguration" progressions at the end of the overture and the opera itself, and perhaps most significantly, the modern practice of performing the work in a single continuous Act.[1] (However much this might have been his original intention, the work was *never* thus performed during Wagner's own lifetime; the practice originated at Bayreuth in 1901, sanctioned by Cosima.)

These changes all serve to hide Wagner's debt to earlier compositional practice and blur our understanding of changes within his own organizational procedures. Wagner's efforts throughout his life to deny musical influences and to rewrite the history of his own musical development so that everything lead to the *Gesamtkunstwerk* have impacted musical scholarship to the present day.[2] Barry Millington's 1984 biography, cast in traditional "life and works" mode, is representative of this Hegelian view of Wagner's development:

> Whereas most of *Die Feen* was written by a young composer content to exercise his abilities within the conventional number form, the scene and aria was an opportunity for Wagner to stretch himself a little. The latter is a complex in which recitative, arioso, and aria are juxtaposed; it was not the invention of Wagner, of course, but it is a fair indication of the direction of his thoughts that he should find it of value. A few years later he was, in *Der fliegende Holländer*, to extend the principle over a larger canvas, so that in a sense the whole opera is a succession of miniature scenes. The final stage of the process was to be the through-composed music drama.[3]

Millington is correct to recognize that Wagner's compositional procedures exhibit features that undermine traditional number-form organization. It is my belief, however, that Wagner worked with discrete set pieces as building blocks in *Der fliegende Holländer* and also to a certain extent throughout his career, and that the formal innovations in *Holländer* and later works merely disguise traditional forms, rather than replacing them. In this chapter, I will attempt to show which aspects of traditional operatic procedure Wagner inherited from classical and early romantic works in his own performance repertoire, and I will enumerate specific techniques he used to extend and undermine the perception of traditional formal units in *Der fliegende Holländer*.

Holländer is the last "number opera" that Wagner composed. The conventions of number opera are most easily understood by looking at an example from Mozart. In *Die Zauberflöte* (1791), Mozart has clearly labeled each number as a self-contained unit with its own key or tonality (Table 4.1). In this particular work, the numbers are generally separated from each other by spoken dialogue; in other number operas by Mozart, *secco recitative* appears between the discrete numbers. An easy way to think of numbers is to consider typical recital or highlights CDs: the excerpts chosen on such recordings, whether overtures, arias, duets, choruses, or others, are generally labeled by the composer as numbers. Numbers, it would seem, are clearly analogous to movements within instrumental works.

This listing exemplifies several of the conventions of a typical eighteenth-century number opera. First, and almost trivially, a number opera is constructed of several discretely labeled numbers, each of which begins and ends in its own key. Second, we note that the key of the overture is the same as the key of the final number. This holds true in many number operas, especially those by German composers, but we should not make too much of this fact. While we are expected to perceive a single dramatic trajectory from beginning to end of the opera, we should not assume an analogous tonal unity across all of the numbers. Again, a comparison to instrumental music is helpful: while the first and last movements of most symphonies and sonatas are in the same key, we do not necessarily expect the intervening movements to share this tonality, nor that we should hear a linear connection through all of the movements. Third, we observe the odd labeling of No. 9a. This number is reproduced in its entirety as Figure 4.1. The "number" is labeled by

Table 4.1: Numbers in W.A. Mozart's *Die Zauberflöte*

Overture—E♭ major

Act I

No. 1 Introduction	C minor ➤ C major
No. 2 Arie [Papageno]	G major
No. 3 Arie [Tamino]	E♭ major
No. 4 Arie [Königen der Nacht]	B♭ major
No. 5 Quintett	B♭ major
No. 6 Terzett	G major
No. 7 Duett [Pamino und Papageno]	E♭ major
No. 8 Finale	C major

Act II

No. 9 Marsch der Priester	F major
No. 9a Der dreimalige Accord	B♭ major
No. 10 Arie mit Chor [Sarastro]	F major
No. 11 Duett [Zwei Priester]	C major
No. 12 Quintett	G major
No. 13 Arie [Monastatos]	C major
No. 14 Arie [Königen der Nacht]	D minor
No. 15 Arie [Sarastro]	E major
No. 16 Terzett	A major
No. 17 Arie [Pamina]	G minor
No. 18 Chor	D major
No. 19 Terzett	B♭ major
No. 20 Arie [Papageno]	F major
No. 21 Finale	E♭ major

Mozart because the orchestra must be cued, but it is not an autonomous piece, as indicated by the idiosyncratic labeling.

Wagner knew the mature operas of Mozart very well by the time he came to compose his *Der fliegende Holländer*. Table 4.2 lists all of the operas that we know Wagner rehearsed or conducted in the 1830s.[4] While I have not been able to examine all of these, those scores that I have looked at conform to the conventions of number opera just described. In this sense, the conventions of number opera were an assumed point of departure for Wagner in 1843.

In the decades between Mozart's death and Wagner's early operas, the conventions of number opera were altered by librettists and composers. I would like to highlight three important ways in which our perception of numbers changes in early nineteenth-century works. While all of these have antecedents in Mozart's own

Figure 4.1: "Der Dreimalige Accord" from Mozart's *Die Zauberflöte*

works, they become more prominent in the early nineteenth century. First, the gradual elimination of *secco* recitative in favor of full orchestral accompaniment blurs the boundaries between numbers: often a number is labeled in the score as beginning with accompanied recitative, but our perception of a single unified key does not encompass this introductory section. A clear example of this is Leonore's Act I aria from Beethoven's *Fidelio* (1805/1814): the recitative "Abscheulicher! Wo eilst du hin?" wanders through several keys, but the aria itself, starting at "Komm Hoffnung, lass den letzten Stern," is tonally closed within the key of E major; that is, it begins *and* ends in that key. Second, the large-scale Finales to each Act are almost always labeled as single numbers, in spite of the obvious scene changes and "additive" or "accumulative" notion of such sections. Mozart himself was famous for this innovation, and a closer examination of the Act II Finale from *Die Zauberflöte* demonstrates the procedure. Figure 4.2 shows that the music encompasses numerous scene changes and changes of keys, and that embedded within the Finale are several discrete pieces that are certainly perceived as separate numbers, including the famous flute

Table 4.2: Stage works rehearsed or conducted by Wagner, 1833–39 (list adapted from Thomas Grey)

Adam	*La Fidèle Berger*
	Le Postillon de Lonjumeau
Auber	*Le Maçon*
	La Muette de Portici
	Fra Diavolo
	Lestocq
	Gustave III, ou Le Bal masqué (seen, not performed)
	Le Philtre (seen, not performed)
Beethoven	*Fidelio*
Bellini	*La straniera*
	I Capuleti e I Montrecchi
	Norma
	I Puritani
Boieldieu	*Jean de Paris*
	La Dame blance
Cherubini	*Les Deux Journées*
Dorn	*Der Schöffe von Paris*
Gläser	*Des Adlers Horst*
Halévy	*La Juive*
Hérold	*Zampa*
Marschner	*Der Vampyr*
	Hans Heiling
	Der Templer und die Jüden
Méhul	*Joseph*
Meyerbeer	*Robert le diable*
Mozart	*Don Giovanni*
	Die Entführung aus dem Serail
	Le nozze di Figaro
	Die Zauberflöte
Paër	*Camilla*
Paisello	*La molinara*
Rossini	*Tancredi*
	Otello
	Il barbiere di Siviglia
Spohr	*Jessonda*
Spontini	*Fernando Cortez* (seen, not performed)
Weber	*Der Freischütz*
	Oberon
	Euryanthe
	Preciosa
Weigl	*Die Schweizerfamilie*
Winter	*Das unterbrochene Opferfest*

m. 1	m. 45	m. 190
Scene 26	Scene 27	Scene 28
3 youthful spirits	Pamina's entrance; suicide attempt and renewed hope	Guardian's chorale; Tamino and Pamina reunited; trials; flute melody; triumphal chorus
E^b major	C minor/E^b major	C minor/major

m. 413	m. 745
Scene 29	Scene 30
Papageno's suicide attempt; Papageno and Papagena reunited and "Pa, pa, pa" duet	Queen of the Night attacks temple; Sarastro's victory; Triumphal chorus
G major	C minor/E^b major

Figure 4.2: *Die Zauberflöte* No. 21 Finale

melody accompanying Tamino and Pamina's trial and the well-known duet, "Pa, Pa, Pa, Pa, Pa." Nevertheless, Mozart's labeling of the Finale as a single number suggests that the additive procedure is to be understood as composing out a progression in a single tonality, in this case E^b major.

This additive procedure in operatic finales found its way into other operatic numbers in the nineteenth century, as seen in works by Carl Maria von Weber and also in many works within the French grand opera tradition. Italian opera also participates in this type of organization: in the opening scene of *Il barbiere di Siviglia* (1816), Count Almaviva's aria is framed by identical music for the chorus and Fiorello, thus creating a structure in which the tonally closed number is nested within a larger tonally closed scene. Several scholars, including Carl Dahlhaus and Barry Millington, see these procedures collectively as a move away from "number opera" and toward something they refer to as "scene opera." Characteristic of this conception is a description of each Act as a series of interconnected groups of numbers.[5]

Wagner's appropriation of this legacy is most obvious in the first four operas: *Die Feen, Das Liebesverbot, Rienzi*, and *Der fliegende Holländer*. All of these works include discretely labeled numbers in the score, and these numbers are generally tonally closed; that is, they begin and end in the same key and should be heard as clearly defined tonal units within their respective keys. In addition, the expansions of number opera conventions described above are all present in these works: accompanied recitatives, additive finales, and the concatenation of subnumbers into tonally unified scenes. A close examination of Act I of *Der fliegende Holländer* will now reveal Wagner's exploitation of all of these features, plus some new techniques that further weaken our perception of the numbers while Wagner continues to work within the conventions.

Wagner labels three numbers within this Act: (1) Introduction; (2) Aria; and (3) Scene, Duet, and Chorus. An outline of the formal organization of the Act is presented in Table 4.3.[6] Yet without seeing these labels in the score, it is unlikely that many listeners would aurally perceive these three numbers as the building blocks of the Act. Wagner uses three means to weaken our perception of the labeled numbers, one previously mentioned and two new means. First, he employs additive procedures within each number; second, linking cadences are introduced to hide the seams between numbers; and third, associative tonal relations across numbers connect units that are tonally separated from each other. I will examine Wagner's use of each of these procedures in turn.

Wagner begins the opera in the midst of a violent storm: Daland's ship has just cast anchor, and the sailors are making the ship secure until the storm blows over. Wagner drops us into this scene by beginning on the dominant chord (F) of his tonic key (B♭ major). We become certain of the key through the choral entrance of the sailors, who provide a clear thematic statement that secures and stabilizes B♭ (15/1/1–15/2/2).[7]

A brief conversation between Daland and the Steersman ensues, after which the Steersman sings his opening aria. This aria is the centerpiece of the first number, and retrospectively we understand the entire passage to consist of three parts, the first two of which are introductory: (1) Storm/Chorus (B♭ major), (2) Conversational Interpolation (several keys), ultimately returning to (3) Aria (B♭ major). The key of the aria is not in doubt; the first strophe begins and ends in that key, and our expectations have been established for a repeated strophic song. However, Wagner pulls the rug out from under us by having the steersman fall asleep, at which point the key dissolves in a transitional passage as the Dutchman's phantom ship comes into view. I will return to this passage later in the chapter.

At this point, the Dutchman sings his lengthy recitative and aria, the second labeled number in the score. This aria is also additive in structure: after a tonally uncertain recitative, the aria proper consists

Table 4.3: Summary of tonality in numbers from Act I of *Der fliegende Höllander*

Act I

1. Introduction: B$^\flat$ major
   - Storm: V of B$^\flat$
   - Chorus: B$^\flat$ established
     - "Hallojo!"
   - Conversation: several keys
     - Acts as introduction to Steersman's Aria
   - Aria (25/4/3)   B$^\flat$ major, second verse dissolves tonally
     - "Mit Gewitter und Sturm aus fernem Meer"

2. Aria: C minor
   - Recitative (29/1/1)   uncertain tonality
     - "Die frist ist um"
   - A section (32/1/1)   closed in C minor
     - "Wie oft in Meeres tiefsten Schlund"
   - B section (35/5/5)   closed in A$^\flat$ minor (major)
     - "Dich frage ich"
   - Retransition   V of C minor (false A$^\flat$ major cadence)
   - C section (38/1/1)   C minor (major)
     - "Nur eine Hoffnung soll mir Bleiben"
   - Coda   E (ghost ship); orchestra closes in C minor

3. Scene, Duet, and Chorus: G minor ⟶ B$^\flat$ major
   - Scene   uncertain tonality, no key signature
   - Duet   G minor ⟶ G major
     - A section (47/3/5)   G minor ⟶ G major
       - "Durch Sturm un bösen Wind verschlagen"
     - B section (58/4/1)   E$^\flat$ major (VI of G minor)
       - "Wohl, Fremdling, hab' ich eine schöne Tochter"
     - Retransition   V of G minor
     - C section (62/3/1)   G minor ⟶ G major
       - "Wenn aus der Qualen Schreckgewalten"
     - Linking cadence   B$^\flat$ major (return to associative key)
       - Conversational introduction to Chorus
   - Chorus (73/2/5)   B$^\flat$ major
     - "Mit Gewitter und Sturm aus fernem Meer"

of three clear sections, as outlined in the chart. Sections A and C are tonally closed in C minor, while Section B is closed in the rather remote key of A♭ minor. A more conventional model would have encompassed a thematic return to accompany the tonal return at this point—in other words, ABA instead of ABC. Here again, Wagner's introduction of new thematic material where a recapitulation is expected further blurs our perception of traditional number procedures. The aria ends with a ghostly echo of the cadence from Section C, this time in E major, but this is "corrected" by an orchestral cadence in C minor which confirms the unity of key for the entire aria; these are shown in Figure 4.3.[8]

The additive structure of the third number is even more explicit than that of the first two and is given away by Wagner's label: scene, duet, and chorus. In fact, the idea of additive structure is present at nested hierarchical levels within this number and arguably across the entire Act. The "scene" is mainly composed of conversational recitative and arioso passages; Wagner does not even provide a key signature here, indicating the transitional, non-closed nature of this passage. The duet between Daland and the Dutchman begins in G minor and consists of three sections: a closed passage that moves from G minor to G major, a quick transition to E♭ major, and then a return to G minor with a close in G major; the three-part structure here is thus analogous to the preceding Dutchman's monologue. The concluding chorus in B♭ major, the relative key of G minor, is perceived as a separate number, especially given that it recapitulates the steersman's song and key and thus effectively frames the entire Act in B♭ major.

The connection between the duet and chorus provides a clear example of my second category of techniques by which Wagner blurs the lines between individual numbers. As we listen to this passage, the rhetoric implies a strong expectation of closure: our knowledge of operatic conventions tells us that the duet is coming to an end, and we will have an opportunity to applaud wildly. Instead, Wagner deceives us with a different type of ending. Conventional music theory refers to the progression shown in Figure 4.4 as a deceptive cadence for obvious reasons: we expect one thing, but the composer provides another. However, Alfred Lorenz, author of the most thorough analysis of musical form in Wagner's mature music dramas, refers to this as a linking cadence because of its dramatic function of beginning something entirely new.[9] In classical theory, the deceptive

Figure 4.3: Conclusion of Dutchman's aria

cadence is eventually replaced with the expected authentic cadence, and we hear the number or movement ending conventionally. With the linking cadence, the duet texture has disappeared, never to be recovered: we are suddenly in the chorus, and our desire for closure in the duet has been denied.

Figure 4.4: Linking cadence between Duet and Chorus

If we search for classical models of this procedure, we can find them readily in the music of Wagner's hero, Beethoven. The third movement of Beethoven's Fifth Symphony never comes to an end, and thus we as audience members are denied the opportunity to fidget and cough. Instead, Beethoven gives us a linking cadence and a transitional passage that takes us directly to the triumphant fourth movement. The same procedure can be found at the conclusion of the third movement and opening of the "Storm" movement in Beethoven's Sixth Symphony. Admittedly, Wagner's procedure is more radical in that his music continues in a different key, whereas in both symphonies, Beethoven keeps the same tonic and merely changes mode.

My third and final category of form-blurring elements in Wagner's opera is his use of associative tonality, a term coined by Robert Bailey in 1969, although the concept is described frequently in scholarly literature throughout the twentieth century.[10] The concept can be illustrated through reference to Figure 4.5, showing three passages from Act I. As we can see, all of these passages are in the same key, specifically B♭ major. They occur at wide temporal intervals across the Act, but our ear associates them both because of

Figure 4.5: Associative tonal relations: B♭ major and the Norwegians
A. The opening of Act I
B. The Steuermann's *Lied*
C. Choral reprise of the Steuermann's *Lied*

the key and because Wagner has associated them specifically with the Norwegian sailors. Throughout the opera, this key is reserved for the Norwegians: the Dutchman and his phantom crew do not live in this tonal world. However, returning to my earlier statement that the Act is framed by B♭ major, it is important to note that B♭ is *not* a hierarchical tonic that controls the entire span. Associative tonal relations are of a different order than the tonal trajectories we expect within a number. They are much more flexible than the hierarchical, chord-by-chord connections we hear within an aria, and they allow the composer to create a web of nonhierarchical relationships across the entire opera. While the entire Act is framed by B♭ major, and the returning themes and motives do provide a sense of unity from beginning to end, the labeled numbers still function as the self-contained tonal units in this opera, similar to movements in a classical instrumental work.

The Dutchman's theme is frequently associated with B minor, a key quite distant from B♭ major, sharing only two out of seven notes. The second verse of the steersman's song shows how the two keys are used associatively and how Wagner undermines our perception of closure within operatic numbers. Figure 4.6 shows how the steersman's B♭ major suddenly gives way to the Dutchman's theme in the key of B minor. The phantom ship drops anchor on F (B♭'s dominant), in effect crashing into Norwegian tonal space. This event half awakens the steersman, but as he returns to sleep, B minor prevails.

Rather than enumerating and describing all of the formal units in Acts II and III of the opera, I will highlight procedures found in one central passage from Act II: Senta's ballad (excerpted from No. 4). Wagner's fourth labeled number is another example of accumulative construction: the number is labeled "Song, Scene, Ballad, and Chorus."[11] The principles of additive construction should be clear by this point; what may be surprising is the apparent tonal incoherence of the number as a whole, with the abrupt move from A major for the spinning chorus ("Song") and "Scene," to the remote key of G minor for Senta's ballad. The solution lies in textual considerations: Senta's ballad originally appeared in A minor and was transposed down to suit the original singer, Wilhemine Schröder-Devrient. Isolde Vetter's edition of the opera, presented as volume 4/1 and 2 in *Richard Wagner. Sämtliche Werke*, restores the original tonality for the ballad, and thus the overall tonal unity of A minor/A major for the entire number becomes apparent. I will refer to the A minor version of the ballad throughout the following discussion.

The ballad itself is presented in three strophes. The first two are very similar to each other, and after a move from A minor to the relative major, the music cadences in A minor. The third verse begins

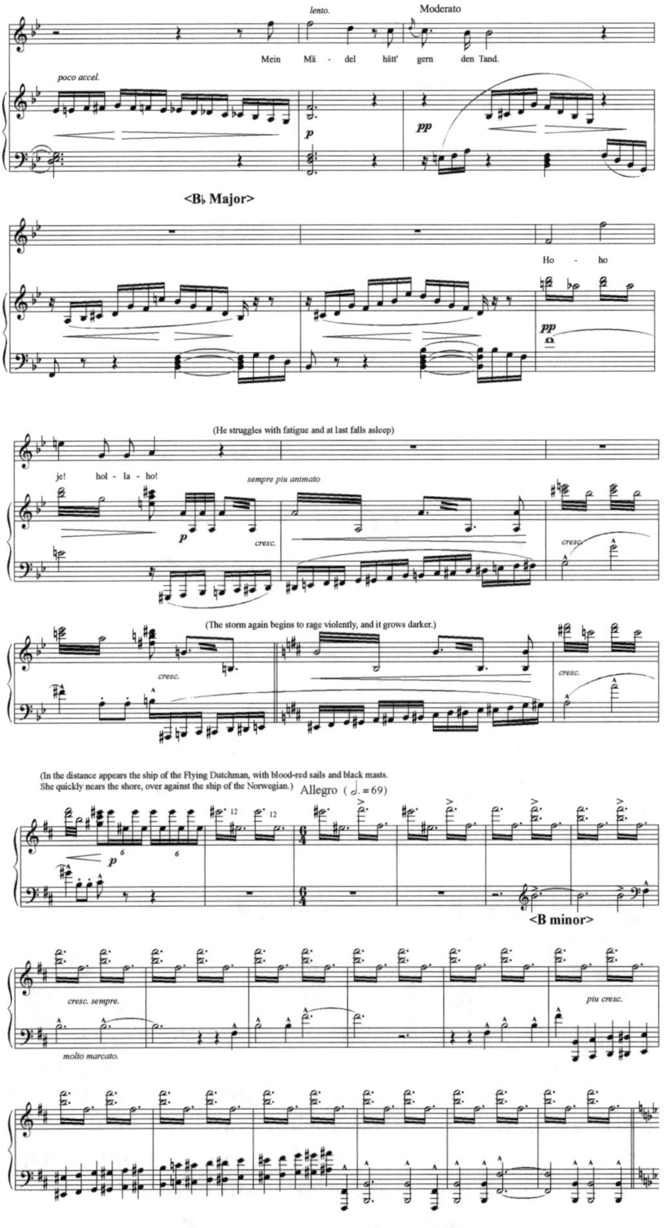

Figure 4.6: Associative conflict between B♭ major and B minor

cont.

Figure 4.6 (continued)

in a similar fashion, but here, Senta refuses to allow the music its "correct" resolution to the tonic chord, and the music stays in C major until the end, marked by a linking cadence (109/1/1).[12]

Wagner's original key scheme is more coherent than the transposed version, not only in the local context of the scene, but also within the global network of associative tonal relationships established in Act I.

If we hear Senta's ballad in G minor/B♭ major, the music is associated incoherently with the keys of Daland, the Norwegians, and Erik. The original key scheme allows strong modulatory moves from A minor to B minor (lines 2 and 4 of each strophe), and later to C major (the second half of each strophe, confirmed in the redemptive coda to the third strophe). B minor is associated throughout Act I with the Dutchman's theme, and C minor/C major is the key of the Dutchman's aria in Act I. In this way, Senta's modulation from A minor to C major represents an escape from the key of the spinning chorus into the Dutchman's key, confirming Senta's role as the Dutchman's redeemer. A further association can be made with Senta's recall of the redemptive cadence during her duet with Erik (134/3/5–135/2/2)—again, in C major.

Since my essay has stressed key relationships across large temporal spans, it seems appropriate to consider the question of perfect pitch, or more accurately, absolute pitch memory. Obviously, readers with absolute pitch memory will be able to make such aural connections quite easily. Does this invalidate these connections for the rest of us? I believe not. First, Wagner provides motivic, orchestrational, and dramatic connections to help us hear the association and return of specific keys. Second, we know that Wagner himself did not have absolute pitch memory, yet it seems clear that he reserves certain keys for specific dramatic purposes across long spans of music—as far as three nights from each other later in his career. Finally, our culture's descriptions of "perfect pitch" are excessively mystical; perfect pitch is nothing more than very well developed memory for sounds that are defined as physical constants. That is, it is a skill that can be learned.[13]

Admittedly, Wagner's use of associative tonality as an organizing principle is inconsistent within this opera, as he does bring some of these themes back in keys other than those I have highlighted; he would refine his use of this technique with each succeeding music drama.[14] Yet even in this early work, by creating aural connections between individual arias, duets, choruses, and connective passages across Acts, Wagner's use of the techniques outlined here calls into question those conventional building blocks of opera, the numbers. Even in his late music dramas, Wagner never completely abandoned the rhetoric of traditional number organization; nevertheless, the process of undermining numbers as structural building blocks is already quite well developed in early works like *Der fliegende Holländer*.

WORKS CITED

Bribitzer-Stull, Matthew. "The A$^\flat$–C–E Complex: The Origin and Function of Chromatic Major Third Collections in Nineteenth-Century Music." *Music Theory Spectrum* 28.2 (2006): 167–90.

Deathridge, John, and Carl Dahlhaus. *The New Grove Wagner.* New York: W. W. Norton, 1984.

Grey, Thomas, ed. *Richard Wagner: Der fliegende Holländer.* Cambridge Opera Handbooks. New York: Cambridge University Press, 2000.

Lorenz, Alfred. *Das Geheimnis der Form bei Richard Wagner, Band I: Der musikalische Aufbau des Bühnenfestspieles Der Ring des Nibelungen.* Reprint ed. Tutzing: H. Schneider, 1966.

Marvin, Elizabeth West, and Alexander R. Brinkman. "The Effect of Key Color and Timbre on Absolute Pitch Recognition in Musical Contexts." *Music Perception* 18.2 (2000): 111–37.

Marvin, William Michael. *Tonality in Selected Set-Pieces from Richard Wagner's* Die Meistersinger von Nürnberg: *A Schenkerian Approach.* Diss., University of Rochester, 2001.

McClatchie, Stephen. *Analyzing Wagner's Operas: Alfred Lorenz and German Nationalist Ideology.* Rochester: University of Rochester Press, 1998.

McCreless, Patrick. *Wagner's Siegfried: Its Drama, History and Music.* Ann Arbor, MI: UMI Research Press, 1982.

Millington, Barry. *Wagner.* Princeton: Princeton University Press, 1992.

———, ed. *The Wagner Compendium: A Guide to Wagner's Life and Music.* New York: Schirmer Books, 1992.

Vetter, Isolde, ed. *Richard Wagner. Sämtliche Werke. Band 4/1-IV: Der fliegende Holländer.* Mainz: B. Schott's Söhne, 1983.

Wagner, Richard. *The Flying Dutchman* (Der fliegende Holländer). Piano–Vocal score. New York: G. Schirmer, 1899.

NOTES

1. For a summary of the various stages of composition in *Der fliegende Holländer*, including all of Wagner's revisions, see Grey, 17–24. Otto Klemperer's 1968 EMI recording presents the earlier three-act version of the opera, without transfiguration cadences, albeit incorporating some aspects of the revised orchestration.

2. See Gottfried Wagner's comments to this effect in Chapter 1 of this book.

3. Millington, *Wagner*, 142. For a similar argument, including a complete listing and description of numbers in *Der fliegende Holländer*, see Grey, 36–64. Grey's formal outline of the opera's numbers is broadly similar to mine, although his descriptions emphasize thematic correspondence and downplay the role of tonal organization within scenes and numbers.

4. Table 4.2 is reformatted from Thomas Grey's chart in Millington, *Wagner Compendium*, 69–70.

5. Deathridge and Dahlhaus, 131–32; Millington, *Wagner*, 162.

6. My numbering follows that of both editions published in Vetter. Many other editions, including the commonly available Schirmer piano/vocal score, label the numbers differently and thus falsify Wagner's conception.

7. Throughout this chapter, all passages from the operas of Wagner are indicated by references to the widely available Schirmer piano/vocal score, in the format page/system/measure within system.

8. The overall structure of the aria can be understood in terms of major third relations on either side of C. For extended discussion of theoretical problems surrounding such tonal procedures, see Bribitzer-Stull, 167–90.

9. "Es wäre aber doch falsch, diese Stellen als 'Trugschlüsse' zu bezeichnen. Denn das Wesen eines Trugschlusses ist eine unerwartete Ausweichung am Ende einer Kadenz, welche aber dann zur Wiederholung der Kadenz und Berichtigung des Schlusses führt oder wenigstens anreizt. Hier aber hat die Kadenz ihre gliedernde Kraft vollkommen ausgewirkt und es tritt (nur trugschlussartig) im gleichzeitigen Einsatz der Dissonanz etwas neues ein. Diese Art wird so zur Manier, daß des Gesangtones wegbleiben kann, ohne den Character dieser Verbindung etwas zu ändern"(Lorenz, 67). This text by Lorenz is translated in McClatchie, 103: "It would, however, be incorrect to label such places as 'deceptive cadences' [*Trugschlüsse*], for the essence of a deceptive cadence lies in the fact that it leads to (or at least indicates) a *repetition* of that cadence and the correction of the close. In this instance, however, the articulating power of the cadence takes full effect, and something *new* (merely *like* a deceptive cadence), enters simultaneously with the dissonance. This type becomes the rule to such an extent that often the melodic close of the vocal part can be omitted without altering the character of this compound in the least" (original italics).

10. See McCreless, 88–89 for a clear summary of Bailey's theories.

11. The Schirmer piano/vocal score divides Wagner's number in two: No. 6 and No. 7, as labeled there.

12. The implications of accumulative musical procedures and of composi-
    tions that begin and end in different keys present significant problems
    for the theory of tonality. For a discussion of some of these issues as
    they relate to Wagner's later music, see William Marvin, 137–94.
13. The published research on absolute pitch is vast and inconclusive. For
    an extensive bibliography, see the citations in Marvin and Brinkman,
    111–37.
14. The most troubling aspect of the analysis here involves the "Steuer-
    mann!" chorus of act III in C major; according to a more consistent
    application of associative tonal relations, this chorus should appear in
    the key of B♭ major. The ensuing quodlibet between the Norwegians
    and the Dutchman's ghost crew would then involve a tonal battle
    between B♭ major and B minor.

CHAPTER 5

NAMING WAGNER'S THEMES

Matthew Bribitzer-Stull

What's in a name? That which we call a rose
by any other name would smell as sweet.
—William Shakespeare

Naming Wagner's themes is not currently in vogue. In fact, the entire practice has been on a steady downhill slide ever since the heady days of Hans von Wolzogen's *Thematischer Leitfaden durch die Musik zu Richard Wagners Festspiel Der Ring des Nibelungen* (*Thematic Guide to the Music of Richard Wagner's* The Ring of the Nibelung [1867]), the first thematic catalogue for Wagner's epic *Ring* cycle. While audiences long to learn of the associative meanings borne by Wagner's musical utterances, scholars have often condemned theme naming as a misleading exercise in futility. Not only does the practice present an oversimplified translation of music into one person's linguistic summary of meaning, but it denies the great transformative power of Wagner's music, the thematic developments that are the hallmark of his mature style.

Opponents of theme names have presented compelling arguments. Carolyn Abbate and Roger Parker, for instance, criticize Ernest Newman and Deryck Cooke's preoccupation with arguing one theme name ("Love") over another ("Flight") for the musical figure presented in Figure 5.1. According to Abbate and Parker, Cooke "drew the wrong moral from the story": the "Love" versus "Flight" question should have served as a warning that associative themes, even in *Der Ring*, do not exhibit lexical precision as their many names might suggest. Rather than solving the problem, Cooke merely "rewrote the dictionary."[1]

Millington concurs with this problematized view of theme names:

> Generations of commentators have contributed to this confused state of affairs by their well-meaning motif-naming guides. As soon as one gives a leitmotif the title "resignation," "futility," or "ambition," one is circumscribing the composer's emotional range. It is dangerous to subject leitmotifs to these limitations, even if some of the labels are appropriate, because the dramatic conditions that call forth a motif are rarely uncomplicated; they are subtle complexes of psychological impulses, and an identical psychological situation will never occur. The gaining of knowledge and experience prevents any precise repetition.[2]

Millington's argument is well taken: naming themes boils down a complex musical entity (or process, really) into its lowest common denominator. While theme names in all the guides are usually accompanied by a melodic musical example and a brief plot synopsis, they often ignore the finer points of harmony, musical context, and thematic development. Figure 5.2, a case in point, is from Newman's *The Wagner Operas*.[3]

In point of fact, Wagner himself critiqued his protégé Wolzogen for limiting his analyses to motif naming:

> Upon the new form of musical construction as applied to the Drama I have expressed myself sufficiently in earlier articles and essays, yet sufficiently merely in the sense that I imagined I had plainly pointed out the road on which a true, and alike a useful judgment of the musical forms now won from Drama by my own artistic labours might be attained by others. To the best of my knowledge, that road has not been trodden yet, and I can remember nothing but the studies of one of my younger friends [Wolzogen] who has viewed the

Figure 5.1: "Love" or "Flight?" Rg/64/1/2–1/3

Figure 5.2: Stereotypical *Leitmotiv* guide excerpt
Declaring himself rested now he starts up and goes to the door, but at a word from
her he halts; ill fate, he warns her, pursues him wherever he goes, and he would not
bring unhappiness on her and her house by staying. He raises the latch, but at an
impulsive cry from her of "Abide thou here! No ill fate canst thou bring where ill fate
has made its home!" he looks searchingly into her face, and, reading what he does
there as she lowers her eyes confusedly and sadly, he returns to her. The sorrow-laden
motive of the Volsungs' Woe:

wells up in the orchestra, followed by that of Sieglinde's Pity (No. 51) and that of
Siegmund (No. 50). "'Woeful,'" he says, is my own name for myself; Hunding here I
will await." He leans against the hearth, looking intently at her with calm sympathy.
She turns her gaze on him again, and during the long silence, during which the
orchestra muses softly on the motives associated with the pair, they look into each
other's eyes with an expression of deepest emotion.

characteristics of what he calls my "Leitmotive" rather in the light of
their dramatic significance, than in that of their bearing on musical
construction.[4]

Wagner's argument against Wolzogen's guide has implications central to our question at hand. Namely, theme naming and theme
guides create a misconceived identity in which the dramatic association of a theme supplants its musical structure. As is often the case,
it is the analyst's, and not the composer's, thoughts that are absorbed by popular culture (not unlike the staying power of editor-
added names to non-programmatic instrumental works [e.g.,
"Lebensstürme" for Schubert's four-hand piano allegro Op. 144]).
Wolzogen's notion of the *leitmotiv* became the word's popular definition and, in turn, spawned wrong-headed criticisms of Wagner's thematic technique, many of which take the theme names at face value
and generalize Wagner's associative themes as one-dimensional, static
entities.[5] Such characterizations include Debussy and Stravinsky's
joking references to "calling cards," Adorno's socio-philosophical
exegesis describing the themes as mnemonic aides for a musically
unenlightened and forgetful bourgeois audience, and Carolyn
Abbate's recent description of Wagner's themes as "music's most
familiar and least interesting narrative competence."[6]

Given its shortcomings, we might question why the practice of theme naming has persisted. Is it possible that naming themes has its advantages? Dahlhaus writes:

> The practice of giving Wagnerian leitmotive names which fix an identity to them once and for all is as questionable as it is unavoidable: questionable, because the translation of musical expression into precise verbal terms is never satisfactory; unavoidable, because the idea of wordless, instinctive understanding of musical motives, without the need for mediation through language, is an illusion. The name that half-misses the object altogether is nevertheless the only way to get at it. But in order to have a clear view of the ramificatory meanings a motive can have, one must start with a basic idea and gradually differentiate it; the infinite wealth of instinctive understanding at which Wagner aimed does not come into existence at the first impact of immediacy, but—if at all—at the second stage, when immediacy has combined with reflection.[7]

To be fair, we must admit that for Wolzogen, his linguistic tags reflected the inner essence, idea, or representation of the music, not the object itself.[8] And even Wagner provided theme names in his sketches on rare occasion. His name for the theme appearing in Act III of *Die Walküre* and at the end of *Götterdämmerung* is simple and logical: "Glorification of Brünnhilde," a name that relates to the dramatic situation at the theme's first statement.[9]

While theme labeling as an end unto itself merits little praise, should theme names be abandoned summarily to avoid oversimplifying the musical-dramatic constructs to which they refer?[10] The names' implications that characters, objects, emotions, and events are *represented* by associative themes is problematic, but this is neither what Wagner intended, nor a necessary consequence of using theme names.[11] The obstacle, however, remains; many of the popular theme names identify objects or characters while the themes themselves embody drama and emotion. Some approaches to Wagner's music have attempted an uneasy compromise between names and no names: the use of numbers to identify each theme. Such practice, adopted by the English National Opera Guides (among others), actually suggests that we fine-tune our original question. We must ask ourselves not only "Must themes be named?" but also "Must themes be labeled at all?" Despite Shakespeare's quote and the evidence presented at the opening of this paper, a strong case can be made in which the merits of theme names outweigh their shortcomings. To support such a case, we must first consider a world without thematic labels at all. Rejecting this, we must then evaluate the strengths and weaknesses of name labels as compared to number labels.

To begin, we are forced to accept that human beings wish to discuss Wagner's themes, which in turn necessitates a method for referring to these themes. If we are to avoid labels altogether, then the only method for referring to themes that bears a hope of intelligibility is to reproduce the music of these themes, either by notation or sound. This, however, presents us with numerous problems. First, musical notation and musical sound are unwieldy or downright impossible in the context of spoken and written communication. Moreover, every variation of a given theme would have to be represented with a separate example, a practical impossibility. Second, such methods of representation still cannot make claims to absolutism since neither the score nor a single performance can actually capture the entirety of a musical thought.[12] In this regard, musical references suffer from the same criticisms applied to labels. Finally, musical representation, like names, admits to a measure of subjectivity; each example must have a beginning and an end, but these thematic boundary points are far from clear-cut. If thematic boundaries were explicit, we could expect most analysts to agree on them. Actually, the opposite is true. Table 5.1 provides a chart of the length of a theme that accompanies the appearance of the giants during the first scene of *Das Rheingold*, as cited by a variety of authors.[13] While all begin at Rg/68/1/1, clearly the endpoint (and the theme label) is debatable.[14] This is by no means an isolated example; many themes from Wagner's works exhibit open-ended boundaries often in service of immediate thematic development or other Wagnerian music-drama constructs like endless melody, musical prose, and the art of transition.

Attempting discourse about Wagner's music without using thematic labels of some kind is not only impractical; it is no more objective than the alternative. Assuming an evaluative stance on Wagner's themes is simply part and parcel of speaking about them, and attempts at denying this in the spirit of objectivity are clearly hollow. This is not to say that musical examples are useless; without them much of our communicative ability is lost. Rather, musical examples,

Table 5.1: Comparative lengths of the theme associated with the entrance of the giants

Author	Theme name	Length
Aldritch	GIANTS	3 bars
Darcy	GIANTS	7 bars
Donington	BRUTE STRENGTH and BRUTAL ASPECT OF PARENTAL AUTHORITY	3 bars (repeated) (bars 7–10)
Gauldin	GIANTS	1 bar
Holman	GIANTS	3 bars
Hutcheson	GIANTS	1 bar
Kobbé	GIANTS	3 bars
Lavignac	GIANTS	3 bars
Newman	No. 16	3 bars
Patterson	GIANTS	2 bars
Spencer, et al.	FASOLT & FAFNER	3 bars
Wolzogen	GIANTS	3 bars
Windsperger	GIANTS	8 bars

be they sound or score, best serve the purposes of discourse when combined with theme labels rather than when they replace them.

Admittedly, it is equally true that theme labels by themselves fail to address the nuances of any theme's musical-dramatic identity or development. By way of example, let us examine two themes associated with Fafner: the first in his incarnation as a giant, the second after his transformation into the dragon. For the purposes of this illustration, the themes will be identified with the names "Giants" and "Fafner as Dragon." In "Giants," shown in Figure 5.3A, the dotted rhythms and scoring for brass and timpani suggest a march topic (probably a funeral march due to the use of the low register, minor mode, and the "Sehr wuchtig und züruckhaltend im Zeitmass" tempo marking). This reinforces the emotions associated with the ominous and plodding approach of the giants and thus blends semantically both connotative (topical) and denotative (associative) meanings when this theme is heard in full for the first time.

In Figure 5.3B we see "Fafner as Dragon," heard during the *Vorspiel* to *Siegfried* Act II (Sg/136/1/2ff) and later in the act during Siegfried's confrontation with the dragon (Sg/185/4/3ff). The musical relationship between "Fafner as Dragon" and "Giants" parallels the dramatic relationship between Fafner in his earlier role as giant and his present role as dragon. The F minor tonality, register,

Figure 5.3: Musical-dramatic relationships between two themes
A. "Giants," Rg/68/1/1ff
B. "Fafner as Dragon," Sg/136/1/1ff

dotted rhythms, falling fourth, and anacrusis smear are common to both statements, but the slower tempo (*Träg und schleppend*), interpolated rests, fragments from the "Dragon" theme of *Das Rheingold*, and augmented (rather than perfect) fourth signify important changes in the semantic content of this theme. During the *Vorspiel* to *Siegfried* Act II, the meaning of these developments may not be readily apparent, at least not to a listener unfamiliar with the music and drama of the upcoming Act. But this theme's recurrence during Siegfried's adventure later in the scene establishes its connection to Fafner as the dragon. The rhythmic changes lend a ponderous quality to the theme and the "Dragon" fragments are an obvious reference to Fafner's new form.[15] At the heart of this development, however, is the intervallic corruption from perfect fourth to augmented fourth. This descending tritone is a marker for Fafner's physical and moral corruption, serving also to corrupt the harmonic fabric of the *Vorspiel* and to embody the sonic representation of Fafner's voice later in the Act.[16] In this way, the tritone motive functions in a fluid and tonally ambiguous way, characteristic of many Wagnerian themes from Ortrud's music in *Lohengrin* forward.

Of note in these examples is that the musical developments of "Giants" parallel the dramatic developments of Fafner's character. The developments allow for the possibility of accumulative association in which music, like language, becomes capable of modifiers— elements that qualify the meaning of an associative theme. Changing a theme into a distinct, but musically and dramatically related theme is but one form of development Wagner uses in *The Ring*. In fact, associative themes are virtually never stated in exactly the same way twice. If each theme has such fuzzy musical and associative values, though, in effect customizable to form potentially limitless realizations of the thematic prototypes, the whole act of naming the themes seems questionable. We would either need thousands of names to reflect every individual theme, or none at all. For the sake of practicality, the degree of thematic development must serve as a guide in our nomenclature.

Carl Dahlhaus divides thematic developments in *The Ring* into two types: those in which the musical relationship remains readily apparent and those in which a musical/dramatic relationship is constructed between two disparate themes.[17] In both cases, these developments modify a theme's musical characteristics to suggest a change in meaning. The techniques Wagner employs in this regard, while decidedly musical, are subtle and flexible enough to rival language's semantic nuances. In Gauldin's words, "The way in which he [Wagner] adapts each thematic recurrence to the dramatic needs of the event at hand, while still managing to maintain its aural identity, is often nothing short of sheer magic."[18] Gauldin likens variants of associative themes to letters from a single person—the author remains the same but the content changes,[19] a process of thematic diversification Wagner termed "*Entwicklung*" (development or evolution).[20] Such diversifications comprise a vast continuum of degrees of intensity. Analysts walk a fine line when distinguishing between modified statements of the same theme and musical relationships between distinct themes. This line, however, is made explicit by the use of theme labels. Labels force any thematic reference to identify with a previous theme by virtue of a shared name or to be distinguished from a previous theme as an object of a different order: different names signal different themes.

Borrowing from Heinrich Schenker, we might invoke an evolutionary metaphor to clarify this distinction.[21] The relatively less intense thematic transformations and concomitant dramatic colorations they imply can be referred to as "mutations" in which a given theme is musically developed without radically altering its associational significance, just as slight genetic mutations affect the DNA but not the species classification of the life form involved. In most cases, this process involves only slight modifications, changing one or two musical parameters while retaining the others. But some developments engage another order of magnitude. In *The Ring* for instance, distinct-but-related themes often evolve out of shared musical materials, just as distinct-but-related species evolve out of shared genetic materials. Each theme has an independent dramatic association, however, and a large number of musical discrepancies between themes can help distinguish this relationship from thematic mutation. Thus, while thematic mutation concerns itself with musical-dramatic differences between variations of the same theme, thematic evolution seeks to find musical-dramatic similarities between different themes as we witnessed between "Giants" and "Fafner as Dragon."

Continuing with our evolutionary metaphor, each theme, like each species, is designated after observation of many individuals with similar features. That is, thematic identity can be understood as comprising a musical-dramatic prototype. On the surface of the actual music, these prototypes are rarely heard. Rather, the listener, hearing multiple repetitions and variations of a theme, forms an abstract prototype of it. By way of analogy we might picture the prototypic bird. While this image will be slightly different for each individual, most people will picture an animal that is small and colorful; has two wings, a beak, and feathers; lives in trees; flies; and sings pretty, high-pitched songs—in sum, something not unlike Siegfried's woodbird. The vast majority of birds do not fit all these categories, and some, like the penguin, fit fewer than half. The category is fuzzy. The prototypic bird exists only in the imagination. Objects can be compared against the prototype to determine their relative bird-ness—high but not perfect for an owl, much lower for a Valkyrie (they fly, but are their high-pitched songs pretty?), and practically nonexistent for a Nibelung.

This notion of prototype is explored in a recent book on cognitive psychology:

> People think in categories, like "furniture," "vegetable," "grandmother," and "turtle." The categories underlie much of our vocabulary—such as the words *turtle* and *furniture*—and they underlie much of our reasoning. We are not dumbfounded by every new turtle we see; we categorize it as a "turtle" and expect it to have certain traits, like being slower than a hare and withdrawing into its shell when frightened. This means that beforehand we did not mindlessly record every turtle we had seen, like a video camera; we must have abstracted what turtles have in common. To understand mental categories is to understand much of human nature.
>
> The members of a category are not created equal, which is what one would expect if they were admitted into the category by meeting the definition. Everyone agrees that a blue jay is somehow a better example of a bird than a chicken or a penguin . . . the best member of all is called the prototype, such as the sparrow for "bird" and a wrench for "tool."
>
> The categories of the mind have fuzzy borders. People aren't quite sure whether garlic, parsley, seaweed, or edible flowers should count as vegetables.
>
> Categories have stereotyped features: traits that everyone associates with the category, even if they have nothing to do with the criteria for membership. When people think of grandmother, they think of gray hair and chicken soup, not of a node in a genealogical tree.[22]

If the notion of a thematic prototype is viable, then not only will it assist us in relating themes to their earlier incarnations, but it will also aid us in conceptualizing pre-appearances of associative themes (proto-themes)—a topic on which relatively little has been written. A three-fold appearance of a rich musical idea from vague sentiment to apotheosis to reminiscence is a typical nineteenth-century gesture; in fact, Wagner suggests that one of music's greatest abilities is to create expectation and longing in the listener and then fulfill that longing in a psychologically satisfying way.[23] Proto-themes presage the appearance of more or less definitive statements of themes in *The Ring*. In terms of Wagner's theories, the orchestra can hint at something as yet unheard or unseen by the vague suggestion of an emotion that is clarified later when it is brought into alignment with the drama.[24] By foreshadowing with proto-themes, the orchestra takes on the role of narrator; it presumes the entire *Ring* drama as past tense, thus allowing the orchestra to allude to future events.[25] Though Wagner's writings emphasize the emotional association of the themes, proto-themes have often been interpreted semiotically as a foreshadowing of objects or events yet to be introduced.[26] This, however, is something of an impossibility. Without the drama to give meaning to the sign, such foreshadowing can only convey the connotations of *topoi*, or word painting, suggesting the emotion that will eventually accompany the full thematic statement.

An example can again be made with the "Giants" music. The march topic, orchestration, register, and characteristic grace-note anacrusis are presaged in dramatically suggestive locations, first in Rg/58/4/1, when Wotan considers the bargain he made with the giants, and later in Rg/64/3/5–64/4/1, during Freia's frantic warning that Fasolt is coming to take her away. This "thematic fore-shadowing," a type of thematic development in its own right, pre-pares the listener for both the dramatic and musical statement of the complete theme to come in Rg/68/1/1. See Figure 5.4.

Wagner's original theory in *Oper und Drama* was to include motives of both presentiment and reminiscence—devices serving equal and complementary function. In the process of composing, reminiscence motives became the more highly developed of the two, though as we noticed, echoes of Wagner's theory of presenti-ment still sound in the *Ring* dramas.[27] These motives were to be a psychological or emotional *preparation* for what was to come, thus making the actual event a *fulfillment* of this preparation.[28] Genesis of an associative theme may occur through development of more primitive elements. Repetition and transformation of these hazy, non-distinct utterances slowly morph into a recognizable, musically and dramatically highlighted theme.[29]

The "definitive" or most prototypical statement of a theme can be difficult to identify, though some clues are available to us. Proto-themes are often motivic in nature and not articulated clearly as dis-crete entities in the musical fabric.[30] And thematic restatements remind the audience of music they have already heard. But defining the point at which the theme crystallizes into a definitive statement is tricky. Given that associative themes function on a prototype model, it is rare that a thematic prototype would actually ever be heard in the music.[31] Often, though, there is one thematic state-ment that fits our idealized prototype better than any other. Such

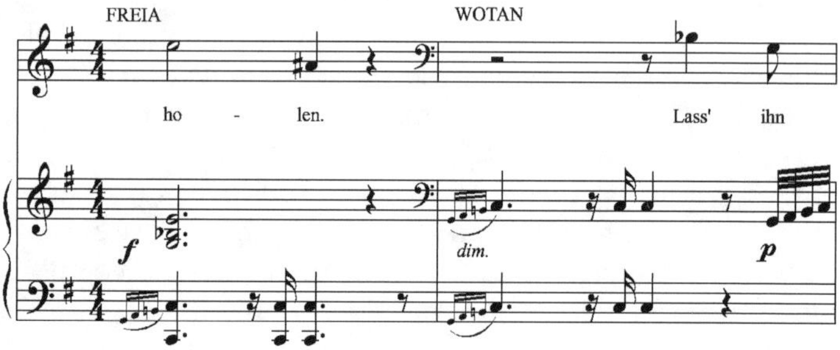

Figure 5.4: Foreshadowing of "Giants"
A. Rg/58/4/1
B. Rg/64/3/5–64/4/1

statements tend to be more or less complete. That is, they are often longer than proto-themes or thematic restatements, and they often fill out complete phrases or periods. Also, these main statements are usually prominent musically, demanding the attention of the listener, while proto-themes and restatements are more likely to be subtly woven into the musical texture. Finally, main statements usually accompany salient and first-time dramatic occurrences, like the actual appearance of the giants on stage in our "prototypical" giants theme (Figure 5.3A). This is the thematic statement most often cited in the theme guides and the one to which other musical statements are compared when considering thematic identity. Wagner himself even suggested performing prototype themes and their later iterations differently. During rehearsals, Wagner is credited with saying, "When a motive is depicting an actual event it should be delivered in a grand style, slowly, and broadly but when serving as a reminiscence . . . it should be slightly faster and with accents less pointed."[32] Even given these specifications, though, identifying the most prototypic occurrence of a theme is a task open to interpretation, dependent on the listener's musical and dramatic understanding.

We are now in a position to appreciate the subtle analytical decisions made in labeling themes. Virtually all theme guides present theme names along with musical examples or score references. Most often, these examples or references are the author's selection of the most prototypical example of a given theme. Though rarely stated explicitly, this prototype selection is an act of interpretation. More importantly, though (and almost never addressed in the theme guides), is the act of using a theme name for the second time. Though no two musical excerpts from any Wagner opera are identical, labeling them the same way implies a measure of equivalence between the two. Likewise, the use of different labels implies a categorical distinction between musical statements. Given the developmental nature of the music in Wagner's music dramas, theme labels provide an irreplaceable analytic statement that clarifies whether two musical excerpts are based on the same or on different prototypes.[33]

Both numbers-as-labels and names-as-labels have the power to make this thematic distinction, but names-as-labels bear benefits that numbers-as-labels do not. Numbers, for all their claim to objectivity, still carry an evaluative stance (at least temporally if themes are numbered in order of appearance), but they cannot illustrate thematic relatedness by label alone without resorting to outright silliness. [Perhaps when themes are combined, their numbers could be added to arrive at the number of the new composite theme? Or dramatically opposed themes could have numbers that were retrogrades of one another?] Associative themes, like words, imply meaning—meaning capable of nuances based on context. Thus, using words to identify the themes not only parallels an associative thematic function but can also illustrate the dramatic relatedness of various themes (as in "Dragon" and "Fafner as Dragon"). Moreover, these names, as words, draw at least some sense of the themes' meanings into the linguistic realm, highlighting subtle thematic developments like the use of irony.[34]

We must also admit that the act of naming is an all-too-human gesture, one imbued with a ritualistic sense of power over the object named in a way that numbering is not.[35] Witness within Wagner's *Ring*, for instance, the power that the names "Wälse" and "Nothung" have for Siegmund, the name "Siegmund" has for Sieglinde, and the name "Nothung," again, has for Siegfried. In each example, the individual, through the act of naming, defines in some way his or her relationship to the thing named. Such is the case with naming themes as well, an act fundamental to musical epistemology. Thomas Grey goes so far as to state that "Wagnerian motives want names, after all, whether or not they behave as leitmotivs."[36] Admittedly, this usage vitiates the potential for standardized theme names common to all Wagner commentators, but, as we realized earlier, the combination of names with musical examples or references will enable us to maintain clarity without sacrificing the individual's evaluative stance with regard to thematic association.

Despite advances in our understanding of associative themes, the typical approach toward identifying and naming them has been entity centered—a one-dimensional mapping between music and meaning. Wagner himself, in response to Wolzogen's thematic catalogue, remarked that the real interest his themes provoked was the manner in which dramatic transformation "opened up a radical new way of developing musical material."[37] While no thematic reference can truly capture this sense of development, theme labels present us with a vehicle for making the categorical distinction between variations of the same theme and related-but-distinct themes. Furthermore, names as labels present an interpretive stance through language, what we imagine all Wagner discourse strives to achieve. Undeniably, theme names must be used carefully; we must remember that alone they communicate little of substance about the music drama, but the appropriate use of names as names (and nothing more) can greatly enrich and facilitate our understanding of Wagner's works. Finally, names appeal to us in a manner that approaches Wagner's art, through the messy subjectivity of symbolism and associative meaning. Thus, there is a parallelism between art and interpretation in the label "Glorification of Brünnhilde" that is missing from "number 40." Wagner's music dramas almost beg us to associate the linguistic with the sonic and, in so doing, to explicitly inject a bit of ourselves, our understanding and interpretation of these

works, into the music that at times suggests such an uncanny understanding of us.

Works Cited

Abbate, Carolyn. *Unsung Voices: Opera and Musical Narrative in the Nine-
teenth Century.* Princeton: Princeton University Press, 1991.
Abbate, Carolyn, and Roger Parker. "Introduction: On Analyzing Opera."
Analyzing Opera: Wagner and Verdi. Ed. Carolyn Abbate and Roger
Parker. Berkeley: University of California Press, 1989. 1–24.
Adorno, Theodor W. *In Search of Wagner.* Trans. Rodney Livingstone.
London: Verso, 1991.
Aldritch, Richard. *A Guide to* The Ring of the Nibelung. Boston: Oliver
Ditson, 1905.
Boretz, Benjamin. "Nelson Goodman's *Languages of Art* from a Musical
Point of View." *Perspectives on Contemporary Music Theory.* Ed. Ben-
jamin Boretz and Edward T. Cone. New York: W. W. Norton, 1972.
31–44.
Bribitzer-Stull, Matthew. "'Did You Hear Love's Fond Farewell?': Some
Examples of Thematic Irony in Wagner's *Ring.*" *Journal of Musicologi-
cal Research* 23.2 (2004): 123–57.
———. *Thematic Development and Dramatic Association in Wagner's* Der
Ring des Nibelungen. Diss. Eastman School of Music, 2001.
Cooke, Deryck. *An Introduction to* Der Ring des Nibelungen. London
Records, 1995. CD 443 581-2. Rerelease of 1969 recording.
———. *I Saw the World End: A Study of Wagner's* Ring. London: Oxford
University Press, 1979.
Dahlhaus, Carl. *Richard Wagner's Music Dramas.* Trans. Mary Whittall.
Cambridge: Cambridge University Press, 1979.
———. "What is a Musical Drama?" *Cambridge Opera Journal* 1.1
(1989): 95–111.
Darcy, Warren. "Rotational Form, Teleological Genesis, and Fantasy-Pro-
jection in the Slow Movement of Mahler's Sixth Symphony." *19th-Cen-
tury Music* 25.1 (2001): 49-74.
———. Unpublished Guide to the Themes of *Der Ring des Nibelungen.* In
Matthew Bribitzer-Stull, *Thematic Development and Dramatic Associa-
tion in Wagner's* Der Ring des Nibelungen. Diss. Eastman School of
Music, 2001. 331–408.
———. *Wagner's* Das Rheingold. New York: Oxford University Press,
1993.

Deathridge, John. "Review of *Richard Wagner and the English*, et al.," *19th-Century Music* 5.1 (1981): 81–89.

Deathridge, John; and Carl Dahlhaus. *The New Grove Wagner*. New York: W. W. Norton, 1984.

Donington, Robert. *Wagner's* Ring *and its Symbols: The Music and the Myth*. London: Faber and Faber, 1969.

Drake, Warren. "The Norns' Scene in *Götterdämmerung*: A Cycle within a Cycle." *Miscellanea Musicologica* 14 (1985): 57–77.

Gauldin, Robert. "Analytical Studies in Wagner's Music." Unpublished typescript, 2000.

Grey, Thomas. *Wagner's Musical Prose: Texts and Contexts*. Cambridge: Cambridge University Press, 1995.

Hacohen, Ruth, and Naphtali Wagner. "The Communicative Force of Wagner's *Leitmotives*: Complement Relations between their Connotations and Denotations." *Music Perception* 14.4 (1997): 445–76.

Hatten, Robert. *Musical Meaning in Beethoven*. Bloomington: Indiana University Press, 1994.

Hepokoski, James. *Sibelius Symphony No. 5*. Cambridge: Cambridge University Press, 1993.

Holman, J. K. *Wagner's* Ring: *A Listener's Companion and Concordance*. Portland, OR: Amadeus, 1996.

Hutcheson, Ernest. *A Musical Guide to the Richard Wagner* Ring of the Nibelung. New York: AMS, 1972.

Kobbé, Gustav. *How to Understand Wagner's* Ring of the Nibelungs. London: William Reeves, 1916.

Lavignac, Albert. *The Music Dramas of Richard Wagner and His Festival Theatre in Bayreuth*. Trans. Esther Singleton. New York: Dodd and Mead, 1926.

London, Justin. "Leitmotifs and Musical Reference in the Classical Film Score." *Music and Cinema*. Ed. James Buhler, Caryl Flinn, and David Neumeyer. Hanover, NH: Wesleyan University Press, 2000. 85–96.

McClatchie, Stephen. *Analyzing Wagner's Operas: Alfred Lorenz and German Nationalist Ideology*. Rochester, NY: University of Rochester Press, 1998.

McCredie, Andrew. "Leitmotive: Wagner's Points of Departure and their Antecedents." *Miscellanea Musicologica* 14 (1985): 1–28.

Millington, Barry. *Wagner*. Princeton, NJ: Princeton University Press, 1992.

Nattiez, Jean-Jacques. *Music and Discourse*. Trans. Carolyn Abbate. Princeton, NJ: Princeton University Press, 1990.

Newman, Ernest. *The Wagner Operas*. Princeton, NJ: Princeton University Press, 1991.

Noske, Frits. "Verbal and Musical Semantics in Opera: Denotation and Connotation." *Die Semantik der musiko-literarischen Gattungen: Methodik und Analyse—Eine Festgabe für Ulrich Weisstein zum 65. Geburtstag.* Ed. Walter Bernhart. Tübingen: Narr, 1994. 35–50.

Patterson, Franklin P. *The Leitmotives of* Der Ring des Nibelungen. Leipzig: Breitköpf & Härtel, 1896.

Pinker, Steven. *Words and Rules.* New York: Basic Books, 1999.

Porges, Heinrich. *Wagner Rehearsing the* Ring: *An Eyewitness Account of the Stage Rehearsals of the First Bayreuth Festival.* Trans. Robert L. Jacobs. Cambridge: Cambridge University Press, 1983.

Schenker, Heinrich. *Neue musikalische Theorien und Phantasien, v. 1: Harmoielehre.* Stuttgart: Cotta, 1906.

Skelton, Geoffrey. *Wagner in Thought and Practice.* London: Lime Tree, 1991.

Spencer, Stewart, and Barry Millington. *Wagner's* Ring of the Nibelung: *A Companion.* London: Thames & Hudson, 1993.

Stein, Jack Madison. *Richard Wagner and the Synthesis of the Arts.* Westport, CT: Greenwood, 1973.

Stokes, Jeffrey Lewis. "Contour and Motive: A Study of 'Flight' and 'Love' in Wagner's *Ring, Tristan,* and *Meistersinger.*" Diss., State University of New York, 1984.

Sumarsam, "Inner Melody in Javanese Gamelan Music." *Asian Music* 7.1 (1976): 3–13.

Tarasti, Eero. *Myth and Music: A Semiotic Approach to the Aesthetics of Myth in Music, Especially That of Wagner, Sibelius, and Stravinsky.* Gravenhage: Mouton, 1979.

von Wolzogen, Hans. *Thematischer Leitfaden durch die Musik zu Richard Wagners Festspiel "Der Ring des Nibelungen."* Leipzig: Feodor Reinboth, 1876.

Wagner, Richard. "Über Frung Liszts Symphonische Dichtungen." In *Gesammelte Schriften und Dichtungen von Richard Wagner.* Leipzig: E. W. Fritzsch, 1871–1883. v. 5, 182–98.

———. "Music Applied to the Drama." In *Richard Wagner's Prose Works.* Trans. William Ashton Ellis. New York: Broude Brothers, 1966. v. 6, 175–91

Windsperger, Lothar. *Das Buch der Motive, Band II.* Mainz: B. Schott's Söhne, n.d.

NOTES

1. Abbate and Parker, 8–9.
2. Millington, 211.

3. Newman, 497–98 (Ex. 54).

4. Wagner, "Music Applied" 182–83.

5. Wagner did not endorse the nineteenth-century German neologism *"Leitmotiv"* in *Oper und Drama*; he preferred *"Melodie"* and later *"Motiv."* See Skelton, 43. Warren Darcy also rejects *"Leitmotiv"* in favor of "associative theme," since he feels "motive" is inadequate to describe the complex nature (harmonization, phrase structure, etc.) of many of the themes (See Bribitzer-Stull, *Thematic Development* 331–32). "Associative theme" also avoids many of the incorrect, stereotyped connotations associated with *"Leitmotiv"* and suggests that the concept of "theme" (rather than "motive") is the prototypical musical entity for these musical-dramatic constructs.

6. Deathridge and Dahlhaus, 112; Adorno, 31; and Abbate, 86.

7. Dahlhaus, *Richard Wagner's Music Dramas*, 61.

8. Ibid. 62. This grew out of Wolzogen's Schopenhauerian belief in *melody* as expression of the will, thus influencing Wolzogen toward *melodic* analysis of Wagner's music.

9. The title in German, found in an unpublished letter from Cosima Wagner to Edmund von Lippman, is "Verherrlichung Brünnhildens." See Deathridge, 84.

10. Proper names for themes are in fact semantically neutral and incapable of summarizing the meanings and formal functions taken by the music they name. For an exploration of this subject, see London, 85–96.

11. Unfortunately, many scholars retain this representational viewpoint. See Cooke, *Introduction*. See also, Tarasti, 188: "The motifs directly concerning some actor in *The Ring* may convey their content in two ways: either they define their object qualitatively when they depict the actor's traits or character, or they define an actor functionally, i.e., depicting his actions in a mythical universe."

12. See Nattiez, 69–70. The act of labeling or naming themes clearly intersects with recent work on musical semiology. While semiotics must, for reasons of scope, remain outside of this article, interested readers are encouraged to consult Nattiez or Hatten for engaging introductions to music and semiotics. See also, Boretz, 31–44, who addresses not only the nature of the musical artwork but also the nature of musical (and linguistic) representation and meaning.

13. The works in which these thematic citations appear are as follows: Aldritch; Darcy, unpublished guides (Darcy's guides to the themes of *The Ring* are included in the appendix to Bribitzer-Stull, *Thematic Development*); Donington; Gauldin; Holman; Hutcheson; Kobbé; Lavignac; Newman; Patterson; Spencer, et al.; Windsperger; and von Wolzogen.

14. Some notes on methodology: All references to scores are given as music drama/page/system/measure and refer to the widely available Schirmer piano-vocal scores (e.g., Sg/184/3/1 = *Siegfried*, page 184, third system, first measure). The abbreviations for the music dramas are as follows: Rg = *Das Rheingold*, Wk = *Die Walküre*, Sg = *Siegfried*, and Gd = *Götterdämmerung*. This convention is maintained even when orchestrational references are made to the full score. All associative themes are capitalized and presented within quotation marks (e.g., "Spear") to distinguish them from the objects, characters, events, moods, and scenes represented by the same word (e.g., spear). Most themes are named using Warren Darcy's nomenclature (see the appendix to Bribitzer-Stull, *Thematic Development*).

15. The "Dragon" theme first appeared during Alberich's transformation in scene 3 of *Das Rheingold* (Rg/150/3/1ff).

16. Most of his lines are sung to tritones. See, for example, Sg/154–56, 185–88.

17. Dahlhaus, *Richard Wagner's Music Dramas,* 136–37.

18. Gauldin, chapter 14, 7.

19. The metaphor is made in distinction to the caricature of the themes as "calling cards." See Gauldin, chapter 36, 3–4.

20. See Wagner's 1857 open letter on Liszt's symphonic poems. Wagner, "Über Franz Liszt's" 182–98.

21. Schenker employs this metaphor (Schenker, 6/6).

22. Pinker, 270ff. Emphasis in original.

23. Drake, 77.

24. Hacohen and Wagner, 445–76 implies that the semantic connotations of the associative themes may be the vehicle for such emotional foreshadowing.

25. Abbate, 169–70.

26. Darcy, *Wagner's* 46–47.

27. Stein, 74.

28. Ibid. 77. Most recently, James Hepokoski and Warren Darcy explore the potential of thematic processes to undergo teleological genesis in nineteenth-century music. See, for instance, Darcy, "Rotational Form" 49-74; and Hepokoski, 26–27.

29. Stokes, 54–72.

30. Similar techniques occur in the music of many different style periods, ranging from the *Vorimitation* of baroque era chorale preludes to similar processes in Debussy's music.

31. A Javanese musician and scholar by the name of Sumarsam has coined the term "inner melody" to describe a prototypical melodic idea that guides or directs performers in their realizations (each realization is constrained by the nature of the instrument being performed on) of

gamelan pieces (*gendhing*). Although he focuses most centrally on the elaborating instruments in the Javanese gamelan, the concept also applies on the more concrete level of *balungan*—one finds slight discrepancies between groups in the realization of the *balungan* of a given *gendhing*, suggesting that as the performers move from the conceptual realm to the reality of performance, there is room for multiple takes on how the concept is crafted into the one-octave constraint of the *balungan*-carrying instruments. Sumarsam's most succinct statement of this concept is found in Sumarsam, 3–13.

32. Porges, 12.
33. In extended cases of thematic evolution, large numbers of themes may be musically and dramatically connected, resulting in what Deryck Cooke calls "thematic families." See Cooke, *Introduction*. The "thematic families" idea has been identified by a variety of names, though the basic concept arises out of Wagner's own writings. The following is drawn from Richard Wagner's essay, "Music Applied," which professes to be about *Holländer*, but is more reflective of Wagner's work on *The Ring* and his efforts to depict himself as Beethoven's heir apparent in the symphonic realm: "This [symphonic] unity then provides the entire work with a continuous web of fundamental themes [Grundthemen] which are contrasted, supplemented, re-formed, separated, and linked together again, just as in a symphonic movement; only here the dramatic action as executed-performed dictates the rules of parting and combination." See Deathridge and Dahlhaus, 72–73; and McClatchie, 64.
34. See Bribitzer-Stull, "Did You Hear," 123–57.
35. As an extreme example of names versus numbers, witness the dehumanizing of Nazi death camp prisoners whose names were eschewed in favor of numbers tattooed on their bodies.
36. Grey, 297.
37. Cooke, *I Saw*, 45.

CHAPTER 6

IN SEARCH OF C MAJOR: TONAL STRUCTURE AND FORMAL DESIGN IN ACT III OF *DIE MEISTERSINGER*

Warren Darcy

The two operas Wagner composed during his long sabbatical from work on *The Ring* are widely regarded as polar opposites.[1] Certainly *Tristan und Isolde* and *Die Meistersinger von Nürnberg* at first appear to inhabit totally different—even mutually exclusive— dramatic/musical universes. However, these apparently irreconcilable works do exhibit at least one common feature: each is based on the elaborate working out of a rather simple harmonic concept. In the case of *Tristan*, the opening dissonance (the famous "Tristan chord") strives for a consonant resolution that is withheld for almost four hours and granted only during the closing bars of the opera; this unresolved dissonance functions as a musical metaphor for the lovers' tormented longing, an insatiable yearning that can be stilled only through death and the extinction of being. The harmonic procedure underlying *Die Meistersinger* is understandably of a somewhat different nature: the entire opera represents a sustained effort to regain its opening key of C major. Having been firmly established by the orchestral Prelude and the first scene of Act I, C major is seemingly abandoned for the remainder of Act I and all of Act II. Only during Act III does this key begin to reassert itself through a series of directed tonal motions. In fact, Act III is literally

engaged in a search for C major, a tonal quest whose goal is defini-
tively attained only during the final scene.

Any discussion of *Die Meistersinger*'s musical structure must
obviously take into account this macrotonal gesture, this search for
C major, and should also make some effort to determine exactly
what Wagner may have meant by it. Music analysis, however fascinating for its practitioner, is here of limited value unless it illumi-
nates some aspect of the drama. Accordingly, this chapter focuses on
Act III of the opera and unfolds simultaneously on two distinct levels of discourse. The first and more technical level explores the
interaction of tonal structure and formal design in an attempt to
provide a meaningful synoptic overview of the Act. The second level
seeks to ascertain exactly how this tonal/formal structure relates to
the work's dramatic content and meaning. In other words, efforts
to explain *what* Wagner does are paralleled by speculation as to *why*
he does it. The chapter concludes with an inquiry into the deeper
meaning of the opera's large-scale tonal quest.

Figure 6.1 displays the tonal structure of the entire opera. Act I
begins solidly in the tonic C major and concludes in F, the key of
the subdominant. Act II centers around G major, the key of the
dominant, with important excursions to its surrounding thirds, B♭
and E. Act III returns to the tonic C in ways that will be demonstrated in the course of this chapter. The work as a whole thus represents an enormous I–IV–V–I tonal progression, a diatonic
background that subsumes all lower-level harmonic fluctuations and
anchors the work on the firm tonal pillars of its opening and closing
scenes.[2]

Act III itself comprises five scenes; the first four are set in Sachs's
workshop and the fifth in an open field. Table 6.1 lists the principal
character and the controlling tonality of each scene. An overall symmetrical pattern is immediately apparent: scenes 1 and 5 are gov-
erned by Sachs and his key of C; scenes 2 and 4 focus on the lovers

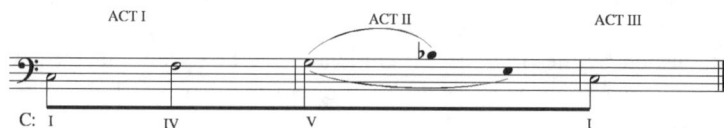

Figure 6.1: Tonal structure of opera

Walther and Eva, whose tonalities of E♭ and A♭ lie respectively a minor third above and a major third below C; while scene 3, the axis of symmetry, features Beckmesser and his key of D major. Such large-scale symmetry is not surprising. "You know my accursed predilection for symmetry," Wagner jokingly wrote Mathilde Maier on December 17, 1864.[3] And symmetrical structures occur throughout the composer's works. Here, the symmetrical effect is somewhat mitigated by the change of locale for scene 5 and by the fact that this fifth scene is twice as long as any one of the preceding four. Perhaps more significant are the tonal relationships: while Sachs is associated with the "neutral" C major, Walther and Eva are both represented by flat keys, and Beckmesser alone by a sharp key. The keys associated with Sachs, Walther, and Eva all stand in consonant relationships to one another, and together they form a major triad. The perfect fifth joining Walther to Eva is, in fact, the strongest harmonic relationship in the tonal system. On the other hand, Beckmesser's D major stands in a dissonant relationship to each of the other three keys. The tritone that separates Beckmesser from Eva has traditionally denoted the most distant tonal relationship, suggesting that the town clerk's hopes of winning Eva's affections are unrealistic in the extreme.

As shown in Table 6.2, the opening scene comprises three formal units: the orchestral Prelude, the dialogue between Sachs and David, and Sachs's famous "Wahn" monologue. This curtain-raising "Prelude, Scene, and Aria" structure is of course no stranger to either Italian or German opera and was used by Wagner himself to

Table 6.1: Outline of Act III

Scene	Principal character	Consonant relationship	Controlling tonality*	Dissonant relationship
1	Sachs		C major	
		Minor 3rd		
2	Walther		E♭ major	Major 2nd
				Minor 2nd
3	Beckmesser	Perfect 5th	D major	Tritone
				Major 2nd
4	Eva		A♭ major	
		Major 3rd		
5	Sachs		C major	

*Not necessarily the initial or concluding tonality

open scene 2 of *Das Rheingold*.[4] On a superficial level, the scene does not appear to be tonally centric; inasmuch as the Prelude establishes G minor/major, the Dialogue expresses D major, and the Monologue progresses by descending thirds toward C. However, Figure 6.2 suggests how this tonal structure may be interpreted as a functional progression within C major. The scene as a whole represents a large dominant-to-tonic motion within C, an authentic cadence at a deep structural level. D major, the key of the Sachs/David Dialogue, is understood as the unfolded upper fifth of G into which D is ultimately absorbed.[5] This explains how Wagner can associate the same key with both David and Beckmesser: the D major of scene 1 is approached from G as its consonant upper fifth, while the D major of scene 3 is approached from E♭ as its dissonant lower neighbor. Both the Prelude and the Dialogue are tonally closed, and each expands its local tonic through a I–V–I arpeggiation; the Monologue, however, is tonally open and descends by thirds from A minor to C major. This monologue should not be taken as an example of "progressive" or "directional" tonality except in the most superficial sense. Controlled at the background level by C major, it simply begins "off-tonic" and moves inexorably toward C, as does, at a deeper level of structure, the entire scene.[6]

The formal designs displayed in Table 6.2 are of some interest.[7] The Prelude, a five-part arch form, exhibits the same structural symmetry as the Act as a whole. The "Wahn" theme that frames the Prelude defines G minor; it originally appeared at this same pitch level in Act II as an orchestral counterpoint to the third strophe of Sachs's Cobbling Song. The Reformation Hymn affirms G major, the key in which the people will later sing it as a tribute to Sachs; however, the hymn's antecedent and consequent phrases are here separated by a sequential development of motives from the Cobbling Song, a parenthetical interpolation that prolongs the dominant (see Figure 6.3 for an interpretation of the harmonic

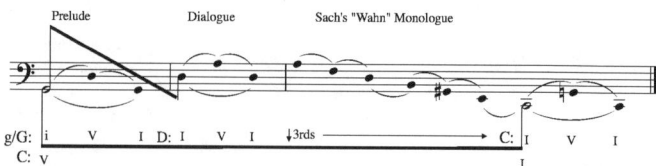

Figure 6.2: Tonal structure of Act III, Scene 1

Table 6.2: Outline of Act III, Scene 1

Section and content		*Harmonic/tonal structure*
I.	Orchestral Prelude	g/G
A	"Wahn" theme	g: i – v^T – I
B	Reformation Hymn (antecedent)	G: I ⟶ V^T
C	"Cobbling" motives (sequential)	G: VI^T – II^T – V^T
B^1	Reformation Hymn (consequent)	G: V ⟶ [I]
A^1	"Wahn" theme	⟶ G
II.	Sachs/David Dialogue	D
A	David pleads for Sachs's forgiveness.	D: IV^T – V – I
A^1	David wonders at Sachs's friendliness.	A (=V^T)
B	David recites his *Johannessprüchlein*.	D
A^2	Sachs makes David his herald.	D: IV – V – I
III.	Sachs's "Wahn" Monologue	To C by descending 3rds
Pt. 1	*Wahn* in the world	a ⟶ V^7/d
Pt. 2	*Wahn* in Nürnberg	F ⟶ d
Pt. 3	*Johannisnacht*	B – G$^{\sharp}$ (A$^{\flat}$) – E
Pt. 4	*Johannistag*	C

Note: The superscript "T" (e.g., v^T) means that the specified harmonic function has been tonicized, or expanded to the status of a temporary tonic.

structure). This Prelude is obviously meant as a psychological portrait of Sachs, and its strong internal contrasts—the uneasy chromatic polyphony of part A, the assured diatonic homophony of part B, and the searching linear sequences of part C—suggest a succession of wide-ranging emotional states.[8]

The Sachs/David dialogue falls into four segments that relate dramatically and musically as A A^1 B A^2; the contrasting third section comprises David's *Johannessprüchlein*, his inset song about John the Baptist. Figure 6.4 uses analytical notation to demonstrate the tonal coherence of this harmonically rich dialogue.

Although in four clearly defined sections, Sachs's "Wahn" monologue does not display an archetypal design and may best be regarded as through composed (see again Table 6.2 and Figure 6.2). Sachs begins contemplating the evil effects of *Wahn ("Madness")* in A

Figure 6.3: Tonal structure of Prelude

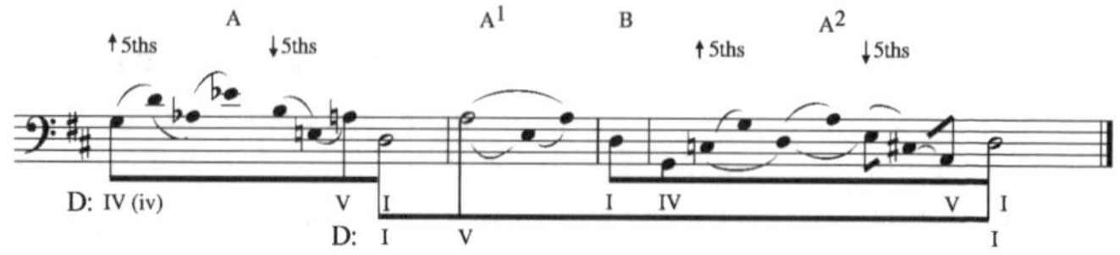

Figure 6.4: Tonal structure of Sachs/David dialogue

minor, a fifth higher from the key of the previous dialogue, but this tonal center soon loses its stability and turns into an active dominant. Sachs's vision of Nuremberg begins confidently in F major, but a recall of the previous night's riot banishes both vision and tonal center with a descent to D minor: Nuremberg's well-established social structure has been seriously undermined. Sachs's explanation of the riot's cause ("Johannisnacht") descends more rapidly by thirds from B through $G^{\#}$ (spelled by Wagner as $A^{\flat}$) to E. Finally, his anticipation of a solution to the problem ("Nun aber kam Johannistag!") completes the descent by thirds with a thrilling arrival at C major.

Scene 1 as a whole thus represents the Act's first large-scale motion toward C major in the form of a gradually unfolded dominant-to-tonic progression. Wagner suggests that Sachs himself intends to lead the music toward C in a manner yet to be determined and that his attempt to bring order out of social chaos will take the musical form of a return to tonal stability.

Scene 2 is tonally closed in $E^{\flat}$. As Table 6.3 shows, its overall formal/tonal structure at first appears unproblematic: a five-part rondo-like design whose two contrasting episodes express the keys of the dominant $B^{\flat}$ and the major submediant C.[9] However, the matter is not quite that simple. The first three sections constitute a coherent A B A^1 ternary form underpinned by a I–V–I tonal progression and an exposition–development–recapitulation thematic process. However, section C does not integrate well into the rest of the structure: its key, length, and closed harmonic/linear structure, as well as its character of a "song on stage," set it off from the preceding sections, with which it shares only a rather tenuous melodic link. In addition, section A^2 sounds less like a well-motivated second recapitulation than a convenient thematic/tonal rounding off. These considerations suggest that the scene is really bipartite: the first part, the A B A^1 design in $E^{\flat}$, constitutes the preparation for Walther's composition of the Prize Song, while the second part contains the act of composition itself in C major. Had Walther completed the third strophe, the scene could well have ended in C; however, his refusal to continue beyond verse 2 forces Sachs to retreat into the original key of E♭. Thus, C major should not be interpreted as VI of a prolonged E♭; rather, the tonal move of the scene is from E♭ to C, a descending minor third that constitutes the Act's second large-scale motion toward C major (see Figure 6.5). The conclusiveness of this move is temporarily thwarted by Walther's refusal to complete his song, a situation that will be rectified in scene 4.

Scene 3, the duping of Beckmesser, is controlled by D minor/ major and comprises three main sections framed by an orchestral Prelude and Postlude (Table 6.4). Each of the three large parts centers

Table 6.3: Outline of Act III Scene 2

Section			Content	Key
A			Discussion of Walther's dream	E♭
B			Sachs explains the importance of the Master's rules.	B♭
A¹			Sachs urges Walther to describe his dream.	E♭
C	Strophe 1:	a	Walther describes his dream, which	C
		[Recit.]	comprises the first two strophes of the	
		a¹	Prize song (each strophe in bar form).	
		[Recit.]		
		b		
	[Recitative]			
	Strophe 2:	a		
		a¹		
		b		
A²			Sachs bids Walter prepare for his wedding day	E♭

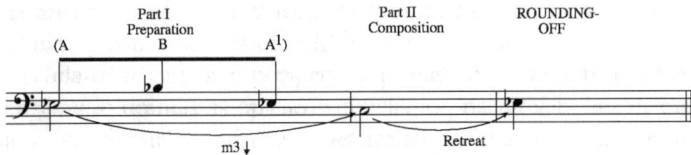

Figure 6.5: Tonal structure of Act III Scene 2

Table 6.4: Outline of Act III, Scene 3

Section	Content	Key
Prelude	Beckmesser's Entrance (pantomime)	d/D: V
Pt. 1 (a)	He thinks of Sachs.	
Pt. 2 (a1)	He thinks of Walther.	
Pt. 3 (b)	He finds the poem.	
Part I		
Dialogue	Beckmesser blames Sachs for last night.	
Solo No. 1	Beckmesser rages at Sachs.	d
Dialogue	Sachs assures Beckmesser he will not woo Eva.	
Part II		
Dialogue	Sachs makes Beckmesser a gift of the poem.	
Solo No. 2	Beckmesser accepts the poem.	D
Part III		
Dialogue Pt. 1	Sachs promises he will not claim the poem.	
Dialogue Pt. 2	Sachs urges Beckmesser to study it well.	
Solo No. 3	Beckmesser is alternately confused and grateful.	D
Postlude	Beckmesser's Exit (pantomime)	D
Transition	Sachs muses over Beckmesser's wickedness.	⟶ C

around a solo sung by Beckmesser: the first (in D minor) expressing his rage over the cobbler's apparent intent to woo Eva, the second and third (in D major) expressing his gratitude for Sachs's gift of the poem. The instrumental framing sections accompany Beckmesser's entrance and exit; the latter is followed by a transitional passage, during which Sachs muses over the town clerk's wickedness and its contribution to his own plan. Each of Beckmesser's tonally centric solos develops out of a harmonically fluid dialogue. These dialogue passages frequently refer to Walther's key of E♭, but invariably absorb the key into Beckmesser's D minor/major as its Neapolitan, a traditionally dark and threatening harmonic region. The solos themselves, while formally impeccable, make no claims to lyric beauty; Beckmesser's mastery of structure cannot conceal the innate poverty of his melodic imagination. As the scene concludes, Sachs's plan for restoring social order is complete: after the town clerk humiliates himself with a predictably grotesque rendition of Walther's Prize Song, the young knight will use the same poem to secure popular approval, win Eva's hand, and reunify society. Beckmesser must thus be sacrificed for the common good. Contemplating this, Sachs leads the tonality yet again toward C, as the orchestra refers point-edly to the conclusion of his "Wahn" monologue. Only two things remain before the plan can be put into action: Walther must complete the Prize Song, and Sachs himself must renounce Eva.

Scene 4, in many ways the emotional core of the drama, exhibits a by-now familiar symmetry (Table 6.5 and Figure 6.6). Eva's entrance is underscored by a striking modulation from C to A♭; as Arnold Whittall has pointed out, this shift of harmonic perspective mirrors the equally striking move from C to E♭ that announced Walther's entrance at the beginning of scene 2.[10] The dialogue between Eva and Sachs proceeds uneventfully in A♭ until this key is suddenly shattered by Walther's dramatic B major appearance at the chamber door. As Sachs grumbles and Eva remains speechless, the music futilely tries to regain its original key; an ineffective attempt to reassert A♭ is literally swept away by the return of C major, as Walther finally sings the third strophe of the Prize Song.

The middle of this scene comprises two crucial episodes: the responses of both Sachs and Eva to Walther's song. Each response is introduced by the "Wahn" theme, and each centers around G—the dominant of C—with an excursion to either its upper or the lower minor third. The shoemaker's grimly ironic utterance expands on his Act II Cobbling Song, while Eva's outburst of affection for Sachs—arguably the most moving moment of the entire opera—chromatically transforms the theme of their initial dialogue into the

Table 6.5: Outline of Act III, Scene 4

Section	Tonal move	Main key
Eva/Sachs Dialogue	A♭ – B – [A♭]	A♭
Strophe 3 of Prize Song (Walther)	C: I – V – I	C
Sachs's Response (Cobbling Song)	g – B♭ – G	G = V/C
Eva's Response (*Tristan* motive!)	G – E – G	
Baptism of Prize Song (Sachs)	D → C	C
Quintet	G♭: I – V^T – I	G♭

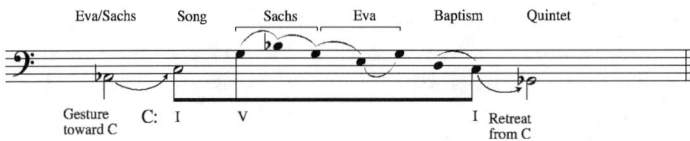

Figure 6.6: Tonal structure of Act III, Scene 4

Sehnsucht ("Longing") motive from *Tristan*. Although this famous interopus citation has been carefully prepared, it always comes as somewhat of a shock—perhaps because it suddenly exposes the sunny diatonicism of *Die Meistersinger* as a fragile veneer, beneath which lurks the tortured chromaticism of *Tristan*. Superficialities aside, the two operas are not that far apart musically, and perhaps not so distant philosophically either, a point that will be considered later. Summoning David and Magdalene as witnesses, Sachs leads the music from G back to C in order to baptize the song. His detour through D major recalls the key of David's *Johannesssprüch-lein*, and the orchestral texture is saturated with references to the C major Baptismal Chorale that opened Act I. Yet Walther's new musical language is man-made, and no divine blessing is invoked: for all its chorales, hymns, biblical allusions, and baptismal imagery, *Die Meistersinger* remains a stubbornly humanistic work.

As Eva proposes to interpret the name of the new mode, "die selige Morgentraum-Deutweise," the music slips into G♭ major for the well-known Quintet. A simple ternary form underpinned by a traditional I–V–I harmonic move, this Quintet supplies the structural pendant to the initial Eva/Sachs dialogue, but it does not share its key. Alfred Lorenz speculated whether Wagner had first sketched the Quintet in A♭, so as to round out the scene tonally, then transposed it down a whole step as a concession to vocal practicality; but this unsupported hypothesis simply misses the point.[11] There can be no return to A♭, the key of Eva's original relationship with Sachs;[12] that relationship has been permanently dissolved, as has the master/pupil relationship between Sachs and Walther. Yet although the pull toward C major is now too strong to be checked, all three characters pause for a moment and pull back from the brink of this tonality toward its tritone counterpole G♭. Dramatic/musical progress is momentarily suspended, as the players postpone, for one timeless moment, what they now understand and accept as their ultimate destiny.

The orchestral interlude between scenes 4 and 5 moves from G♭ through a descending circle of fifths to V^7 of C; however, the expected resolution is thwarted by the entrance of the Guilds who detour into the subdominant F. C major is also avoided by the apprentices, who merrily dance into the still deeper subdominant waters of B♭; but the arrival of the Mastersingers signals the long-awaited resolution to C and with it the goal of the Act's extended tonal quest. Formally, scene 5 is quite complex, which is why Table 6.6 sketches only the bare outlines of its overall symmetrical structure. Dramatically, however, little occurs except what is now felt as inevitable: Beckmesser humiliates himself and is hooted off the stage, while Walther, compressing his original tristrophic song into one extended lyric paean, wins both popular acclaim and Eva's hand. Although the scene's central segment—the song contest—arpeggiates C in various ways, the tonal outcome is no more in doubt than the dramatic one. The only minor surprise comes when Walther, at first rejecting entrance into the Masters' Guild, retreats musically toward both the key and the theme of the Quintet. However, Sachs takes the young artist firmly in hand and leads him back to C major, across whose bright tonal surface the minor modality of the cobbler's warning against foreign influences casts only a fleeting shadow.

Having sketched the tonal progress of Act III, the main points of which are summarized in Figure 6.7, it is now appropriate to inquire into the deeper meaning of this large-scale quest for C major. Why does the opera begin in C, why is this key soon abandoned, and why is Act III devoted to its recapture? One is tempted to remark that *Die Meistersinger* is, after all, a comedy, that a comedy typically begins and ends in a state of social stability, and that C major, with its absence of chromatic complications, might well function as a key of comic resolution. The opera opens on the solid tonal foundations of the Baptismal Chorale; as the dramatic complications

Table 6.6: Outline of Act III, Scene 5

Section	Tonal move
Transition (change of scene)	$G^\flat \longrightarrow V/C$
Entrance of Guilds and Mastersingers (march themes from Act I Prelude)	$\longrightarrow C$
The people hail Sachs (Reformation Hymn).	G
Sachs addresses the people and masters (assembly music from Act I, Scene 3).	G
Preparation for Beckmesser's Song (3 parts)	$C - E^\flat - C$
Beckmesser's Song	$e \longrightarrow G$
Response to Beckmesser's Song	$\longrightarrow V/C$
Preparation for Walther's Song (2 parts)	$C - E - D - F - G^7$
Walther's Song	C
Response to Walther's Song (3 parts)	C
Sachs addresses Walther and the people.	$C - c - C$
The people repeat Sachs's words and hail him.	C
[March themes from Act I Prelude during last two segments]	C

begin to multiply—as *Wahn* is let loose in the world—C major yields to a variety of other tonal centers, and when social order is restored—when the customary reconciliation of opposing generations takes place—the original key returns. Such an explanation, although correct as far as it goes, is rather too pat to do justice either to Wagner or the richness of his work. The remainder of this chapter proposes a somewhat different interpretive stance.

Scholars who search for a thematic link among the various components of the Wagnerian canon generally opt for the notion of *Erlösung*, or redemption. Without minimizing the importance of this concept, it is possible to discern yet another common thread: the conflict between the individual and society. Although the exploration of this conflict is most properly the subject of comedy, it recurs throughout Wagner's dramatic oeuvre. Usually the individual is an outsider who represents a certain threat to the established social order: the Dutchman in Daland's house, Tannhäuser at the Wartburg, Lohengrin in tenth-century Antwerp, Siegfried at the court of the Gibichungs, and Parsifal in the Hall of the Grail. Furthermore, Wagner almost invariably uses C major to represent entrenched society: the chorus of Norwegian sailors, the public assemblies on the bank of the Scheldt, the arrival at Cornwall, the rallying of the Gibichung vassals, and the first Grail ceremony. Generally the conflict is not so much resolved as terminated in one of two ways: either the individual transcends the social world (as do the Dutchman, Tannhäuser, Siegfried, and Brünnhilde), or he merges with and becomes a part of it (as does Parsifal). The *Tristan/Meistersinger* dichotomy neatly illustrates this: in *Tristan*, the lovers transcend the phenomenal world by surrendering their individuality and merging with each other and the universe; in *Die Meistersinger*, the main characters surrender their individuality in order to merge with a newly reconstituted society.[13]

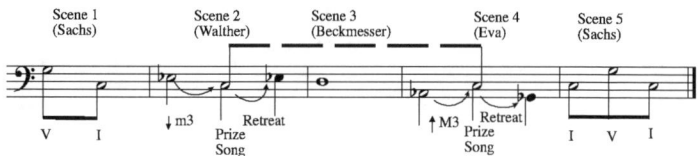

Figure 6.7: Tonal structure of Act III

More specifically, *Die Meistersinger* explores what happens when the will of the individual begins to threaten the welfare of society. Most of the characters act contrary to established social mores: Eva and Walther plan to elope, Beckmesser woos a woman much younger than himself, and even Sachs briefly contemplates marriage with a daughter-figure. Festering discontent finally erupts into a full-fledged riot that shakes the social structure of Nuremberg to its foundation. Clearly the will of the individual, a potentially destructive force, must be checked if social order is to be reestablished—if society is to be healed—and Sachs determines to achieve this through the agency of artistic creation. If the concept of renouncing the will through art sounds vaguely Schopenhauerian, it should. *Tristan* and *Die Meistersinger* are really two sides of the same Schopenhauerian coin: in the former, renunciation of the Will allows the individual to transcend society, in the latter, to merge with society.[14]

We can now appreciate the deeper implications of the opera's search for C major. At the opening of Act I, the C major chorale represents an anonymous, if somewhat smugly complacent, society; the lyrical interludes that accompany Walther's silent entreaties to Eva—chromatic passages played on solo instruments—suggest the individual will beginning to assert itself in opposition to this society. By the conclusion of scene 1, C major has been seriously weakened and the dramatic entanglements set in motion. The clash of opposing wills culminates in the Act II riot, which causes Sachs to ponder the problem in universal terms. His description of *Wahn* reminds one of the Schopenhauerian Will—always at war with itself, forever causing individuals to act against their common interest. He decides that social order must be restored—C major must be regained—even though it means renouncing his feelings for Eva. Walther, on the other hand, must bow to society's demands to the extent of participating in the song contest and allowing his artistic inspiration to be tempered by the Masters' rules. Beckmesser, however, has no place in the redeemed society; in fact, his humiliation amounts to a public execution.[15] Yet however desirable a return to social stability might be (however necessary that final C major), it comes at quite a price—the voluntary loss of individuality—and we cannot censure the characters for their temporary retreat into G♭ major. It also carries a rather high price tag for the audience, who have come to know and care about, not the threatened society of Nuremberg, but the very individuals who represent that threat, all of whom are ultimately absorbed into a massive, undifferentiated C major sonority. Wagner's stage directions are unambiguous: "All present join in the song of the people"; the final chorus is "to be sung by all, finally also by Walther and Eva."

The repression of the individual will for the good of society and the expulsion from that purified society of all undesirable elements are dangerous concepts, especially when they find expression in a march-like chorus with distinctly militaristic overtones.[16] Instead of further exploring these rather disturbing implications, this chapter concludes with the following observation: Interpretive studies of *Die Meistersinger* have mainly pursued two courses: an examination of Wagner's sketches and drafts for the poem, demonstrating how his original conception underwent substantial modifications, and an explication of the poem itself in the light of the composer's political essays *"über Staat und Religion"* and *"Deutsche Kunst und Deutsche Politik."*[17] Valuable though such studies may be, they can never serve as anything more than preliminaries to an analysis of the final musical setting[18]—by which I do not mean a headlong plunge into the puerilities of *leitmotiv* exegesis.[19] The interpretation suggested above, although in some respects opposed to the traditional view of this opera, is fully consonant with the text; however, it was not reached by a consideration of that text alone, but through a careful *musical* study of tonal structure and formal design.

WORKS CITED

Bailey, Robert. "An Analytical Study of the Sketches and Drafts." In
    *Richard Wagner, Prelude and Transfiguration from "Tristan und
    Isolde."* Ed. Robert Bailey. New York: W. W. Norton, 1985. 113–46,
Beckett, Lucy. *Richard Wagner: "Parsifal."* New York: Cambridge University Press, 1981.
Darcy, Warren. "The Metaphysics of Annihilation: Wagner, Schopenhauer,
    and the Ending of the *Ring.*" *Music Theory Spectrum* 16.1 (1994):
    1–40.
———. *Wagner's Das Rheingold.* New York: Oxford University Press,
    1993.
Forte, Allen, and Steven E. Gilbert. *Introduction to Schenkerian Analysis.*
    New York: Norton, 1982.

Komow, Ray. *The Genesis and Tone of* Die Meistersinger von Nürnberg. Diss., Brandeis University, 1991.

Lorenz, Alfred. *Das Geheimnis der Form bei Richard Wagner.* 4 vols. Tutzing: H. Schneider, 1966.

Magee, Bryan. *The Philosophy of Schopenhauer.* New York: Oxford University Press, 1983.

Marvin, William. *Tonality in Selected Set-Pieces from Richard Wagner's Die Meistersinger von Nürnberg: A Schenkerian Approach.* Diss., University of Rochester, 2001.

Puri, Michael. "The Ecstasy and the Agony: Exploring the Nexus of Music and Message in the Act III Prelude to *Die Meistersinger von Nürnberg.*" *19th-Century Music* 25.2–3 (2001/2002): 212–36.

Schenker, Heinrich. *Free Composition.* Trans. Ernst Oster. New York: Longman, 1979.

Scholz, Hans, ed. *Richard Wagner an Mathilde Maier (1862–1878).* Leipzig: T. Weicher, 1930.

Turner, Richard. "*Die Meistersinger von Nürnberg:* The Conceptual Growth of an Opera." *Wagner* 3.1 (1982): 2–16.

Whittall, Arnold. "A Musical Commentary." *Richard Wagner.* The Mastersingers of Nuremberg, ENO Opera Guide No. 19. Ed. Nicholas John. London: John Calder, 1983. 15–26.

NOTES

1. Wagner finished the first complete draft of *Siegfried* Act II on July 30, 1857, and the second complete draft on August 9, after which he set the opera aside (he did not, as once claimed, suspend work at the point where Siegfried first reclines under the linden tree). He completed the full score of *Tristan und Isolde* on August 6, 1859, and that of *Die Meistersinger von Nürnberg* on October 24, 1867. On September 27, 1864, he resumed work on the second full score (the fair copy) of *Siegfried* Act I, and on December 22 he began the first full score of Act II, which he completed on December 2, 1865. He did not finish the second full score of Act II until February 23, 1869, after which he began the composition of Act III (March 1). Thus the oft-repeated remark that Wagner suspended work on *The Ring* for twelve years (1857–1869) is false unless one chooses to ignore his work on the first and second full scores of Acts I and II.

2. The reduction of a four and a half-hour opera to a four-chord harmonic progression obviously entails a high degree of musical abstraction, whose underlying theoretical assumptions cannot be elucidated here.

3. "Du kennst meinen unseligen Hang zur Symmetrie" (Scholz, 190). Wagner was referring to the arrangement of his household furnishings.

4. The orchestral rendition of the "Valhalla" theme functions as a prelude, the Wotan/Fricka dialogue as a little scene set in recitative/arioso, and Wotan's apostrophe to the fortress as a miniature aria. It is characteristic of this structure that the music of the "Prelude" recurs during both the "Scene" and the "Aria," as does the "Wahn" theme in *Die Meistersinger* Act III scene 1. For a more detailed discussion of this passage, see Darcy, *Wagner's Das Rheingold* 130–35.

5. The Austrian music theorist Heinrich Schenker (1868–1935) coined the term *Ausfaltung* (unfolding); it refers to the temporal linearization of a conceptually vertical interval. In this case, the perfect fifth between the root and fifth of the G major harmony (dominant of C) is unfolded at a middle ground level of structure; the fifth D (dominant of G) then supports its own middle ground harmony. The D major harmony would also qualify as an "applied divider," a backwards-relating dominant. At the background level, this projected fifth D is absorbed into the structural dominant on G. See Schenker, 50–51, 83–84 for a discussion of unfolding. See also Forte and Gilbert, 159–65, 257–60.

6. The term "progressive tonality" was coined by Dika Newlin, who used it to refer to the situation in which a piece or movement begins in one key but ends in another (a large-scale example would be Mahler's Second Symphony, which begins in the "tragic" key of C minor, but strives toward and concludes in $E^\flat$ major, the key of spiritual redemption). Robert Bailey developed this into his far more sophisticated concept of "directional tonality," which features an interplay between two different tonal centers, both of which can function as tonic. For an explication of the so-called "double tonic complex," see Bailey "An Analytical Study." Bailey's theory offered an attractive alternative for those who found Schenker's concept of monotonality inadequate to cope with the complexities of much nineteenth-century music. Bailey's theory was embraced and developed further by his students William Kinderman, Christopher Lewis, Patrick McCreless, and Deborah Stein. In my opinion, many examples of so-called "directional tonality" are really large-scale instances of what Schenker called the "auxiliary cadence" (Schenker, 88–90), that is, a background progression that begins harmonically with something other than the tonic (e.g., III–V–i). Although the "Wahn" monologue is not such an instance, it progresses so inexorably and logically towards C that it may certainly be understood as monotonal: the passage is controlled by C, even though this tonal center does not actually materialize at the foreground level until the final section. The V–I progression underlying

the entire scene may be understood as an auxiliary cadence at the background level.

7. It is hoped that the information contained in these musical examples and figures will prove sufficient to orient the reader armed with a vocal or an orchestral score. Because scores differ widely in their pagination and because no reader can reasonably be expected to number the measures of Act III, neither page numbers nor measure numbers are provided. The analytical notation employed in some of these examples presupposes some background in Schenkerian analysis.

8. For an important recent study of the Act III Prelude, one that brilliantly synthesizes analysis and hermeneutics, see Puri, 212–36.

9. This is the way the scene was analyzed by Alfred Lorenz. However, as Lorenz noted, the five sections display a marked disproportion in length: 107 + 67 + 31 + 159 + 46 measures. By contrast, the bipartite structure suggested here divides the scene exactly in half: 205 + 205 measures! See Lorenz, vol. 3, 131.

10. Whittall, 23–24.

11. Lorenz, vol. 3, 148.

12. In this book, see Chapter 2 by Robert Gauldin, who discusses the role of $A^\flat$ in all of Wagner's operas and music dramas.

13. The literal outsider in *Die Meistersinger* is, of course, Walther von Stolzing, whose aristocratic lineage and artistic license threatens the bourgeois, conservative society of Nuremberg. However, Sachs, Eva, and Beckmesser also threaten this rather complacent society (as suggested in the following paragraph) and therefore function metaphorically, if not literally, as "outsiders."

14. Lucy Beckett goes so far as to describe *Die Meistersinger* as "Wagner's most fully Schopenhauerian work" (134). For a discussion of the effect of Schopenhauer's philosophy on the ending of *The Ring*, see Darcy, "Metaphysics of Annihilation" 1–40. The best general discussion of the Wagner-Schopenhauer relationship remains that by Bryan Magee (see Magee, 326–78, Appendix 6).

15. This is underscored by the people's comment after Beckmesser's second stollen: "Bald hängt er am Galgen!" (Soon he will hang on the gallows!). After such an exhibition, Beckmesser will never again be able to hold up his head in Nuremberg; he has been effectively ruined for life. Although some directors have attempted to "redeem" Beckmesser (thereby letting both Sachs and Wagner off the hook), this was clearly not the composer's intent: while the orchestra encourages both the people and the audience to laugh at Beckmesser, the town clerk "verliert sich unter dem Volke" (loses himself among the people) and is not seen again.

16. These themes are further examined by Paul Rose's chapter in this book (Chapter 10).
17. A typical example, one that combines both these approaches but does not say word one about the music, can be found in Turner, 2–16.
18. For two recent large-scale musical studies of *Die Meistersinger*, see Komow; and Marvin.
19. Note that Matthew Bribitzer-Stull's chapter in this book (Chapter 5) makes a case for the analytical implications involved in naming Wagner's themes.

PART 2

WAGNER AND SOCIETY

CHAPTER 7

LINGERING DISCOURSES: CRITICS, JEWS,
AND THE CASE OF GOTTFRIED WAGNER

Marc Weiner

The spirit of Adolf Hitler continues to haunt postwar Germany. Just
when the endless discussions of the guilt of the fathers, the suppressed trauma of the postwar generation, and the problems of
"coming to terms with the past" appeared to have taken their
course and had given way to the political laissez-faire of the post-
modern age, National Socialism once again seemed to function as a
central feature within the formation of modern German identity.
That the Nazi past still constitutes what the Germans call "ein
wunder Punkt" (a "sore spot") within the public arena is clear not
solely from the emergence of the neo-Nazi skinheads—who sys-
tematically exploit their country's sensitivity regarding its racist
heritage—but also from a host of highly publicized debates and
controversies in the recent past. These include, for example, the
Historikerstreit ("The Historians' Debate") from the late 1980s;
the Goldhagen affair of the mid-1990s;[1] the debates surrounding
the Jewish memorial in Berlin; the publication of Botho Strauss's
"anschwellender Bocksgesang;" Martin Walser's "Paulskircherede"
("Speech at St. Paul's Church") and the ensuing debate with Ignatz
Bubis concerning the author's resentment regarding his country's
association with the Holocaust; Daniel Barenboim's public controversy with the Berliner Staatsoper (especially when Klaus Land-
owsky, leader of the ruling Christian Democrats in the Berlin Senat

[state parliament], referred to the conductor as "der Jude Barenboim" [the Jew Barenboim] and juxtaposed him to his colleague,
"der Deutsche Thielemann" [the German Thielemann], which created quite a stir); the German reception of the work of Norman
Finkelstein (author of *The Holocaust Industry: Reflections on the
Exploitation of Jewish Suffering*), a publishing event so polarizing
and inflammatory that it was characterized in *Der Spiegel* as a second *Historikerstreit* (more on *Finkelstein later*);[2] and, most recently,
the widespread furor (ranging from vituperative rejection to impassioned defense) over the comments of the late FDP (*Freie
Demokratische Partei* [Free Democratic Party]) representative Jürgen Möllemann regarding Jewish complicity in the growth of anti-
Semitism, and the publication of Martin Walser's allegedly
anti-Semitic novel, *Tod eines Kritikers* (*Death of a Critic*).

All of these controversies suggest that Germany's sensitivity to its
National Socialist past has not only failed to diminish, but has even
escalated over the last few years. Even after more than fifty years
since the Holocaust, those demanding absolution and atonement
are experiencing a new license or liberty granting both sides in the
debate over Germany's Nazi past an unrestricted forcefulness in
their public pronouncements that had been unheard of only a few
years before. This is not to say that the feelings involved were not
just as intense in the 1960s, 1970s, and 1980s, but that a shift in the
contours of the public sphere now makes their expression more
acceptable and widespread.

This is borne out by what I perceive to be a relatively recent
development: a shift in a mode of discourse and argumentation
found in discussions concerning the life and works of Richard Wagner, the most hallowed and hated, revered and reviled, exemplar of
nineteenth-century German culture, whose works—fairly or
unfairly—have come to be inextricably linked in the public consciousness with the Nazi regime, owing to that regime's enthusiasm
for Wagner's music dramas, his anti-Semitic writings and the summer festivals in Bayreuth devoted solely to the performance of Wagner's works for the stage.

I wish to focus on what I perceive to be a new feature in Wagner
research because, though it is less well-known, I believe it evinces
much of the heated affect, resentments, and assumptions found in the
other controversies concerning modern German identity I have just
cited, and thus provides us with a locus for their concrete analysis.

For it is my belief that disagreements in the Wagner debate have much to do not only with questions of aesthetic judgment and a discomfort brought about through the besmirching of hallowed works of art—though these often constitute the manifest content of the discussion—but also with the current social and political function of Wagner in contemporary Germany as a hallmark of cultural and political heritage, and that means, for many, German identity per se. In this sense, the Wagner debate is representative of deep-seated, larger issues of cultural identity that, since the 1980s, have emerged in other cultural controversies associated with the Nazi past in general and with the Holocaust in particular.

For a decade I have been arguing that there is a connection between Wagner's works for the stage and the repertoire of anti-Semitic images found throughout his writings and in the culture in which he worked.[3] And just as I believe that an entire repertoire of anti-Semitic associations contributed to the conceptualization of many of Wagner's dramatic figures whom the composer never explicitly labeled as Jews (Mime, Alberich, Hagen, Beckmesser, Klingsor, Kundry, etc.), so I also discern, in the rhetoric and arguments of some recent scholarly and popular discussions of Wagner and the Bayreuth festival, the phantasmatic image of the Jew as a figure threatening the sanctity of the Wagnerian heritage. In other words, some of Wagner's assumptions regarding the Jew can still be discerned—alarmingly—behind the methodologies, arguments, and discourse of a small group of writers currently involved in public discussions defending Wagner, the Wagner family, and the Bayreuth festival. In their writings, this threatening, phantasmatic figure is only occasionally explicitly labeled as a Jew, but whether overtly identified as such or not, he consistently bears the traces of the being Richard Wagner most despised and feared.

Since the end of World War II, and especially since the late 1960s, the question of the degree to which Wagner's anti-Semitism should play a role in our understanding of his works for the stage has been the most contentious issue within Wagner studies, and the way it has been discussed helps us to recognize three phases in post-war Wagnerian scholarship: the first, from the end of World War II to the late 1960s, characterized primarily by silence or denial on the subject of the composer's racism; the second, from the late 1960s to the late 1990s, in which the subject was so forcefully articulated by a host of scholars that it could no longer be ignored—from Robert

Gutman and Hartmut Zelinsky from the late 1960s to the late 1980s, to Paul Lawrence Rose, Barry Millington, Stewart Spencer, and David Levin in the late 1980s and throughout the 1990s.[4] The third phase is characterized by the aforementioned new level of vituperousness in the last decade. In this phase, it was also addressed, though forcefully dismissed, by a much larger group of established scholars, most notably Curt von Westerhagen, Carl Dahlhaus, Peter Wapnewski, Martin Gregor-Dellin, Dieter Borchmeyer, Jakob Katz, Michael Tanner, and many others as well.[5] What I am describing as a more recent phenomenon actually constitutes a development based on many of the assumptions of the more defensive scholars in the 1980s and 1990s, and has only emerged in the past few years in the writings of a much smaller group, since roughly 1997. It is characterized for me by a shift in both the content and the conceptual frame of its public pronouncements.

Throughout the 1980s and 1990s, it was clear that disagreements about Wagner's anti-Semitism often resulted from the fact that the participants were interested in and were talking about vastly different things and from the fact that they were basing their arguments on nearly incompatible aesthetic paradigms.[6] These methodological disagreements dovetailed with and often masked different ideological positions. At the risk of oversimplification, one could say that when one was defending Wagner, Wagner's champions focused on the material of the aesthetic object, while those interested in the anti-Semitic implications of Wagner's works focused on the social and historical contexts—something Wagner's defenders also did in their work on the figure and his music dramas, but not when the issue was anti-Semitism.[7] When Hartmut Zelinsky argued that *Parsifal* was a product of Wagner's anti-Semitism, Joachim Kaiser replied that "*Parsifal* contains no anti-Semitic word, no somehow unequivocally anti-Semitic constellation!" (*Parsifal* enthält kein antisemitisches Wort, keine irgendwie eindeutig antisemitische Konstellation!).[8]

Of particular interest here is the conflation of a paradigm of literal reading, based on the assumption that meaning must be immanently manifest to be deemed valid, with a position that rejects an interpretation of Wagner's music dramas as anti-Semitic.[9] Time and again, reference is made in defenses such as this to the purportedly philologically unverifiable nature of the claims made by Wagner's critics in an attempt to discredit their readings as all too speculative,

associative, and metaphorical in nature. This is the very strategy or
mode of reading that informs the work of Dieter Borchmeyer, who
has both repeatedly defended Wagner's works against the charge
of racism and, in his capacity as editor of the ten-volume edition of
Wagner's *Dichtungen und Schriften* published by the Insel press in
1983, chose to omit most of the anti-Semitic essays from the collection and did so, as he stated in print, gladly.[10] In a lecture presented
the following year to the Richard-Wagner-Verband in Brunswick
and subsequently published in the 1986 edition of the *Richard-
Wagner-Handbuch* (translated into English in the early 1990s),
Borchmeyer argues in a fashion similar to that of his fellow philologically oriented, apologetic literal reader Kaiser:

> It must be said that, in all of Wagner's innumerable commentaries on
> his own works, there is not a single statement which would entitle us
> to interpret any of the characters in the music dramas or any of the
> details of their plots in anti-Semitic terms, or even to interpret them
> as allusions to Jews. The attempt to interpret the Nibelungs, and
> especially the figure of Mime, as mythic projections of the Jews—an
> interpretation based on Wagner's description of the physical appear-
> ance and speech patterns of Jews in his 1850 essay ("Das Judentum
> in der Musik"—"Judaism in Music")—is no more than an unverifi-
> able hypothesis. . . . We are bound to ask ourselves why, in spite of his
> violently anti-Semitic polemical writings, there is not a single trace in
> Wagner's music dramas of any similar tendencies (a claim which is
> philologically unassailable, notwithstanding speculative suggestions
> to the contrary).[11]

This defense of the artworks through a paradigm of literal reading
became a repeated hallmark of the writings of a number of other
Wagnerian critics as well and reemerged in Professor Borchmeyer's
most recent and popular book on the figure, *Richard Wagner:
Ahasvers Wandlungen* (Ahasvers' Transformations). So, this is a
methodological issue that has by no means disappeared.[12] It also is
central to the writings of a number of other Wagnerian critics as
well, especially Hans Rudolf Vaget, who, writing in a similar vein,
has made such arguments as the following:

> Any attempt to ascertain the textual existence of a "Jewish" Beck-
> messer, a "Jewish" Alberich, a "Jewish" Klingsor must come to grips
> with the following questions: Is it not reasonable to assume that the

absence of any *clearly and unmistakably* Jewish attributes indicates the innocence of Wagner's work on this score? . . . And what about the *semantic indeterminacy* of the art of music: Does it not really *preclude* the musical articulation of anti-Semitism, even in so fanatical an anti-Semite and sophisticated a composer as Wagner? . . . Those of us who . . . insist on making distinctions and balanced judgments *on the basis of incontrovertible evidence*, are scorned for our unenlightened views. . . . What [this] shows is that while the alleged Jewish figures in Wagner may have a certain contextual existence, they have, strictly speaking, no textual existence.[13]

The emergence of this paradigm in defense of Wagner's works is particularly ironic given the fact that it is readily comparable to Wagner's understanding of a kind of superficial, literal aesthetics he associated with Jews, an aesthetics that locates meaning in the material of the sign and that fails to discern the implications and associations to which the sign also can refer. In "Deutsche Kunst und deutsche Politik" ("German Art and German Politics"), Wagner characterizes this distinction as that between "Realismus" and "Idealismus," and he associates the former with the superficial art of the mime and with what he calls "die kosmopolitische Synagoge der Jetztzeit" (the "cosmopolitan synagogue of the modern age"), while he associates the latter with the German artist's purported ability to discern meaning behind the sign, between the lines, as it were. It is my belief that Wagner dramatized this notion in the confrontation between the Nibelung dwarf Mime—an artist who invents the *Tarnhelm*, a device that allows one to take on the appearance of others, and hence a metaphor for mimicry—and the German superhero, Siegfried.[14] In other words, if Wagner were reading these debates today, he would characterize his defenders as Jews and his detractors as Germans, a historical irony indeed.

Another methodology used in defense of Wagner and his works against the charge of anti-Semitism is what I would call a kind of mind-boggling positivism. It emerges clearly, for example, in the work of Dieter David Scholz, who trained with Peter Wapnewski and Jakob Katz and who now regularly writes for the Bayreuth Festivals' summer programs. In an article entitled "Wagner im Zwielicht" ("Wagner in the Twilight"), published in 1997 in the Sender Freies Berlin's journal *Triangel*, Scholz engages in a remarkable

methodological exercise that recalls both Richard Wagner's preoccupation with his own racial heritage and Wagnerian scholarship
from the Nazi period.[15] It is positivism par excellence.

Scholz seeks to refute the characterization of Richard Wagner as
a racist, the reading of his works as anti-Semitic, and criticism of the
Bayreuth Festival's tainted past by arguing that Wagner could not
have been a Jew! In other words, according to Scholz, if Wagner
were not a Jew, any discussion of his racism would be beside the
point. The assumptions and the implications of this argument are
worth considering.

Ever since Nietzsche's pun that "an eagle [Adler] is almost a vulture [Geier]" (based on the assumption that anyone named "Adler"
must be Jewish), Wagner scholarship has often posed the question
of whether the composer himself wondered if he might have been
the illegitimate son of Ludwig Geyer (the German pronunciation of
which is identical to that of the word for "vulture"), whom Wagner
may have suspected of being a Jew. The evidence on this issue is not
hard and fast, but quite provocative and was made much of by the
English scholar Ernest Newman in the 1930s and later by Adorno
in his pioneering book, *Versuch über Wagner*.[16] Throughout the
writings of virtually all of the major Wagner critics, this issue has
arisen repeatedly, either as a provocative reflection on the motivation for Wagner's anti-Semitism or as an irritant that must be dismissed in the writings of those who wish to minimize the
composer's racism or to segregate it from a discussion of his works.
I think of it as a nearly racist preoccupation, and Richard Wagner
was not the only one to worry about the matter.

Given the racist program of the National Socialists, it makes
sense that scholars under this program sought to put this rumor to
rest by documenting the racial purity of both Wagner's official
father, Carl Friedrich Wilhelm Wagner, and the man who Richard
Wagner may have suspected of being his biological progenitor, Ludwig Heinrich Christian Geyer, whom Wagner's mother married following the death of her first husband, just six months after Wagner's
birth. The most famous example of this kind of study is Walter
Lange's *Richard Wagners Sippe: Vom Urahn zum Enkel* (Richard
Wagner's Tribe: From Ancestor to Grandson), published in Leipzig
in 1938. But the Nazi's racist agenda did not disappear in 1945; it
resurfaced in 1985 in an exhibit at Bayreuth organized by the director of its archives, Dr. Manfred Eger, and published as *Wagner und*

die Juden: Fakten und Hintergründe: Eine Dokumentation zur Ausstellung im Richard-Wagner-Museum Bayreuth.[17] Here, Eger went to some lengths to lay to rest the questions concerning both Geyer's having been Wagner's true father and (just in case?) Geyer's racial pedigree. These were the "facts" that were designed to put an end to troubling speculation regarding Wagner's identity.[18]

Clearly, Lange's motivation was outright racist, while Eger's may have resulted from the need felt by the directorship of the Bayreuth festival to downplay the racism of both the man and the music with which the festival is associated. If so, the Bayreyth administration made the assumption that Wagner's racial pedigree was inherently related to his feelings toward Jews, though it is unclear whether that assumption is based on some late-nineteenth-century notion of genetics as the basis of identity, on a psychoanalytic model of identity formation, or simply on a personal antipathy about the notion that Wagner may have been Jewish. Whatever their motivation, they clearly felt the need to point out that Richard Wagner was no Jew.

And this is apparently precisely the motivation behind Scholz's work—he goes to great lengths to demonstrate that the area in which Geyer lived was not a *Judenviertel* (Jewish quarter), and he does a good deal of racially interested genealogical research designed to exonerate Wagner's racial pedigree. Scholz clearly believes that if he can prove that Wagner's paternal heritage is *judenfrei* (free of Jewish ancestry), any discussion of Wagner's racism is unfounded and beside the point, but he does not say why. Does he believe that if we know that Wagner was not Jewish, Wagner must have known this as well? Or does he feel that this is some kind of ex post facto exoneration (that would let Richard off the hook)? The implication is that any discussion of the composer's racism in general, or any suggestion that Wagner drew upon an arsenal of anti-Semitic imagery when creating his works for the stage, would be without not only any philological or even positivistic, biographical foundation, but perhaps even without a biological one as well. But it is hard to say what the motivation is—whether one, two, or all of these reasons play a role—because Scholz does not feel it necessary to explain why he is making this claim.

This kind of statement regarding the racial identity of Richard Wagner and of the Wagner clan crops up repeatedly in the writings of those associated with Bayreuth, an *idée fixe* found, for example, in Wolfgang Wagner's autobiography, *Lebensakte* (1994), when he writes of Cosima Wagner's mother, Marie de Flavigny, and describes her as "a banker's daughter from the house of Bethmann in Frankfurt am Main (arian!) [*arisch!*]."[19] I find this clarification—this aside in brackets—revealing. Those who defend Bayreuth don't like people speculating about Richard Wagner's potential Jewishness, nor that of any of the other Wagners, apparently.

Things would not be so bad if the reemergence, within recent scholarship, of Wagner's notion of Jewish aesthetics, sensibilities, and even genetically determined identity were limited to the use of antiquated, philologically oriented aesthetic paradigms and positivism on the part of some defensive critics trying to protect Wagner, his works, and the festival with which he is associated from the charge of anti-Semitism. In fact, it might be kind of funny. But things get a bit worse when some of the other features Wagner associated with the Jew reemerge in public debates about Wagner, his works, and the Bayreuth festival as well.

Wagner thought of the Jew as avaricious, out to belittle great works for personal gain; as uncreative, merely adept at copying or mimicry; as psychologically imbalanced, so anxious and malicious as to verge on insanity; and as a figure who, longing to be accepted by a society that excludes him, attempts to make his foreignness invisible. All of these are stock nineteenth-century anti-Semitic clichés central to Wagner's writings about Jews and their place in European culture, and they all reappear in some recent attacks on a figure who has criticized Wagner's music dramas and the Wagnerian tradition in Bayreuth, a figure who is described as avaricious, irreverent, uncreative, and psychologically imbalanced.

I wish to make clear that I am *not* claiming that the scholars I am about to discuss, whose writings employ such character assassination, are themselves necessarily anti-Semitic, nor that their audience will automatically recognize their attacks as propelled by Judeophobia. What I am claiming is that the discourse of the Wagner debate, like the recent and very popular discussion of the work of Norman Finkelstein (described below) and of Martin Walser's literary portrayal of the Jewish critic Marcel Reich-Ranicki,[20] evinces many of the features Richard Wagner explicitly associated with the Jew, and it does so in connection with a figure some have seen as acting like, or even of actually himself *being*, a Jew.

That figure is Gottfried Wagner, son of the current festival director, Wolfgang, great-grandson of the composer Richard Wagner, and indisputably the black sheep of the Wagner clan. My argument is that Gottfried Wagner has been turned into a Jew, that he functions for some much as the Jew did for Wagner. Gottfried Wagner is described as bearing the features and traits his great-grandfather discerned in his most despised racial and aesthetic nemesis—as greedy, without requisite awe and piety, and obviously off his rocker.

In what follows, I will be discussing Gottfried Wagner not because I wish to defend him, but to show that he functions as what one might call an occasion or a space around which an affect-laden discursive phenomenon has emerged. Gottfried Wagner constitutes an irritant within the discussion of Richard Wagner, and it is illuminating to observe how different participants, responding to him for different reasons, have resorted to a similar rhetorical and characterological repertoire once associated explicitly with anti-Semitism.

In his 1997 autobiography, *Wer nicht mit dem Wolf heult* (*Twilight of the Wagners: The Unveiling of a Family's Legacy*), and elsewhere, Gottfried Wagner has written extensively of his father's and the Bayreuth festival's close ties to the Nazi past, of the function of Richard Wagner's artworks as signifying both the composer's and the National Socialists' racism, and of his family's culpability vis-à-vis Israel and the Jews.[21] Such arguments were initially received by Wolfgang Wagner in silence and then in angry denunciation of his son, something that is lamentable, but perhaps at least understandable.

Beginning in the summer of 1997, however, the aforementioned Dieter David Scholz engaged in what I can only describe as a highly public campaign of character assassination directed at Gottfried Wagner. And since then, he and others have continued to reject Richard Wagner's great-grandson within the forum of public debate, not by addressing his arguments, but through a strategy of detailed personal invective and slander that I believe draws upon a repertoire of clichés that, in the nineteenth and early twentieth centuries, were openly anti-Semitic. Scholz contributed to a climate of character assassination that drew on this repertoire by implying that Gottfried Wagner's criticism of his father and of the Bayreuth festival is primarily driven *by a desire for financial gain*. He did so first in a radio interview with the Sender Freies Berlin and again in the aforementioned article in *Triangel*, in which he wrote the following: "If Gottfried, Wagner's great-grandson, wants to make it his private life's mission to drag his father's and his great-grandfather's family history through the mud, *from which he lives well*, so be it" (Wenn

Gottfried, der Urenkel Wagners, es sich zu seiner privaten Leben-saufgabe macht, die Familiengeschichte seines Vaters und seines Urgroßvaters in den Schmutz zu ziehen, *wovon er gut lebt*, sei ihm dies unbenommen).[22]

Scholz's accusatory "From which he lives well" is a reference to Gottfried Wagner's visibility as author, media personality omni-present in discussions of Bayreuth on the radio, in television, and in the newspapers, and to the fact that, both as a critic and lecturer, he receives an honorarium, as do most others involved in the same pro-fessional activities, including of course Scholz himself. It is signifi-cant that this kind of statement is found not only in Scholz's writings, but throughout the negative reception of the Gottfried Wagner's autobiography, most famously perhaps in a 1997 review not by a right-wing, conservative reactionary, but by Henryk Broder, who, as a trenchant observer of German politics and a chronicler of the Jews in Germany, has been a thorn in the side of the German Establishment for over thirty years. His review appeared in *Der Tagesspiegel Berlin* and opened with a statement nearly identical to the one just quoted, describing the book as "a documentation of the life and suffering of the great-grandson of Wagner, who for many years *has been making a living* by unmasking his great-grandfather as an anti-Semite, an anti-democrat, and as someone who prepared the way for the Nazis" (eine Dokumenta-tion über das Leben und das Leiden des Wagner-Urenkels, der *seit vielen Jahren davon lebt*, daß er seinen Urgroßvater als Antisemiten, Anti-Demokraten und Nazi-Wegbereiter entlarvt).[23] So Scholz's statement should be seen as representative of a pervasive response, and it is remarkable just how often reviews of the book link Got-tfried Wagner's writings and his livelihood in an obvious attempt to discredit his criticism. Indeed, they do so largely in place of engag-ing in a discussion of the merits—or lack thereof—of Gottfried Wagner's arguments.

Scholz makes this kind of remark not once, but twice in the *Tri-angel* article, for not long after the passage just cited, he continues with the following: "Gottfried Wagner (like many other one-sided polemicizing Wagner ideologues) completely ignores [a host of] facts, in order to keep his effect-laden and lucrative intellectual con-struct from collapsing." (Gottfried Wagner ignoriert [wie manche anderen einseitig polemisierenden Wagner-Ideologen] diese Tat-sachen völlig, um sein effektvoll-lukratives Gedankengebäude nicht

einstürzen zu lassen).[24] This is a repeated topos: Wagner criticism as
a lucrative enterprise that only brings gain, apparently, to those who
have negative things to say about the Master and his works, whereby
the critic emerges as a Judas-like figure whose gold is tainted.

What's more, that purportedly avaricious critic is also calumniated as suffering from mental imbalance. Now, to be sure, Gottfried
Wagner's autobiography, *Wer nicht mit dem Wolf heult* often evinces
evidence of psychological trauma, but the criticism of which I am
speaking goes well beyond merely taking note of this feature within
a discussion of the author's arguments. When Gottfried Wagner
appeared in Bayreuth during a lecture tour in Germany in the summer of 1997, he was asked by a member of the audience, "How
much time have you spent in mental institutions?" and a prominent
review of his autobiography, by Horst Seferens from the summer of
1997, bore the title "Was Gottfried Wagner seinem Therapeuten noch
sagen wollte . . . " (which can be roughly translated as "And another
thing that Gottfried Wagner wanted to tell his therapist . . . ").[25] In an
official response to the book by the city of Bayreuth, the lord and
vice-mayors wrote of the author's "offenkundige Persönlichkeit-
sprobleme" (obvious character disorders).[26] Seferens also characterizes
the autobiography as "an occasionally embarrassing document of
avaricious or obsessive [*besitzergreifenden*] philosemitism" and writes
of "a specific, infantile philosemitism that does not mark the stages of a
maturation process, but rather the fortified refuge [*Fluchtburg*] of a
failed German search for identity after the Holocaust."[27]

Here, pop psychology reduces Gottfried Wagner's motivation to
the needs of a whining child who can never get enough and whose
fears, desires, and ingratitude are the typical hallmarks of a spoiled
brat. Moreover, throughout the material under discussion, a subtext
is palpably manifest regarding the question as to who gets to qualify
as a victim and who is labeled as occupying the position of perpetra-
tor—the very issues involved, moreover, in the recent controversies
surrounding Jürgen Möllemann and Martin Walser mentioned
above. Such remarks go hand-in-hand and are linked with those
regarding Gottfried Wagner's purported avarice and mental instability, and they take the place of a detailed analysis of his arguments.

These character traits emerge as part of a purported syndrome
that is seen to reveal identity, and that identity is implicitly limited
not solely to one's psychological makeup, but even to one's genetic

lineage as well. This was the case, of course, in the writings of Richard Wagner, where the link between a catalogue of anti-Semitic stereotypes and racial identity was explicit. One passage of Scholz's text suggests that that may be the case here as well, though here the connection is only implied.

The link between character and heritage emerges in Scholz's work from 1997 and from the summer of 2000, in his book *Richard Wagners Antisemitismus: Jahrhundertgenie im Zwielicht* and in his responses to Gottfried Wagner's charges of anti-Semitism in Wagner's life, works, and in the history of the Bayreuth Festival, published in the article in *Triangel.* His aforementioned remark concerning the "facts" about Richard Wagner's non-Jewish heritage that Gottfried Wagner is said to ignore *immediately precedes* Scholz's repeated charge that the composer's great-grandson is engaging in criticism of the Bayreuth festival in order to make money. Here, again, is the passage already cited: "Gottfried Wagner (like many other one-sided polemicizing Wagner ideologues) completely ignores these facts [i.e., concerning the probability that Geyer was not Wagner's father and that neither Geyer nor Carl Friedrich Wilhelm Wagner was Jewish], in order to keep his effect-laden and lucrative intellectual construct from collapsing." The implied connection here, within the rhetorical movement of Scholz's text, between Wagner's non-Jewish paternal lineage and the characterization of Gottfried Wagner as money-grubbing is both obvious and horrific, incredible and laughable at the same time. For by saying that Richard Wagner wasn't Jewish, the logic of Scholz's text implies that the composer was free of traits stereotypically associated with Jews, while the other Wagner, Gottfried, exhibits precisely those traits the composer repeatedly calumniated as the opposite of the generous and selfless, communally minded German. Here, the Jew is airbrushed out of the image of Richard Wagner, if only to reappear in that of his great-grandson who is accused of bearing a host of stereotypical features publicly linked to the Jew in an earlier phase of German culture. The point is that Scholz and his publishers find such arguments as these persuasive and assume that an audience of readers and opera-goers will find them so as well (and perhaps they do). One of their assumptions is that the question of racial identity is somehow related to the veracity of the arguments of Wagner's critics, and these are the "facts" of which Scholz writes, recalling the title of Manfred Eger's exhibit at Bayreuth on Wagner and the Jews: "Fakten und Hintergründe."

But how direct is the connection between racial identity and the criticism of Bayreuth? Is it only implied—not only in the remarks of Scholz, but of others as well—or is it more explicit? In other words, is the Jew evoked primarily as a metaphorical construct replete with specific character traits, or is the notion of identity more firmly anchored in biology and genetic conceptualizations of race and lineage? An answer is suggested in an important book from 1998 by Gottfried Wagner's cousin Nike, daughter of the famed director Wieland Wagner (Wolfgang Wagner's brother who died in 1966) and herself, for a time, an aspirant to the directorship of the Bayreuth Festival. In *Wagner Theater* (translated into English as *The Wagners: The Dramas of a Musical Dynasty*), she makes it clear that her family went so far as to suggest *explicitly* that Gottfried may in fact *be* a Jew. She writes, "There was a persistent family rumour that his [Gottfried's] maternal grandmother, Thora, had been of Jewish origin: this may have intensified his feelings of personal involvement." (Hartnäckig hielt in der Familie sich das Gerücht, daß seine Großmutter mütterlicherseits, Thora mit Namen, jüdischer Herkunft gewesen sei).[28] Nike Wagner makes no mention of his sister, Eva Wagner-Pasquier, despite the fact that she is from the same gene pool, presumably because that inconsistency was never mentioned, or recognized as a contradiction, by the other members of the Wagner family of which she writes. Now, if Gottfried Wagner is Jewish owing to his maternal grandmother, why isn't his sister? Presumably because Eva was no outspoken critic of Bayreuth. Apparently, the Wagner family believed that there had to be something Jewish about you for you to engage in criticism of the anti-Semitic history of that hallowed institution, and thus Eva escapes the racial epithet, while her brother does not. No wonder Winifred Wagner, Gottfried's grandmother and, to the moment of her death, an outspoken and unrepentant admirer of Hitler, described her grandson as the "friend in the family of Jews and Bolsheviks."[29]

Gottfried Wagner is Richard Wagner's Jew—a being too close for comfort, someone resembling the family but not really part of it, and thus remarkably similar to Richard Wagner's description of the assimilated, Western Jew—a Heine- and Meyerbeer-like figure who must be revealed for what he is: someone who looks like a member of the family, but is a dangerous, greedy, and critical schemer, an imposter who should not be taken too seriously, whose foreignness must be recognized, lest he be given too much credibility.[30] Nike's remarks serve the purpose of making explicit something that I feel is lurking beneath the other statements regarding Gottfried Wagner's character I have just cited.

I'd like to make clear that I am not concerned with the veracity of these statements—whether Gottfried Wagner really is greedy, is clinically imbalanced, does identify with Jews as victims, or even had a Jewish grandmother, for that matter—but I am concerned with the fact that these issues are used to avoid a discussion of his arguments on the assumption that such rhetorical moves, such invective (which often includes a biological, racist subtext), will persuade a large audience today, an assumption apparently shared by Scholz's publishers. Gottfried Wagner's points are discredited through calumniation, and the specific content and nature of that calumniation evoke a repertoire of character traits that had hitherto been associated with anti-Semitic portrayals of Jews in the nineteenth and early twentieth centuries. Moreover, it occurs at a time when other German discussions of anti-Semitism and the Holocaust have also evinced a similarly affect-laden strategy of personal ridicule drawing upon similar clichés.

Now, in the recent discussion of Martin Walser's *Tod eines Kritikers*, the question was repeatedly asked whether the repertoire of anti-Semitic clichés discernible in the novel makes it or its author or both anti-Semitic—obvious questions, perhaps, but ultimately unproductive and something that each reader must decide for him or herself. My purpose has been to point out a feature of recent Wagner criticism that constitutes, I think, an expansion of earlier manifestations within the Wagner debate of characteristics the composer associated with Jews, precisely because the figure of the Jew is one of the central issues of these discussions, and because these features have gone unnoticed.

In the 1980s and early 1990s, the traits Wagner associated with Jews reappeared in the reliance on a kind of literal interpretive paradigm used by Wagner's modern defenders. Since the late 1990s, more characterological traits have reemerged as well in the writings of those defending Richard Wagner and the Bayreuth festival against the criticism by Gottfried Wagner. Precisely because these reintroduced neo-Wagnerian Jewish stereotypes have gone unnoticed, one could justifiably argue that they are not anti-Semitic, or certainly were not intended as such, and personally I am not at all concerned about what such authors as Scholz, Seferens, and others I have cited think about Jews or about their own relationship to them. I am not saying that they are anti-Semites, and frankly, I do not care if they are. What does interest me is the conceptual and rhetorical tradition in which both the figure they are discussing and their own mode of argumentation can be seen.

I do not wish to fall into the philological trap of saying that a statement is only anti-Semitic if it is overtly so, for that is precisely the defense that has been put forth by such slippery and politically adept figures as Jörg Haider and Jürgen Möllemann, who understand quite well that a given cultural context will lend specifically racist overtones to statements that a philologist would have to label as free of overtly racist meaning. But perhaps this example goes too far, because what I am referring to is not so much intention as a question of cultural resonance. What I would call a given cultural vocabulary may provide the associations that turn manifestly inoffensive statements—and dramatic images, for that matter—into innuendo, thereby making the question as to what constitutes an anti-Semitic remark and image by no means one that can be addressed by those such as Kaiser, Borchmeyer, and Vaget, who insist on a hermeneutics of literal reading. By comparing Scholz, Seferens, and Broder, I am drawing attention to thinkers who span the entire intellectual and political spectrum and whose work seeks to address vastly different projects. They are not all alike, but precisely for this reason, their argumentative assumptions, rhetorical moves, and even simple statements allow us insight into a widespread discursive phenomenon that may resonate in different ways difficult to determine.

I have stated above that some of the most recent writing in the Wagner debate shares a particularly heated affect with other recent controversies related to the Holocaust—with the discussions about the Holocaust memorial, the Goldhagen and Walser affairs, Barenboim's position as a public Jewish figure, and others still. Therefore, I would like now to shift not the focus, but the material of the discussion and pursue just one of these examples in order to underscore the similarities involved—that is, to show that the Wagner discussion really is representative of a larger discourse. To different degrees, the other controversies evince a similar defensive and angry affect and, occasionally, a similar tendency toward character assassination. These

are most obvious, however, in the reception of the work of Norman
Finkelstein, which I therefore would like to trace very briefly.

When Finkelstein's *Holocaust Industry* was first discussed in the
German press (a half year before it appeared in German translation),
critics dismissed the book by lambasting its author as mentally
unstable and out for financial gain. As Leon de Winter put it in *Der
Spiegel*, in a review from August 2000 entitled "Der Groll des
Sohnes" ("The son's burning resentment"), Finkelstein still lives in
the apartment left to him by his deceased parents, he is motivated
by revenge on behalf of his mother who was insufficiently compen-
sated by the Conference on Jewish Material Claims against Germany for her time in the death camp Majdanek, and he is merely a
lecturer at Hunter College, a position roughly comparable, de Winter says, to that of an elevator attendant at the City University of
New York, an institution, as the *Spiegel* author put it, "nicht sonder-
lich angesehen" (not particularly prestigious), all fairly calumniating
statements in the unforgiving climate of fetishized professional
accomplishment in Germany.[31] Omar Bartov had engaged in similar
assaults on Finkelstein's character when he reviewed the book in *the
New York Times*. He wrote, "There is something sad in this warping
of intelligence, and in this perversion of moral indignation. There is
also something indecent about it, something juvenile, self-righteous, arrogant and stupid. . . . This book is, in a word, an ideological fanatic's view of other people's opportunism."[32] And Bartov
even went so far as to suggest that Finkelstein was aligning himself
with "the bastions of Western capitalism" by denouncing those who
exploit Jewish suffering for financial reparations, a claim that once
again raises the issue of financial gain within the arena of public
exchange in order to invalidate an opponent's arguments.

De Winter's review in *Der Spiegel* is less a discussion of Finkelstein's book than of the man himself and claims, for example, that
The Holocaust Industry, a "curious book," is "basically nothing
more than the obscure product of an emotionally driven extremist."
(Finkelsteins kuriose[s] Buch [ist] . . . im Grunde nichts als das
obscure Produkt eines von Gefühlen geleiteten Extremisten). De
Winter concludes his review by saying that "Finkelstein does not
catalogue the unadulterated truth. He cannot do otherwise,
because he wishes to justify the radical beliefs and feelings of his
deceased mother. That he did not secure the attention of a good
therapist, but instead found the interest of the world press, is quite

an accomplishment." (Finkelstein zeigt nicht die unverblümte Wahrheit auf. Er kann nicht anders, weil er die radikalen Ansichten und Gefühle seiner verstorbenen Mutter rechtfertigen möchte. Dass er sich damit nicht etwa der Aufmerksamkeit eines guten Thera-peuten versichert, sondern das Interesse der Weltpresse gefunden hat, ist schon eine reife Leistung).[33] We have only to recall the title of Horst Seferens's aforementioned review, "Was Gottfried Wagner seinem Therapeuten noch sagen wollte . . . ," to realize that we are dealing here with a pervasive topos.

The critics in the Wagner debate and Finkelstein's detractors share much with the participants in the other debates I have men-tioned, in that all of their polemical exchanges—albeit to differing degrees—evince a shift in a public discourse that constitutes a mis-understanding or an exploitation of the introduction of the personal within discussions of identity politics. Nor are they alone in this regard, as even a cursory look at Gottfried Wagner's and Finkel-stein's own rhetoric will demonstrate (given the former's focus on the ideological implications of his father's biography and the fact that if ever there was a tome replete with ad hominem invective, it is *The Holocaust Industry*). But that is the point. These most recent discussions of the Holocaust and of cultural artifacts indirectly related to it are often discussions not about these events and aes-thetic objects, but about those who speak about them.

I believe that the image of the Jew has accompanied many of these scholarly exchanges. In the Wagner debate of the 1970s and 1980s, it was usually unacknowledged (or perhaps one could even say "repressed," functioning as an irritating subtext), thereby con-tributing to the tension and resentments of the debate, while in the third, most recent phase, the Jew has emerged as associated with traits deemed objectionable. In the Finkelstein debate, it is a bit more complicated because Finkelstein is arguing for an expanded notion of Jewish identity (divorced from support of Israeli politics). One could argue that here we find the opposite of what unfolds in the Wagner debate, in that some of Finkelstein's critics argue that, in terms of identity, Finkelstein is not really a Jew at all, but a traitor to them. My point, however, is that both debates evince a repertoire of epithets and affect recalling earlier anti-Semitic invective, as seen in the fact that Finkelstein emerges as bearing the very traits assigned to Gottfried Wagner as a critic of Bayreuth.

What might account for this shift in the public discourse in Germany that allows for the calumniation of one's opponents through recourse to a discourse once associated with attacks on Jews, both within the rarified confines of the Wagner debate and within the other more public recent controversies I have referred to? One explanation might be found in the need to speak more loudly within the increasing and increasingly competitive noise of the media, in which one must seek more forcefully than ever before to gain the listener's and reader's attention if one is to be heard at all.[34] In other words, to speak in Marxist terms, perhaps there is a material substructure—the recent proliferation of media within German-speaking Europe—that propels a proliferation of attempts to shock the audience in order to gain its attention.

That would suggest, however, that such statements as those I have been discussing really are seen as shocking, and yet I have also been arguing the opposite, that they appear to have become *salonfähig* (acceptable), or at least tolerated, within the public sphere. So perhaps we are dealing here with a contradiction central to the emerging contours of that sphere at this moment—the fact that what is shocking only appears to be so or purportedly functions as such, even though it actually has come to be tolerated and perhaps even expected within public discussions in Germany. This explanation would be far more in keeping with the tenets of the culture industry thesis, according to which the content of the discussion is secondary to the structure—that is, the media—within which it unfolds. Seen in this light, the debates I have been discussing appear as distant cousins of TV afternoon talk shows, in which the audience is "shocked, shocked!" by guests lambasting each other with character assassination. And perhaps it is no coincidence that such shows began to appear widely on German television in the late 1990s, around the time that the shift in the discourse of the Wagner debate became manifest. Both are examples of the same phenomenon.

A different possible explanation is more psychological in nature. If ever a psychoanalytical theory of culture were appropriate to a discussion of postwar Germany (as the Mitscherlichs maintained in the 1970s, as Habermas suggested, once again, in the *Historikerstreit*, and as Erik Santner has articulated more recently),[35] the Wagner debate and the other controversies I have just alluded to would be an ideal place for it. Reading these exchanges through the Mitscherlichs' interpretive matrix, one can see that in Germany the obviously painful interaction with the charge of anti-Semitism suggests deep-seated issues of personal, social, and perhaps even national identity.

But the psychoanalytical healing process pleaded for by the Mitscherlichs has proven far less persuasive. They felt that the repressed trauma of a generation would be healed if it could be openly acknowledged, and this belief has demonstrably proven unfounded. For as Freud pointed out, the patient has to want to change in order to benefit from the "Trauerarbeit" (work of mourning) that breaks down mechanisms of repression, and that process cannot be dictated if it is to be successful. If there are those who resent and refuse the self-indicting therapy demanded of them by their opponents, no campaign of guilt and atonement, public or otherwise, will bring about the result the Mitscherlichs so desired (In Germany, this was made particularly clear in the Walser/Bubis controversy).

The most recent phase of the Wagner debate, as well as its comparison with earlier phases, suggests that it would be illusionary to hang on to the dream of a democratic heterogeneity, masking the homogeneity of like-minded, philo-Semitic brethren engaging in the kind of egalitarian exchange that would bring a smile to the face of Jürgen Habermas. In place of a psychological model of open confession bringing forth suppressed trauma, we are faced today with a battle for the status of victim that evinces no signs of widespread psychological healing, but only a continuation—albeit far more unabashed and open—of the very wounds the Mitscherlichs discerned in the 1970s. For political correctness never persuaded the more resentful and more defensive Wagnerians; it only kept them quiet for a time and made their reliance on a host of rigid and antiquated methodologies all the more understandable. But now they are followed by the new Wagnerians who are saying more than they may realize. Their discourse suggests that they are the true followers of Wagner. And in this sense, they are indeed symptomatic of others in Germany today.

In Germany, it seems particularly difficult to admit that one can take enjoyment from something that can be deemed anti-Semitic, and this has doubtless contributed to the vituperation and anger of the Wagner debate. But surely, there must be a way to make the discussion less contentious and less polarized—or at least one would hope so, for such polarization constitutes a modern version of Wagner's way of thinking. A different way of approaching his moving, enigmatic, and thought-provoking works of art would be to acknowledge the traces of racism discernible within them, even as we admire and take enjoyment from them, traces also found in the history of the theatrical institutions with which they have been associated. Perhaps I am just falling back into the trap of sounding like one of the Mitscherlichs, but I feel it would be ideologically beneficial if a public discussion of the anti-Semitism discernible both in Wagner's works and in the history of the Bayreuth festival could acknowledge the presence therein of features once deemed anti-Semitic, while still insisting that the music dramas are masterpieces well worth studying and enjoying. They are tainted masterpieces, perhaps, but are far more rich and fascinating because of their more nefarious aspects than the whitewashed versions so many of Wagner's defenders would seem to prefer. Nike Wagner's work—like that of David Levin, Michael P. Steinberg, Stewart Spencer, Barry Millington, and others—provides an example of the kind of scholarship that criticizes the ideology of such institutions while appreciating the aesthetic makeup of the art works as well. Wolfgang Wagner's work, on the other hand—like that of his many sycophantic followers—most certainly does not. In his eyes, the artworks rise above and are separated from the petty, cold, avaricious, egotistical, impious, and imbalanced traits others would discern in them, traits that Wagner's defenders perceive to be not defining features of the works they so vociferously defend (seeking to wash them clean of any "evidence" of a nefarious character), but of the critics who they fear would belittle these glorious accomplishments. In other words, it is not only the spirit of Adolf Hitler that continues to haunt postwar Germany—it is the spirit of the Jew as well.

WORKS CITED

Adorno, Theodor W. *In Search of Wagner*. Trans. Rodney Livingston. London: New Left Books, 1981.

Bartov, Omar. "A Tale of Two Holocausts." *New York Times* Aug. 6, 2000.

Borchmeyer, Dieter. "Nachwort zu dieser Ausgabe." In *Richard Wagner, Dichtungen und Schriften*. 10 vols. Frankfurt am Main: Insel, 1983. 10:182–89.

———. "The Question of Anti-Semitism." Trans. Stewart Spencer. In *Wagner Handbook*. Ed. Ulrich Müller, Peter Wapnewski, and John Deathridge. Cambridge: Harvard University Press, 1992. 166–85.

———. *Richard Wagner: Ahasvers Wandlungen*. Frankfurt am Main: Insel, 2000.

———. "Wagner-Literatur—Eine deutsche Misere. Neue Ansichten zum 'Fall Wagner.'" *Internationales Archiv für Sozialgeschichte der deutschen Literatur* 3. Sonderheft, Forschungsreferate 2. Folge (1992): 1–62.

Broder, Henryk M. "Gerade Linie von Uropa zu Urenkel." *Der Tagesspiegel Berlin* 8 (March 1997): n.p.

Dahlhaus, Carl. "Erlösung dem Erlöser." *Richard Wagner. Parsifal: Texte, Materialien, Kommentare*. Ed. Attila Csampai and Dietmar Holland. Reinbek: Rowohlt, 1984. 262–69.

Deathridge, John. *The New Grove Wagner*. London: Macmillan, 1990.

de Winter, Leon. "Der Groll des Sohnes." *Der Spiegel* 28 (August 2000): 198–200.

Eger, Manfred. "Muß den Hut zurückgeben." *Nordbayerischer Kurier* 1.2 (May 1997): n.p.

———. *Wagner und die Juden: Fakten und Hintergründe: Eine Dokumentation zur Ausstellung im Richard-Wagner-Museum Bayreuth*. Bayreuth: Druckhaus Bayreuth, 1985.

"Erklärung." Signed by Dr. Dieter Mronz (Oberbürgermeister), Bernd Meyer (2nd Bürgermeister), and Wolfgang Kern (3rd Bürgermeister). 10 March 1997.

Finkelstein, Norman G. *The Holocaust Industry: Reflections on the Exploitation of Jewish Suffering*. New York: Verso, 2000.

Goldhagen, Daniel Jonah. *Hitler's Willing Executioners*. New York: Knopf, 1996.

Gregor-Dellin, Martin. *Richard Wagner: Sein Leben—Sein Werk—Sein Jahrhundert*. Munich: Goldmann, 1980.

Gutman, Robert W. *Richard Wagner: The Man, His Mind, and His Music*. New York: Harcourt, Brace, Jovanovich, 1990.

Habermas, Jürgen. "Concerning the Public Use of History." *New German Critique* 44 (1988): 40–50.

———. "A Kind of Settlement of Damages (Apologetic Tendencies)." *New German Critique* 44 (1988): 25–39.

Kaiser, Joachim. "Hat Zelinsky recht gegen Wagners *Parsifal*?" *Richard Wagner. Parsifal: Texte, Materialien, Kommentare*. Ed. Attila Csampai and Dietmar Holland. Reinbek: Rowohlt, 1984. 257–59.

Katz, Jacob. *The Darker Side of Genius: Richard Wagner's Anti-Semitism*. Hanover, NH: University Press of New England, 1986.

Lange, Walter. *Richard Wagners Sippe: Vom Urahn zum Enkel*. Leipzig: Max Beck Verlag, 1938.

Levin, David J. "Reading Beckmesser Reading: Anti-Semitism and Aesthetic Practice in *The Mastersingers of Nuremberg.*" *New German Critique* 69 (1996): 127–46.

———. *Richard Wagner, Fritz Lang, and the Nibelungen: The Dramaturgy of Disavowal.* Princeton, NJ: Princeton University Press, 1998.

Malte Fischer, Jens, ed. *Richard Wagners "Das Judentum in der Musik": Eine kritische Dokumentation als Beitrag zur Geschichte des Antisemitismus.* Frankfurt am Main: Insel, 2000.

Millington, Barry. "Nuremberg Trial: Is there Anti-Semitism in *Die Meistersinger?*" *Cambridge Opera Journal* 3 (1991): 247–60.

———. "*Parsifal*: A Wound Reopened." *Wagner* 8 (1987): 114–20.

Mitscherlich, Alexander, and Margarete Mitscherlich. *Die Unfähigkeit zu trauern: Grundlagen kollektiven Verhaltens.* Munich: Piper, 2001.

Müller, Ulrich, and Peter Wapnewski, ed. *Richard-Wagner-Handbuch.* Stuttgart: Alfred Kröner, 1986.

Newman, Ernest. *Wagner as Man and Artist.* London: Victor Gollancz, 1963.

Nietzsche, Friedrich. *Werke: Kritische Gesamtausgabe.* Ed. Giorgio Colli and Mazzino Montinari. Berlin: de Gruyter, 1967.

Piper, Ernst, ed. *Gibt es wirklich eine Holocaust-Industrie? Zur Auseinandersetzung um Norman Finkelstein.* Zurich: Pendo, 2001.

Rose, Paul Lawrence. *Wagner: Race and Revolution.* New Haven, CT: Yale University Press, 1992.

Rosenfeld, Alvin. H. "Feeling Alone, Again: The Growing Unease Among Germany's Jews." *International Perspectives* 49 (2002): 1–27.

Santner, Eric L. *Stranded Objects: Mourning, Memory, and Film in Postwar Germany.* Ithaca, NY: Cornell University Press, 1993.

Scholz, Dieter David. "Wagner im Zwielicht: Eine Korrektur und eine Antwort auf Gottfried Wagner." *Triangel* (September 2000): 24–26.

Seferens, Horst. "Was Gottfried Wagner seinem Therapeuten noch sagen wollte . . ." *Allgemeine jüdische Wochenzeitung* May 2, 1997.

Sloterdijk, Peter, and Hans-Jürgen Heinrichs. *Die Sonne und der Tod: Dialogische Untersuchungen.* Frankfurt am Main: Suhrkamp, 2001.

Steinberger, Petra, ed. *Die Finkelstein Debatte.* Munich: Piper, 2001.

Tanner, Michael J. *Wagner.* London: Harper Collins, 1996.

Vaget, Hans Rudolf. "Imaginings." *Wagner Notes* 18.6 (1995): n.p.

———. "Sixtus Beckmesser: 'A Jew in the Brambles'?" *Opera Quarterly* 12.1 (1995): 35–45.

———. "Wagner, Anti-Semitism, and Mr. Rose: *Merkwürd'ger Fall!*" Review of *Wagner: Race and Revolution,* by Paul Lawrence Rose." *The German Quarterly* 66.2 (1993): Forum Section, 222–36.

Wagner, Gottfried. *Twilight of the Wagners: The Unveiling of a Family's Legacy.* Trans. Della Couling. New York: Picadot, 1999.

————. *Wer nicht mit dem Wolf heult: Autobiographische Aufzeichnungen eines Wagner-Urenkels*. Cologne: Kiepenheuer & Witsch, 1997.

Wagner, Nike. *The Wagners: The Dramas of a Musical Dynasty*. Trans. Ewald Osers and Michael Downes. Princeton, NJ: Princeton University Press, 1998.

————. *Wagner Theater*. Frankfurt am Main: Suhrkamp, 1999.

Wagner, Wolfgang. *Lebensakte*. Munich: A Knaus, 1994.

Walser, Martin. *Tod eines Kritikers*. Frankfurt am Main: Suhrkamp, 2002.

Wapnewski, Peter. *Der traurige Gott: Richard Wagner in seinen Helden*. Munich: Beck, 1978.

Weiner, Marc A. "Reading the Ideal." *New German Critique* 69 (1996): 53–83.

————. *Antisemitische Fantasien: Die Musikdramen Richard Wagners*. Berlin: Henschel, 2000. Translated by Henning Thies as *Richard Wagner and the Anti-Semitic Imagination*. 2nd ed. Lincoln: University of Nebraska Press, 1997.

————. "Über Wagner sprechen: Ideologie und Methodenstreit." *Richard Wagner im dritten Reich*. Ed. Jörn Rüsen and Saul Friedländer. Munich: Beck, 2000. 339–59.

Weiner, Marc A., and William Rasch. "A Response to Hans Rudolf Vaget's 'Wagner, Anti-Semitism, and Mr. Rose.'" *The German Quarterly* 67.3 (1994): 400–410.

Zelinsky, Hartmut. "Der Plenipotentarius des Untergangs." *Neohelicon* 9 (1982): 145–76.

————. "Der verschwiegene Gehalt des 'Parsifal'." *Richard Wagner. Parsifal: Texte, Materialien, Kommentare*. Ed. Attila Csampai and Dietmar Holland. Reinbek: Rowohlt, 1984. 244–51.

————. "Die deutsche Losung Siegfried: oder die 'innere Notwendigkeit' des Juden-Fluches im Werk Richard Wagners." *In den Trümmern der eignen Welt: Richard Wagners Der Ring des Nibelungen*. Ed. Udo Bermbach. Berlin: Reimer, 1989. 201–50.

————. "Rettung ins Ungenaue: zu M. Gregor-Dellins Wagner-Biographie." *Richard Wagner: Parsifal*. Ed. Heinz-Klaus Metzger and Rainer Riehn. *Musikkonzepte* 25 Munich: Text & Kritik, 1982. 74–115.

————. "Richard Wagners letzte Karte." *Richard Wagner. Parsifal: Texte, Materialien, Kommentare*. Ed. Attila Csampai and Dietmar Holland. Reinbek: Rowohlt, 1984. 252–56.

Notes

1. Cf. Goldhagen. A useful source for reviews of Goldhagen's book can be found at http://www.normanfinkelstein.com/content.php?pg=2.

2. See Finkelstein; Steinberger; and Piper. For earlier German reactions see http://www.normanfinkelstein.com/content.php?pg=2.

3. See Weiner, *Antisemitische Fantasien.*

4. See Gutman; Zelinsky, "Richard Wagners" 252–56; Zelinsky, "Die deutsche" 201–50; Zelinsky, "Der Plenipotentarius" 145–76; Zelinsky, "Rettung ins Ungenaue" 74–115, see also note 8; Rose; Millington, "*Parsifal*" 114–20; Millington, "Nuremberg Trial" 247–60; Levin, "Reading Beckmesser" 127–46; and Levin, *Richard Wagner* 86–95, 152n12, 169–70n88.

5. See Dahlhaus, 262–69, containing a vituperative attack on Zelinsky's work; Wapnewski, 65–67, in which Wapnewski excoriates Gutman on a comparatively minor philological issue found in his book (see note 4) that openly discusses Wagner's racism; and Gregor-Dellin. Zelinsky has claimed that Gregor-Dellin minimizes Wagner's anti-Semitism. See Zelinsky, "Rettung ins Ungenaue;" on Borchmeyer, see notes 10, 11, 12; and Katz. The central argument of this text is that Wagner's racism was not unusual for his time, but was always out of step with the development of German-Jewish relations. Above all, Katz insists that the composer's undeniable racism has nothing to do with his aesthetic production. See Tanner, *ix–x*, a text that, among other things, both downplays the composer's anti-Semitism and is concerned with explaining why it is irrelevant to an understanding of Wagner's art works.

6. This is the subject of Weiner, "über Wagner sprechen" 339–59.

7. This is a point made in Weiner and Rasch, 400–410, responding to Vaget, "Wagner, Anti-Semitism" 222–36.

8. Zelinsky, "Der verschwiegene Gehalt" 244–51; and Kaiser, 257–59. Unless otherwise noted, all translations are my own.

9. Portions of the following discussion can be found in Weiner, "Reading the Ideal" 53–83.

10. See Borchmeyer, "Nachwort" 185.

11. Borchmeyer, "Question of Anti-Semitism" 183–84, originally as "Richard Wagner und der Antisemitismus" 137–61. See especially the section "Antijüdische Spuren in den Musikdramen?"159–61. See also Borchmeyer, "Wagner-Literatur" 1–62, esp. 36–41, see also note 8.

12. Borchmeyer, *Richard Wagner.*

13. Vaget, "Imaginings" n.p. See also Vaget, "Wagner, Anti-Semitism" 226; and Vaget, "Sixtus Beckmesser" 43. Emphasis added.

14. Borchmeyer, *Richard Wagner, Dichtungen und Schriften* vol. 8, 265. For a more detailed analysis of this text, see Weiner, "Reading the Ideal."

15. Scholz, 24–26.

16. See Nietzsche, VI/3: 35n. On the question of Wagner's Jewish ancestry, see Deathridge, 1–5; Gutman, 4–9; Newman, 387–414; and Adorno, 24–25.

17. Eger, *Wagner und die Juden.*
18. Gottfried Wagner publicly criticized the exhibit, and in an open letter responding to this criticism, Eger made a point of citing the many Jewish journalists and Rabbis who praised it. The implication is either that, if Jews like it, it must be good—an indication that this is a sensitive issue—or that Eger felt he needed his Jewish supporters as fig leaves, as token Jews to shield himself and his exhibit from criticism. See Eger, "'Muß den Hut zurückgeben.'"
19. Wagner, 51.
20. See Walser. On this and the Möllemann controversy, see Rosenfeld, 1–27.
21. Gottfried Wagner, *Wer nicht*; and Gottfried Wagner, *Twilight.*
22. Scholz, 24. Emphasis added.
23. Broder, n.p. Emphasis added.
24. Scholz, 26.
25. Seferens, n.p.
26. "Erklärung," 10 March 1997, signed by Dr. Dieter Mronz (Oberbürgermeister), Bernd Meyer (2nd Bürgermeister), and Wolfgang Kern (3rd Bürgermeister).
27. Seferens, n.p.
28. Nike Wagner, *Wagners: The Dramas* 291; and Nike Wagner, *Wagner Theater* 407. The psychological clarification—"this may have intensified his feelings of personal involvement"—is not contained in the original German version, but was added by its author, or by its translators and presumably approved by its author, in the recent past as the English version of the book went into production. The topos of psychological instability emerges elsewhere in this book as well when the author writes of her cousin's "identification with the victim" as evidence of an Oedipal conflict (*Wagner Theater* 406).
29. Seferens, n.p.
30. See, for example, Richard Wagner, "Das Judentum in der Musik," in Malte Fischer, 167–69, 172.
31. de Winter, 199.
32. Bartov.
33. de Winter, 200.
34. In his analysis of the controversy surrounding his lecture "Regeln für den Menschenpark," Peter Sloterdijk has argued that modern societies constitute "theme exchanges" (like stock exchanges, but trading in topics for widespread discussion and excitement) that are held together by the media. See Sloterdijk and Heinrichs, 74–76, 86.
35. Mitscherlich and Mitscherlich; Habermas, "Kind of Settlement" 25–39; Habermas, "Concerning" 40–50 (This is a special issue devoted to the *Historikerstreit* and contains a number of important essays on the subject); and Santner.

CHAPTER 8

WAGNER'S EMBLEMATIC ROLE: THE CASE OF HOLOCAUST COMMEMORATION IN ISRAEL[1]

Na'ama Sheffi

Translated from the Hebrew by Martha Grenzeback

> No need for fine distinctions here. There is no doubt that in the popular mind Wagner has become the classic symbol of anti-Semitism and the spiritual father of Nazism. There is nothing to argue about here, and we could line up a thousand proofs, but even if we don't agree, this is what happened and it is an inalienable part of the culture of the State of Israel. The first boycott of Wagner was begun by the people in the art world themselves, by the Philharmonic Orchestra of the State of Israel, when, after *Kristallnacht*, it canceled its performance of a Wagner piece. This means that the musicians themselves felt they just could not do it.[2]

This pronouncement by Knesset Member Shaul Yahalom at the opening of a special meeting of Knesset Education, Culture and Sports Committee highlighted Wagner's unique status in Israeli culture as a symbol of anti-Semitism in general and National Socialism in particular—and accordingly as a part of the Israeli collective memory of the Holocaust. The subtext of Yahalom's speech was as interesting as the speech itself. The fact that such a debate was even taking place in the Knesset was a measure of the degree of political involvement in the subject, and Yahalom's membership in the National Religious Party suggested that the debate over Wagner reflected broad cultural characteristics of Israeli society. Even the date of the speech, May 8, 2001, was significant, inviting reflections on the fraught relationship between Israel and Germany. On the day that Europe was celebrating the fifty-sixth anniversary of the Allied victory over Nazi Germany, the organizers of the Israel Festival were asked to cancel a concert at which Act I to Richard Wagner's *Die Walküre* was to be played. The Berlin State Orchestra and its musical director, Daniel Barenboim, had been planning to perform the work in Jerusalem.

In this context, I would like to examine and analyze the process by which Wagner became a symbolic part of the commemoration of the Holocaust in Israel. After reviewing some of the stages in that process, many of which coincided with climactic moments in the public discussion of the Holocaust, I will argue that the means by which Wagner became a symbol was closely related to the nature of Holocaust commemoration in Israeli culture.[3] Moreover, I see a definite parallel between the character of the Wagner debate and the way that public debate on the Holocaust has been conducted. In both cases, the debate began among Holocaust survivors and the relatives of those murdered, and then expanded to the general public. In other words, each debate involved a transition from the private memories of those personally affected by the Holocaust to the collective memory of all Israelis, who see the Holocaust as a shared national experience. The issue is also a focus for yet another significant correlation between the development of ideology and the gradual formation of national identity. In other words, the Wagner debate has served as a catalyst in the creation of that specific part of the Jewish-Israeli identity that is related to the collective experiences of Holocaust survivors and their impact on Israeli society.[4] Similarly, the public debate concerning the status Israel should assign German culture in general and Wagner in particular on occasion overflowed into concerns over the shaping of Israeli culture. In this respect, it is notable that Israeli society tends to identify ideological opposition to the Nazi heritage and the duty to remember the Holocaust, on one hand, with the perception of these ideas as a unifying element in modern Hebrew-Jewish culture, on the other. Finally, I will examine Wagner's status as part of the Israeli collective memory of the Holocaust today and try to determine whose memory the collective memory really is.[5]

Most of the rounds of the Wagner debate in Israel have coincided with other debates concerning the Holocaust and relations between Israel and Germany or between Israelis and Germans. In my view, this is not by chance. Criticism of Wagner focused primarily on his anti-Semitic attitudes, which he expressed both privately and in a vituperative article entitled *"Das Judentum in der Musik"* ("Judaism in Music"), published initially under a pen name and later under his own name.[6] In addition, the nationalistic interpretation given to his musical works both during his lifetime and after his death, his adoption by the Nazis, and his characterization—refuted only in recent years—as the composer whom Hitler admired were the more significant factors in his lasting rejection by Israelis.[7] These points against him were further reinforced over the years by the testimony of Holocaust survivors, for whom the sounds of Wagner's music could never be dissociated from the image of Jews being marched to their deaths in the concentration camps.[8]

As Knesset Member Yahalom mentioned, Wagner was taken off the program of the Palestine Symphony Orchestra (which would later become the Israel Philharmonic Orchestra) for the first time immediately after *Kristallnacht* in November 1938. The program of the concert that was to open the season three days after *Kristallnacht* was changed at the request of the orchestra management. The conductor, Arturo Toscanini, himself a voluntary exile who had refused to put his art at the service of the Fascist regime in Italy, replaced the overture to *Die Meistersinger von Nürnberg*—a work popular at Nazi party conventions—with another piece.[9] Plans to play Wagner compositions in Israel were subsequently canceled on many occasions, always for ideological reasons.

In the 1950s and 1960s the Wagner issue was coupled with the controversy over Richard Strauss, the first director of the Nazi propaganda ministry's music division. Toward the end of 1952, about ten months after negotiations over German reparations to Israel were announced, the Jewish state was rife with rumors that the Israel Philharmonic Orchestra (IPO) was going to perform pieces by Wagner and Strauss, an idea that stirred up great public turmoil.[10] In the spring of 1953, in the same week as the Day of Remembrance of the Holocaust and Heroism, the Jewish violinist Jascha Heifetz played Strauss's Sonata for Violin in the course of a series of recitals he was giving in Israel. He was fiercely attacked by the press and ultimately physically assaulted on the street.[11] In the summer of 1966, a year after the establishment of diplomatic ties with West Germany and six years after the renowned trial of the Nazi war criminal Adolf Eichmann,[12] the IPO printed an article in its concert programs announcing its intention to play works by Wagner and Strauss. The ensuing public uproar led the IPO to cancel this plan.[13]

Another similar declaration of intent rekindled the conflict in the winter of 1981, a time when Prime Minister Menachem Begin was embroiled in a grim battle with the West German chancellor, Helmut Schmidt. This phase of the controversy also featured elements of xenophobia and general pronouncements on the significance of adopting Western culture in the State of Israel.[14] A new attempt to lift the boycott exactly one decade later again elicited protests. This time an aggravating factor was the recent Gulf War, during which newspapers in Israel had often compared Saddam Hussein to Adolf Hitler and the modern threat of gas warfare to the horrifying use of Zyklon B in the past.[15] In the spring and summer of 2001, the issue was not only the performance of Wagner's music in itself, but also the fact that it was to be performed by a German orchestra in the Israeli capital. It should be remembered that over the last twenty years, Israeli society has undergone a process of fragmentation in which emphasis has been placed on the disparities between secular and religious Jews, Jews and Arabs, urban areas and peripheral settlements. This trend of segregation may reflect in part the eruption of tensions that had been suppressed for years by artificial social and economic solutions dictated by the ideal of the "melting pot," a concept that dominated the first decades of statehood. Another reason for this fragmentation may be the revision of the electoral system and the establishment of direct voting for prime minister.

On all these occasions, and on others not directly linked to other debates on the Holocaust and Israeli-German relations, the issue of Holocaust survivors was a central factor. The survivors expressed clearly their feeling that performing Wagner's works was an insult to the memory of the dead who had been marched to their doom to the strains of his music. At the very least, Wagner was beyond the pale by virtue of his proto-Nazi ideology, which had influenced National Socialism itself. The degree of Wagner's anti-Semitism has been seriously discussed in Israel only in the last twenty years, since the renewal of the controversy in 1981 and the publication of the first Hebrew translation of Wagner's diatribe against Jews, "Das

Judentum in der Musik," in 1984.[16] Even before that, quite a few caustic articles had been published associating Wagner with anti-Semitism in such terms as "the horrible influence that Wagner's music exercised on the German beasts of prey,"[17] or, with respect to Strauss, "the sounds of spiritual and moral degeneracy arose from the magical violin [of Jascha Heifetz] and entered Jewish ears that *remained* attached to their heads after ten years of total annihilation."[18]

Some of the authors of these harsh articles were themselves Holocaust survivors or relatives of those who had died. In recent years, as their active lives as journalists and politicians have drawn to an end, some of them have been moved to appeal to Israeli courts for injunctions against the performance of Wagner's music in Israel. From September 2000 to May 2001, survivors took court action against Wagner's music both as individuals and through the umbrella organization of Holocaust survivors no fewer than five times.[19] This development would seem to be a natural extension of the significant increase in legal actions in Israel in the last decades and of the heavy involvement of the courts—especially the Supreme Court—in Israeli public life. Now, however, other survivors have broken the unity of the past to complain that they would no longer serve as tools in the hands of those who saw themselves as the representatives of all survivors.

This declaration underlined a very problematic factor in the Israeli attitude toward Holocaust survivors: Up to that point, and despite the theoretical recognition that every survivor had his or her own personal story, survivors had been perceived as a monolithic body in Israeli society. But now, in letters sent primarily to musical institutions and, less frequently, to the press, some survivors have expressed contempt for those who have "made a career out of being a Holocaust survivor. They exploit every opportunity to shout and cry . . . I, too, am a Holocaust survivor, left disabled after Nazi persecution. The Nazis murdered part of my family. Yet, despite that, I keep myself sane, distinguish between past and present, emotion and sense, and politics and art."[20] Thus, it appears in fact that survivors' declining public activity and the courts' increasing involvement in public life were not the only reasons for more frequent recourse to the law. To a large extent, the open dissension among the survivors, their decreasing numbers, and their fear of radical erosion of their special status in Israeli society, accorded for so many years, were their real reasons for taking legal action. These may also have been the reasons for the increasing involvement of politicians in the issue, an idea I will return to later.

Survivors had reacted strongly to the Wagner issue before this. In 1981 Dov Shilansky, the deputy minister in the prime minister's office and a Holocaust survivor, made some very insulting remarks about Zubin Mehta, the IPO musical director who was determined to conduct Wagner's music in Israel. In a radio interview, Shilansky recommended that Mehta go back to where he had come from—India.[21] This xenophobic message was in tune with some of the articles in the press, one of which, written by another Holocaust survivor, asked, "How would Zubin Mehta and his people react if, for example, they were all brought into some place in which there were sacred cows, and someone stood up and said: 'We are about to slaughter the cows. Anyone who doesn't want to see it should leave.' Does that seem all right to Zubin Mehta?"[22] Thus, on the public level, Holocaust survivors and relatives of the dead seemed to be insisting on an Israeli monopoly on the right to make decisions concerning Wagner, and they were not willing to entrust this right to a foreigner—even a faithful friend of Israel, as Mehta was described in other articles.[23]

Ten years later it became apparent that not only foreignness bothered the survivors. When Daniel Barenboim, identified as an Israeli, took up the daunting challenge of breaking the boycott on Wagner, he discovered that there were other factors that disqualified people from discussing the subject. Barenboim had led the anti-boycott movement since 1989, and, ultimately, after conducting a special concert of Wagnerian works at the end of 1991, he was attacked on account of his excessive youth—as someone who had been only a child at the time of the Holocaust and was therefore unqualified to debate issues connected with it, in this case, the performance of Wagner's music in Israel.[24] Only then was it evident that nationality was not enough to entitle anyone to discuss Wagner; you had to be part of the right generation as well. In this respect, the 1991 conflict reflected Holocaust survivors' eagerness to appropriate an exclusive franchise on decisions concerning Wagner and, perhaps, to retain the great power they had held during the initial debates over the Day of Remembrance of Holocaust and Heroism in Israel. It should be remembered, however, that most of the publicists writing on the subject at the time were too young to have gone through the Holocaust themselves, and some of them did not even have any relatives who had. At this point, an interesting contradiction was evident between the ambition to turn the Holocaust into a collective historical experience and the desire to maintain it as a private, personal experience.

Yet Holocaust survivors are not the only people who have tried to prevent Wagner's infiltration of Israeli society, nor are they the only ones accused of emotional manipulation with respect to this issue. The controversy has been fueled to a huge extent by politicians across the political spectrum. In the 1950s and 1960s Herut and Mapam party members played the most prominent role, bitterly opposing Prime Minister David Ben-Gurion's diplomatic gestures toward Germany—or "the other Germany," as he called it. Since the 1980s they have been joined by Labour and National Religious Party Knesset members. They all have pursued the matter in the Knesset by means of interpellations or debates in the Knesset Education, Culture and Sports Committee. They all have made authoritarian, manipulative use of the Holocaust to resolve the Wagner-Strauss issue and to take it off the public agenda once and for all. Following a 1956 interpellation by Knesset member Esther Raziel-Naor (Herut) on the subject of Strauss, during which she demanded that the orchestra lose its state funding if it played a work by Strauss, Knesset member Menachem Begin, the head of her own party, intervened. He argued that the Education Ministry's policy of nonintervention in the issue undermined the commemoration of the Holocaust.[25] Subsequent discussion in the Knesset followed the same lines, except that from the 1980s onward, personal notes were injected—for example, by survivor Dov Shilansky, and by Knesset member Hagai Meirom (Labor) who cited his mother's persecution by the Nazis in order to justify the ban on Wagner's music in Israel.[26] As Begin had pointed out back in the 1950s, Israeli education ministers' basic policy on Wagner was nonintervention. Every education minister, regardless of political party affiliation, tried to avoid taking a stand on the issue, the sole exception being Professor Ben-Zion Dinur, one of the founders of the Yad Vashem institution; he appealed to Jascha Heifetz personally to stop playing Strauss in Israel.[27] In general, the Wagner issue has given politicians a conduit for ideas and feelings that they usually have to suppress at the political level for pragmatic reasons. Thus, Israeli politics are responsible both for the rational measures taken with respect to Germany and for the emotional responses to German culture.

Of course, political pragmatism and cultural emotionalism cannot be compared. Economic or diplomatic decisions exist on a different plane from cultural rapprochement, which is emotionally based. Yet the perception of culture as unique in this respect merits further examination. Almost from the beginning, the Wagner controversy has also symbolized a struggle over the nature of Israeli culture, and to a large degree it has shown that an internalized resistance to German heritage has played an essential role in the formation of the new Jewish-Hebrew identity. An excellent definition of this role was written in 1991 by an Israeli publicist, Ariel Hirschfeld, who argued that "abstaining from Wagner is one of the few truly cosmopolitan acts carried out here in the musical field, an act that does not resemble the provincial, imitative sycophancy typical of musical life here and of the Philharmonic in particular."[28]

This attitude dovetailed with the ideas that had already been expressed generally in the 1950s and 1960s and which were recycled from the 1980s on, mostly at the initiative of religious Jews. In the 1950s and 1960s, the managers of the IPO were not only compelled to defend the orchestra's decisions with respect to Wagner and Strauss on the grounds that artistic considerations were involved, but they were also called upon to address other issues directly connected with the shaping of modern Israeli culture in any national context that had some link to the Holocaust. I am referring to their direct involvement in the decisions made during the 1950s and 1960s in response to the controversies over, respectively, vocal concerts in the German language—a language whose use on stage had been banned by the Film and Theater Review Board—and performances of Christian liturgical music.[29] During those years, it was very clear that cultural affairs were closely linked with national issues, including the significance of the Holocaust in Israeli public discourse. The clearest evidence of this in the context of our subject was the censorship exercised against public use of the German language.

It may have been the demise of that censorship, or else fears that the slowly receding memory of the Holocaust would vanish altogether, that reawakened the polemic in the 1980s. This time the standard bearers of the cause were mostly publicists and politicians from the religious sector. This faction's newspapers presented the controversy over Wagner as evidence supporting their demand that every effort be made to foster the Hebrew character of the state. The ultra-Orthodox attacked secular Jews who complained that they, the ultra-Orthodox, did not respect the annual siren calling for a moment's silent remembrance of the victims of the Holocaust; generally, their attitude was, "how dare you accuse us, when you listen with enjoyment to the music of an anti-Semite, Wagner?"[30] In the latest clash, during the summer of 2001, the religious dimension of the debate achieved new prominence in a letter to the editor by a member of Professors for a Strong Israel, a group identified with the Israeli right wing. After remarking that "undoubtedly Germany, with all its institutions, is trying to cleanse itself of the sins of the Holocaust, and there is no place like Israel to do that," the letter's author added, "How symbolic it is that precisely on the eve of 17 Tammuz, the date on which a fast-day was declared to commemorate the destruction of the walls of Jerusalem, the representatives of German culture managed to undermine the walls of Jewish culture and honor, and, by playing Wagner, placed a German cultural icon on an Israeli stage."[31]

The increasingly shrill tone of the debate concerning the general cultural context of playing Wagner's music in Israel is, I think, linked not only to the growing combativeness of public expression in Israel in general, but also to the fears I have already mentioned. The increasing remoteness of the Holocaust, which might have been expected to moderate emotional attitudes toward it, is producing the exact opposite effect. I believe that this can be attributed to the fear that memory and the mechanisms of its conservation, imprinted in Israeli society and culture, are being eroded. One clear indication that this fear exists can be found in the highly varied range of activities focusing on the Holocaust that are based not only on a multifaceted approach to the subject over time, but also on the need to preserve the Holocaust as a living memory no matter how tired of the subject people become.

Another issue, no less central, concerns both the changing composition of Israeli society and the processes of commemorating the Holocaust that this society has internalized to date. In the 1950s, one fourth of all Israelis were Holocaust survivors; but today those numbers are naturally declining in society in general and in public life in particular. Yet in the sixty years that have passed since the beginning of the Final Solution up to today, the commemorative process has changed character twice. Initially, Holocaust awareness

erupted from the personal memories of survivors into the Israeli
collective memory—and in this respect, the central role played by
the Eichmann trial testimony is well known. Later, the comprehen-
sive memory of the Holocaust returned to the personal mention of
Holocaust victims in the framework of the projects grouped under
the slogan "Unto Every Person There Is a Name."[32]

In these respects, the debates on Wagner in Israeli society and the
changes they have undergone over the years are very similar to
the debates on the nature of Holocaust commemoration in Israel.
For example, in the 1950s—the decade that the Knesset twice
enacted laws defining the character of the national Holocaust
remembrance day as well as the Law for the Punishment of Nazis
and their Collaborators, the decade that the Yad Vashem museum
was founded, the years when Israeli society was watching the Kapo
trials and the more publicized Grünwald-Kasztner case—the Wagner-
Strauss issue came up three times and in one instance went all the
way to the Knesset.[33] In the 1960s, when the Israeli public was
coping with both the chilling testimony of the Eichmann trial and
the establishment of full diplomatic relations with West Germany,
there was talk of relaxing the ban on the performance of Christian
liturgical music and vocal works in German even before the perennial Wagner controversy broke out again. Israel's redefinition of
itself with respect to the Holocaust—definitions conditioned by the
Six-Day and Yom Kippur Wars and that oscillated between fear of
annihilation and an intoxicating sense of power—led to a certain
moderation of the Wagner controversy as well. Everything that had
seemed to be part of a rational process paralleling the move away
from the Holocaust itself was undermined in the 1980s with respect
to both Holocaust remembrance in Israel in general and the Wagner
controversy in particular.

Since the 1980s, and particularly in the 1990s, there has been a
growing awareness of the processes of Holocaust commemoration.
Although the standard official ceremonies have remained
unchanged, other forms of remembrance have multiplied alongside
them: survivors are invited to school classrooms and special semi-
nars to tell their stories, trips to the death camps are organized,
intensive media attention is paid to the feelings of second-genera-
tion survivors, and there has been an outpouring of works in various
artistic media on the subject of the Holocaust. Meanwhile, particularly fierce rounds of the Wagner conflict took place in 1981 and

again in 2001. As mentioned, I attribute the intensive renewed activity in the field of shaping Holocaust memory both to the anxiety aroused by the increasing remoteness of the Holocaust experience and to the sweeping involvement of the entire Israeli society in the process of remembrance. Wagner, who had become a symbol in Israel in the early days of statehood because of his ideas, his writing on art, and the way he was viewed after his death, has, in more recent years, also served as a brick in the edifice of Holocaust remembrance; these years have shown that not only survivors see him as a symbol, but so does the wider public, some of whom view the Holocaust as a collective historic experience rather than a personal one. Thus, the Wagner debate has come to reflect a strange and interesting juxtaposition of ideology and the part of Israeli identity that is based on the Holocaust.

In conclusion, I would like to raise a question concerning what participants in the Wagner debate view as "the ownership" of the decision to lift the boycott or not. As I said earlier, the last twenty years have seen an increasingly evident determination on the part of Holocaust survivors to keep the decision-making power in their own hands on the grounds that only someone who lived through the horror can understand the musical and ideological implications of what Wagner represents. In the public debate that took place in November 2001 in Tel Aviv, a Holocaust survivor expressed this poignantly: "Wait a few more years, until we've left the world, and then go back to discussing the Wagner issue among yourselves." She said this with a simple candor that even the great cynics sitting in the auditorium could not withstand.[34]

Nevertheless, this attitude raises a number of important questions. One of them is whether, after going through the whole process of instilling the memory of the Holocaust in the entire Jewish population of Israel, it is reasonable to leave the task of coping with the painful past solely to the survivors who live among us. Will we not doom ourselves to that same threatening process of amnesia and oblivion once the Holocaust survivors pass away, as they are bound to do? Moreover, since it is clear to everyone that the Wagner issue cannot be divorced from the memory of the Holocaust, will waiting another ten or twenty years to discuss it permit a different kind of debate? Is this a problem inherent in Israeli society, a problem closely linked to the way it wants to form its identity?

Undoubtedly the answers to these questions—like the entire Wagner debate—depend on our perspective. We might believe that preserving the memory of the Holocaust need encompass no more than it does right now—familiarity with the events of the Holocaust, honoring the memory of those murdered, and treating survivors with special marks of distinction—or we might believe that this is not enough and that further essentials include understanding the very short road that links the blatant verbal anti-Semitism exemplified by Wagner with acts that can lead to genocide, or the even shorter path that permits a democratic society to change overnight into a violent, totalitarian society. In my mind, suppressing discussion of the Wagner issue repeats the same mistake that Israeli society has already made by artificially separating discussion of the lessons offered by German history from discussion of the lessons that Jewish society learned from industrialized genocide. In addition, having given Holocaust survivors a special place in Israeli society, how can we then brazenly wait for their deaths in order to discuss more freely the difficult experiences that they carried around with them all their lives? We must consider whether Wagner is the right symbol for clarifying Holocaust awareness in Israel.

WORKS CITED

Alther Podlowsky and Gedaliahu Appel v. Rishon Letzion Symphony Orchestra. Misc. Civic Appeal No. 27053/00. Israel. October 18, 2000.

Alther Podlowsky, Gedaliahu Appel, and Israel Silberberg v. Rishon Letzion Symphony Orchestra. Misc. Civic Appeal No. 27228/00. Israel. October 24, 2000.

Alther Podlowsky, Gedaliahu Appel, Israel Silberberg, Center of Organizations of Holocaust Survivors in Israel, and Simon Wiesenthal Center Fund v. Rishon Letzion Symphony Orchestra. Misc. Civic Appeal No. 6280/01. Israel. March 4, 2001.

Alther Podlowsky, Gedaliahu Appel, Israel Silberberg, Center of Organizations of Holocaust Survivors in Israel, and Simon Wiesenthal Center Fund v. Rishon Letzion Symphony Orchestra. Supreme Court Appeal No. 7700/00. Israel. October 25, 2000.

Arie (Louis) Garb v. Israel Broadcasting Authorities. Supreme Court Appeal No. 6032/00. Israel. August 24, 2000.

Balabkins, Nicholas. *West Germany and the Reparations to Israel*. New Brunswick, NJ: Rutgers University Press, 1971.

Carlebach, Azriel. "Manners of a Guest [Hebrew]." *Ma'ariv* Apr. 13, 1953.

Daddy, Come to the Fair. Dir. Shmuel Vilozny and Nava Semmel. Fatherland Productions, 1995.

Divrei HaKnesset May 12, 1953: 1310–14.

Divrei HaKnesset May 18, 1953: 1331–53.

Divrei HaKnesset Aug. 19, 1953: 2402–09.

Divrei HaKnesset Nov. 8, 1989: 334–36.

Don't Touch My Holocaust. Dir. Asher Tlalim. Tlalim Films, 1994.

Drei Schwestern [Three Sisters]. Dir. Tsipi Reibenbach. Israel Broadcasting Authority (Channel 1), 1998.

Eaziel-Naor, Esther. "Interpellation 7." *Divrei HaKnesset* Dec. 10, 1956.

Fenelon, Fania. *Playing for Time.* New York: Atheneum, 1977.

Film and Theater Review Board. Letter to the Israel Philharmonic Orchestra Management. May 6, 1952. Israel Philharmonic Orchestra Archives. "Miscellaneous" file.

Funkenstein, Amos. *Perceptions of Jewish History.* Los Angeles: University of California Press, 1993.

Gilead, Itzhak. "Public Opinion in Israel on Relations between the State of Israel and West Germany in the Years 1949–1965 [Hebrew]." Diss. Tel Aviv University, 1984.

Girlfriends. Dir. Yoel Kaminsky. Yarkon Procuctions, 1994.

Gutfroind, Amir. *Our Holocaust* [Hebrew]. Tel Aviv: Zmora Bitan, 2000.

"Hok le-Asiat Din be-Nazim u be-Ozreihem (The Law for the Punishment of Nazis and their Collaborators)." *Divrei HaKnesset* April 12, 1951: 1655–57; *Divrei HaKnesset* March 10, 1959: 1385–90; *Divrei HaKnesset* April 8, 1959: 1992–93.

Hoch, Moshe. *Return from the Inferno* [Hebrew]. Hadera: Knesset Protocol, 1988.

Hugo. Dir. Yair Lev. Distributed by the director, 1989.

Kliger, Noah. "Consideration for Feelings [Hebrew]." *Yediot Aharonot* Oct. 21, 1981.

Knesset Education, Culture and Sports Committee. *Protocol No. 268.* Israel, May 8, 2001.

———. *Protocol No. 316.* Israel, July 24, 2001.

Köhler, Joachim. *Wagners Hitler: Der Prophet und sein Vollstrecker.* Munich: Karl Belssing Verlag, 1997.

Liebe Perla [Dear Perla]. Dir. Shahar Rozen. Eden Productions, 1999.

"Life without Wagner [Hebrew]." *Yom Hashishi* Dec. 27, 1991.

Litvin, Rina, and Hezi Shelach, ed. *Who's Afraid of Richard Wagner: Different Aspects of the Controversial Figure* [Hebrew]. Jerusalem: Keter, 1984.

Nevenzal, Israel. "A German Icon in the Temple of Music [Hebrew]." *Ha'aretz* July 15, 2001.

"Now the Feelings of Secular Jews Are Being Hurt, Too [Hebrew]." *Yated Ne'eman* Dec. 20, 1991.

Rose, Paul Lawrence. *Wagner: Race and Revolution.* Boston, MA: Faber and Faber, 1992.

Rosenblum, Herzl. "To Zubin Mehta, with All Due Respect [Hebrew]." *Yediot Aharonot* Oct. 19, 1981.

Sachs, Harvey. *Toscanini.* New York: Weidenfeld and Nicholson, 1988.

Sheffi, Na'ama. "Between Collective Memory and Manipulation: The Holocaust, Wagner and the Israelis." *Journal of Israeli History* 23, no. 1 (Spring 2004): 65–77.

———. *The Ring of Myths: Wagner, The Israelis, and the Nazis.* Brighton: Sussex Academic Press, 2001.

Shilansky, Dov. Interview. *The Voice of Israel.* Radio 1. Oct. 23, 1981.

"The Overt Simplicity of that Honor [Hebrew]." *Ha'aretz* Dec. 27, 1991.

"The Time Has Come for Wagner to Be Just Music Again [Hebrew]." *Ha'aretz* Dec. 16, 1991.

Toeplitz, Uri. "On the Importance of Wagner [Hebrew]." Israel Philharmonic Orchestra Program. June 1966.

Wagner, Gottfried. *Twilight of the Wagners: The Unveiling of a Family Legacy.* Trans. Della Couling. New York: Picadot, 1999.

Wagner, Richard. "Judaism in Music." *Stories and Essays.* Trans. Charles Osborne. London: Open Court, 1973. 23–39.

Weiner, Marc A. *Richard Wagner and the Anti-Semitic Imagination.* Lincoln: University of Nebraska Press, 1997.

Weitz, Yechiam. "Political Dimensions of Holocaust Memory in Israel during the 1950's." *Israel Affairs* 1.3 (1995): 129–45.

"With or without the Richards [Hebrew]." *Davar* Dec. 1, 1952.

Yerushalmi, Yosef Hayim. *Zakhor: Jewish History and Jewish Memory.* Seattle: University of Washington Press, 1982.

Yishai, David. "Degenerate Music Burst Forth on Holocaust Memorial Day [Hebrew]." *Herut* Apr. 16, 1953.

Zuckerman, Moshe. "The Abuse of Holocaust Commemoration [Hebrew]." May 7, 2001 http://www.y-net.co.il.

———. *Shoa in the Sealed Room: The "Holocaust" in the Israeli Press During the Gulf War* [Hebrew]. Tel Aviv: 1993.

NOTES

1. This article originally appeared in a somewhat different form as Na'ama Sheffi, "Between Collective Memory and Manipulation: The

Holocaust, Wagner and the Israelis," *Journal of Israeli History* 23, no. 1 (Spring 2004): 65–77. Used by permission.

2. Knesset Education, Culture and Sports Committee, Protocol No. 268. Following that meeting, the Israel Festival Board and conductor Daniel Barenboim decided to replace the Wagner concert with another. At the end of it, Barenboim and the Berlin State Orchestra played a short excerpt from *Tristan and Isolde*, provoking yet another fierce debate about public performances of Wagner in Israel. Finally, the Knesset Education, Culture and Sports Committee declared Barenboim to be a "cultural persona non grata" in Israel. See Knesset Education, Culture and Sports Committee, *Protocol* No. 316. During the 16th Knesset in 2005, the committee became known as the Education, Culture and Sports Committee, heretofore the Education and Culture Committee.

3. For a detailed discussion on the Wagner debate in Israel, see Sheffi.

4. The last two decades have seen numerous studies on the shaping of national identities. Outstanding examinations of the special Jewish identity and modes of commemoration can be found in Funkenstein; and Yerushalmi. I wish to thank Yosefa Loshizky for her interesting comment on the idea-identity issue.

5. For further perspectives, see Weitz, 129–45.

6. The essay was first published in 1850 under the pseudonym K. Freigedank and again in 1869 under Wagner's own name when he was already a successful composer. See Richard Wagner, 23–39.

7. This general impression, harbored by many Israeli publicists, is supported by research. See, for example, Köhler; Rose; and Weiner. See also Gottfried Wagner.

8. Despite general testimony by survivors indicating that Wagner's music was played in the concentration camps, two important witnesses give evidence to the contrary. See Fenelon; and Hoch.

9. On Toscanini, see the biography by Sachs, especially 196–269.

10. On the reparations agreement, see Balabkins.

11. The attack caused a radical change in press attitudes towards Heifetz. See, for example, *Hador* and *Ma'ariv* on the day after the incident, April 17, 1953. It is important to note that most of the Hebrew press in Israel had taken part in the debate (*Davar, Ha'aretz, Herut, Haolam Hazeh, Ma'ariv, Haboker, Hador*, and *Yediot Aharonot*), as had the foreign language press (*Jediot Hadashot, Emeth, Jerusalem Post, Yediot Hayom*). Reports had also appeared in foreign papers such as *New York Post, New York Herald Tribune, Herald Tribune* (Paris), and *Buenos Aires Herald*.

12. Adolf Eichmann was kidnapped from Argentina and brought to trial in Israel in May 1960. The trial began a year later and included a long list

of witnesses who illuminated, for the first time, what Hannah Arendt defined as "The Banality of Evil". Eichmann was found guilty in crimes against humanity and was hanged in Israel in May 1962.

13. The debate erupted after the publication of an article by first flutist and board member Uri Toeplitz on the IPO's plans to play Wagner and Strauss. His original article claimed that "a change has taken place in the nation's attitude to the exterminators of our people." The public uproar that followed the article's publication led him to revise the passage to read, "We feel the time has come for a change, not only because of the paramount demands of artistic freedom, but also because the opposition to Wagner has become a mere gesture. Why should we go on denying ourselves some of the greatest music by forbidding the playing of Wagner, a loss that cannot be replaced by the works of any other composer, while a mere convenience like the German Volkswagen, with all its associations from the Hitler era, is allowed to crowd our streets? . . . Accordingly, this time we must take a rational and courageous stand and allow Wagner's music to be played, thereby reopening the door to works included among the best of the music composed in the nineteenth century" (See Toeplitz).

14. This time the press discussed the matter for several weeks and even more extensively; local and special interest magazines, flourishing at the time, jumped on the bandwagon, as did the electronic media, which had previously avoided the subject.

15. Zuckermann, *Shoa*.

16. The essay appeared in Litvin and Shelach, 203–18.

17. "With or without."

18. Original emphasis. Yishai, "Degenerate Music."

19. See *Arie (Louis) Garb v. Israel Broadcasting Authorities; Alther Podlowsky and Gedaliahu Appel v. Rishon Letzion Symphony Orchestra; Alther Podlowsky, Gedaliahu Appel, and Israel Silberberg v. Rishon Letzion Symphony Orchestra; Alther Podlowsky, Gedaliahu Appel, Israel Silberberg, Center of Organizations of Holocaust Survivors in Israel, and Simon Wiesenthal Center Fund v. Rishon Letzion Symphony Orchestra*, Supreme Court Appeal No. 7700/00; and *Alther Podlowsky, Gedaliahu Appel, Israel Silberberg, Center of Organizations of Holocaust Survivors in Israel, and Simon Wiesenthal Center Fund v. Rishon Letzion Symphony Orchestra*, Miscellaneous Civil Appeal No. 6280/01.

20. This undated letter was sent by Shmuel Santo, a Holocaust survivor living in Rishon Letzion, to the managers of that city's symphony orchestra right after the performance of the *Siegfried Idyll* in October, 2000. See also Zuckerman, "Abuse," http://www.y-net.co.il.

21. See Shilansky.

22. Kliger.

23. See the comment made by the editor in chief of *Yediot Aharonot* in Rosenblum: "This whole problem is an internal problem of our own, a problem that must be discussed inside our own house, and no foreigners, even if they are our friends, should enter into it. . . . This is also true for our dear friend Zubin Mehta, who loves us with all his soul, and we him, but he *read* about Auschwitz, and we were *taken* there. . . . He must leave us to ourselves, and not try to tell us what to do."

24. "Time Has Come."

25. Eaziel-Naor, 429. A copy of the question and its answer can be found in the IPO Archives, Wagner and Strauss file. IPO Archive, 1 Huberman St., Tel Aviv, Israel.

26. In his proposal, Meirom detailed the history of Wagner's anti-Semitism, noting that the composer had "lived in Germany between the years 1813 and 1883. He was born and grew up in the city of Leipzig. One hundred years later in the city of Leipzig my mother was born, and persecuted." He went on to explain that the idea of playing Wagner in Israel was wrong, criticizing those "who try to take us out of our provincial attitude and to bring into our home the geniuses who lay the foundations for the racist creed" (*Divrei HaKnesset*, November 8, 1989, pp. 334–36).

27. Heifetz was described as a guest with poor manners, and the editor of *Ma'ariv*, Dr. Azriel Carlebach, expressed his displeasure in an editorial: "The education minister, Professor Dinur, requested that no Strauss be played. And the justice minister, Dr. Rosen, seconded that request (despite his different personal views on the identification of an artist with his art). . . . Yet Jascha Heifetz received the request from two ministers of Israel, shoved it into his pocket, said whatever he said about opposing musical censorship and refused to comply. He played Strauss in Haifa, and afterwards in Tel Aviv as well." See Carlebach.

28. "Overt Simplicity."

29. The Film and Theater Review Board (the state's cultural censor) intervened in the question of whether to allow performances in the German language on Israeli stages following a concert by singer Kenneth Spencer in 1950. The board also sent a memorandum to the IPO before the performance of *Das Lied von der Erde* by Gustav Mahler. The Kenneth Spencer affair is described in Gilead, 32. On the censorship board's request, see Film and Theater Review Board.

30. This sentiment was evident in several articles appearing in the religious press. See, for example, "Life without Wagner"; and "Now the Feelings."

31. Nevenzal.

32. The gradual personification of Holocaust survivors is notable in many artworks of the last two decades. See, for example, the growing numbers of personal documentaries, such as *Hugo* (Yair Lev, 1989); *Don't*

Touch My Holocaust (Asher Tlalim, 1994); *Girlfriends* (Yoel Kaminsky, 1994); *Daddy, Come to the Fair*, (Shmuel Vilozny and Nava Semmel, 1995); *Drei Schwestern* [Three Sisters] (Tsipi Reibenbach, 1998); and *Liebe Perla* [Dear Perla] (Shahar Rozen, 1999). This trend is also evident in literature, the most recent example being Gutfroind's *Our Holocaust*.

33. See "Hok le-Asiat." For Knesset debates on the establishment of Yad Vashem, see *Divrei HaKnesset* 14 (May 12, 1953): 1310–14, (May 18, 1953): 1331–53, and (Aug. 19, 1953): 2402–9.

34. The open debate took place on November 15, 2001, at the Felicja Blumental Music Center and Library in Tel Aviv. Some of the papers delivered at the conference appeared in the *Tel Aviver Jahrbuch für deutsche Geschichte*, 2003.

CHAPTER 9

RICHARD WAGNER AND
DISABILITY STUDIES

Alex Lubet

INTRODUCTION

What's it all about?
—Burt Bacharach, "Alfie"

The field of Disability Studies privileges personal narrative perhaps
more than does any other field, and so it is with a personal concern—
shortly to become political as well—that I begin. When Matthew
Bribitzer-Stull and I started this project, to be joined later by Gottfried Wagner, my role on the team was simply that of the only University of Minnesota faculty member with appointments in both
Music and Jewish Studies—a Jew playing the not uncharacteristic
role of middleman in organizing the international conference whose
presentations form a nucleus of this volume, but no Wagnerian of
either the musical or cultural/historical stripe. As the project
evolved, I increasingly internalized its importance (feeling what I'd
always *known*) and became increasingly driven to make my own
scholarly contribution. Given our cast of notables from Music Theory, Musicology, Literature, and History—Wagner specialists all—I
decided I could best serve this enterprise using the tools of Disability

Studies, rarely applied to music by anyone other than me, in interrogating Wagner's artistic and polemic creations. Embarking on a methodologically new project, I pose here appropriately fundamental questions. What might extant research on Richard Wagner offer the field of Disability Studies? What insights can Disability Studies provide about Wagner? How might contemplating Wagner from a disability perspective shed light on broader issues?

Disability Studies examines culture and society through a disability perspective, largely analogous to the methods of feminist, queer, and critical race theory. While research that is overtly about people with disabilities is obviously central to this project, the ubiquity of the condition and concept of disability—which touch nearly every human life and death—renders a disability standpoint widely valuable in the examination of social and cultural phenomena.

While broadly interdisciplinary, Disability Studies is not without core theoretical underpinnings; foremost of these is the social model of disability. The social model proposes that disability is a social construct rooted in biological impairment, roughly analogous to the relationship between gender and sex in gender studies and to related perspectives on race and sexual orientation. The Disability Studies perspective is arguably the most radical of these social critiques insofar as its assertion—that the (largely disadvantaged) position of the disabled subject resides primarily in social praxis, rather than in the individual's impaired body—has gained far less acceptance than the (still far from perfect) acknowledgment that achieving sexual and racial equality are fundamentally civil projects and not impossibilities fated by biological destiny. While the reticence to confer social equity on people with disabilities cannot be condoned, it can be understood in that even common parlance that has not been rejected by the disability rights movement or scholars of Disability Studies—*dis*ability, *im*pairment—carries indisputable negative connotations.[1]

How Wagner Studies Can
Inform Disability Studies

*Disability is everywhere in history, once you begin looking
for it, but conspicuously absent in the histories we write.*
—Douglas Baynton

Extant research on Wagner and close reading of the composer's theoretical and musical works afford considerable insight into contemporaneous attitudes toward disability. One fundamental work of
scholarship is Marc Weiner's 1995 (additional postscript, 1997)
Richard Wagner and the Anti-Semitic Imagination. Weiner convincingly demonstrates that the composer's anti-Semitism, so viru-
lently propounded in his theoretical writings, is also made manifest
in his music dramas. Although Jews are never referenced explicitly or
literally in Wagner's operas, familiar anti-Semitic stereotypes of his
time pervade the staging, libretti, and music associated with his
antagonists, particularly in *Die Meistersinger*, *Der Ring*, and *Parsifal*.

Jews were commonly defined principally in nineteenth-century
Germany as a racial—thus physical—type, rather than as a religious
group, ethnicity, nation, or people. The Jewish body was regarded
as inferior to the German, in terms that prominently include numerous references to disability, dysfunction, disease, and degeneration.
As Weiner demonstrates, much of Wagner's portrayal of Jews (and
his characterization in general) is through iconography of the body
(whose various parts, functions, and conditions form the organizational principle that guides Weiner's chapter organization). Mal-
adies commonly attributed to Jews in Wagner's time—some since
the Middle Ages—that the composer applies to such villains as
Beckmesser (*Die Meistersinger*); Mime, Alberich, and Hagen (*Der
Ring*); and Klingsor and (villianess) Kundry (*Parsifal*) include dis-
eases of the eyes and skin, aphasia, malodorousness or scent of
seduction, effeminate and immature vocal range and tessitura, castration, dwarfism, deformed feet/ambulatory impairments, and
general degeneration and deterioration of kinds associated in Wagner's time with onanism and syphilis. As Weiner observes, "Every
Jewish stereotype in Wagner works, as in his culture, is defined by
his or her damaged body and is given away by features deemed idio-
syncratically different and inferior to those of the German."[2]

Wagner's pathologization of Jewishness would have less importance were it only the artist's idiosyncrasy rather than the prejudice
lifted from centuries-old icons of German anti-Semitism whose
awful resonance would peak under Adolf Hitler, well-known to be a
Wagnerian of the first order. Wagner's racism, far from iconoclastic,
exemplified his place and time. The rise of German anti-Semitism is
all the more disturbing for having flourished in a larger context of
increasing Western racism, the rise of eugenics, and exclusionary
legislation in immigration and human rights.

It is useful to compare the conclusions one draws from Weiner's
research as read from a disability perspective to historian Douglas
Baynton's article, "Disability and the Justification of Inequality in
American History." Baynton examines a different nation and a
longer period than Weiner (roughly from American independence
through the 1920s), though his focus is the middle to late nineteenth century, Wagner's time. The sociobiological and eugenic
praxis Baynton chronicles in the United States was pervasive
throughout the West, including, of course, Wagner's Germany, and,
as has been noted previously here, Weiner emphasizes in no uncertain terms that the composer's racist ideas and iconography were far
from unique or original; his anti-Semitic images were common in
German parlance, some dating back to medieval times.

From a disability perspective, Baynton demonstrates with numerous and varied examples incidences of (successful and unsuccessful)
calls for restrictions of immigration and civil and human rights not
only of Americans with (what would today be regarded as) disabilities, but also women, gays and lesbians, ethnic and racial minorities,
and immigrants through *disability arguments* grounded in biological inferiority, defects, and deviances. Between Weiner and Baynton
and historians of nineteenth-century race and disability, respectively,
a picture emerges of an era in Western society in which Social Dar-
winist thinking,[3] grounded in corporeal imageries of archetypes of
the superior and the defective (which I shall term standard/deviant)
predominates.[4]

Wagner and many of his *Landsmen* were fixated on the opposed
binaries of an idealized German *Volk* and the demonized, cosmopolitan Jew (whose stereotypical imageries were nearly always syncretized
with male antagonists in the music dramas—Kundry, in *Parsifal*, was
the notable exception). Baynton observes that nineteenth-century
America was a time and place in which a transformation in thinking

occurred regarding the precise nature of standard/deviant types—from natural/monstrous to normal/defective.[5] It is the latter (and historically later) opposition that will concern us. Baynton's observation will prove pivotal to our next concern: the application of disability theory to Wagner.

Disability Theory and Wagner Studies

My future is my past.
—Mose Allison, "Lost Mind"

I will apply disability theory to the question of whether Wagner should be regarded as a "forward-looking" artist. My goal is not a final word on this subject but is merely intended to demonstrate how Disability Studies can contribute to this discussion. "Forward-looking" is a term I have chosen carefully, eschewing the approximate synonyms:

1. "Revolutionary" and "of the future": Wagner's own self-aggrandizements, overwrought with historical and egotistical baggage
2. "Progressive": A term with unhelpful political connotations (and certainly not an adjective one would use today to describe Wagner's racist, proto-Nazi ideology)
3. "Late Romantic," "Modernist" (or "Pre-Modern"): Quite specific to musical styles and epochs that may inhibit a larger perspective and context

Given the broad agreement that Wagner was a musical and theatrical original, one might well question my pursuit of this line of investigation. But even Wagner's own characterization of his work as "revolutionary" and "of the future" might not necessarily connote innovation. A restoration of traditional values (or more likely—and more typical of revival movements in general—an *imagined* restoration of traditional values) is also a possibility, one Wagner implies in his numerous references to the German *Volk*. Despite the common categorization of Wagner as the archetypal late Romantic composer, his polemical writings reveal him, in his ardent calls for a restoration of the values of ancient Greek civilization and in particular its theatrical tradition, to have also been a staunch neo-classicist in the most literal sense.

Despite wide recognition of the innovative aspects of Wagner's creations, one notable critic, drawing on a famous observation by an important composer, reads Wagner quite differently. Referring to *Tristan und Isolde* in *Music, Society, Education*, Christopher Small observes that:

> This seemed to be about as far as the resources of tonal functional harmony could stretch without breaking altogether. If we see in tonal-harmonic music a metaphor for the rationalistic and individualistic temper of Western man, Wagner presents to us, in genuinely mythic form, his situation in the later years of the 19th century, which was about as far along the rationalist-individualist road as it was possible to travel at that time period. Debussy, thirty years later, said that Wagner was a sunset that thought it was a sunrise, and we can see now that he was right; Wagner stands at the end of an old tradition, not, as he himself thought, at the beginning of a new.[6]

Small and Debussy do not exactly deny Wagner's innovations, but they certainly circumscribe the limits of his achievement, characterizing *Tristan* as a sort of valedictory address for tonality, celebrating its accomplishments in broad terms, and then dismissing it to make way for the new class of more authentic modernists. Wagner might thus be heard as having moved forward stylistically himself, although only to the farthest perimeter of the boundaries of harmonic tonality. His musical praxis reflects upon the past, rather than staking out the future. To Small and Debussy, Wagner may have stepped slightly forward, but while gazing backward.[7]

The case for Wagner as "retro" is certainly consistent with the composer's neoclassical theatrical aspirations. It is important to, like Weiner, at least hypothesize consistency between Wagner's theories and the praxis of his *Gesamtkunstwerk*. However simpler and more comfortable it may be to ignore everything we find odious about Wagner and concern ourselves only with "the music" (as if that were ever possible or desirable) in the manner of those whom Weiner terms "apologists," this would simultaneously deflate our estimation of his formidable artistic and intellectual gifts and negate his influence on one of history's worst moments.

There is a clue to where disability theory takes our analysis in Small's characterization of Wagner's music dramas as "in genuinely mythic form." While Small notes Wagner's employment of myth only in *Tristan*, arguably all the operas (certainly nearly all) are based on archetypes from either myth or the distant past—and thus easily mythologized—rather than the realism (broadly construed here to include all works that treat human subjects from recoverable recent history) that was increasingly prevalent in Italian opera repertoire as early as Mozart (*The Magic Flute* in German is a notable exception) and continuing at least through Puccini, Mascagni, and Leoncavallo.[8]

It requires only a small theoretical leap across idioms that utilize text to associate "realistic" opera with the novel, a literary genre that emerged in eighteenth-century Europe, first in England and later France, as essential to and emblematic of the foundations of modernism as industrialization.[9] It is important here to view the novel not with contemporary eyes, but as it was seen at its origins. Disability literary theorist Lennard Davis quotes Clara Reeve in 1785: "The Novel is a picture of real life and matters, and of the times in which it is written. The novel gives a familiar relation of such things, and has every day before our eyes, such as may happen to our friend, or to ourselves."[10] This contemporaneous definition of the novel, a, perhaps *the*, progressive literary genre in its time, is hardly what one sees in a Wagner music drama. Davis, in terms stunningly evocative of Baynton, speaks of the novel as departing from literary models based on "the ideal" and "linked ideologically to structures of kingship and feudal society," embracing instead "that most perfect of subjects—the average citizen."[11] Significantly (and again remarkably consistently with Baynton), "the word and concept of 'normal' enter the English and French languages at this time. Novels were novel precisely because they were a form engaged in depicting this average or normal life, as Reeve and Dunlop noted in their own time."[12] And "on some profound level, the novel emerges as an ideological form of symbolic production whose central binary is normal-abnormal."[13]

While from our own perspective it may be possible to read Wagner's music dramas as *formally* novelistic—narratively linear, essentially conflictual, and asymmetrically arched toward dramatic musical climax—the perspective of those who witnessed the emergence of the genre identified its most prescient innovation as something quite different and unrelated to design and schematic characteristics: the emergence of the average citizen as protagonist. Certainly, the signature prose genre of the Industrial Age was identified in its early decades by its subject matter, which bore nothing in common with Wagner's choice of mythic/folkloric (that is, *volkisch*) topics. As a dramatist, Wagner aligned himself not with the new literary genre from England and France—whose cultures he disdained as tainted by Jewish influence—but with the theatrical model of ancient Greece, and he was right.

It would be wrong to deny any similarities between Wagner's literary imagination and that of early novelists. There is both significant commonality and important difference. An important commonality is nascent nationalism. According to Davis, "there are few novels from 1720 to 1870 whose main characters, the ones with whom we identify and sympathize, are not national stereotypes. And, as such, these characters also have bodies and minds that signify this averageness."[14] The protagonists of these early novels, while average, were also "virtuous" in ways that embodied the national ideals of their author's homelands.[15] While, of course, Wagner in his music dramas also epitomizes the concepts of virtue and nation (or virtue *in* nation), these concepts are portrayed in the guise of protagonists who are mythic, larger-than-life, and villains, who are considerably smaller, or at least bent, like the Jewish stereotypes of the day, and thus disabled to boot.

Wagner's music dramas thus stand removed from the process of modernization elected by many of Wagner's literary contemporaries, initially and largely non-German. He was not alone in this, having Weber as an operatic precedent, Humperdinck as an operatic contemporary, and the Brothers Grimm as his compatriots in the recasting of *Volk*-tales. In contrast, the foremost exponents of musical theater in nineteenth-century Britain, one of the novel's vanguard states, were Gilbert and Sullivan who were, unlike Wagner, almost exclusively purveyors of comedies that, like the novel (*Mikado*, a notable exception), largely portrayed commoners, usually British.[16] Despite the profound and obvious differences between these nineteenth-century musical/dramatic genres, each was in its own way a national—and nationalistic—theater, a commonality I will revisit later.

Disability theory finds Wagner non- or even anti-modern. Recall Douglas Baynton's observation, seconded in only slightly different terms by Davis, that the standard/deviant model of human assessment shifted in nineteenth-century America (and throughout the West) from natural/monstrous to normal/abnormal. The former, and by then largely archaic, natural/monstrous binary is, to all extents and purposes, identical to the ideal versus demonic binary of Wagner's Germans and Jews in his polemics and, as Weiner asserts, German and Jewish surrogates in the music dramas.

Heretofore, the connection between Davis's theory of the early novel and disability may have been less than clear. Simply put, the emergence of the virtuous "normal," that is, the "average citizen" of "the nation," was at the expense of the "abnormal," a label that Baynton reminds us is always de facto "subnormal" when it is raised as a red flag of concern or fear and of advocacy for exclusionary and discriminatory practices and policies. Davis observes that "this project of cultural typicality has to be seen for what it is—the incipient impulse of the tendency that would later be called eugenics."[17]

By the late nineteenth century, the era in which reified eugenic thinking emerged when Darwin's theory of the evolution of species was rendered sociobiological (by Wagner, among others), the novel adopts disability as a signifier of two potential targets of eugenics: the "immoral or negative," such as Ahab, and the "utterly innocent," like Tiny Tim.[18] Only when the "standard" changes from an ideal individual sovereign or tiny feudal class to a ruling collective entity as large as the "normal" citizenry (typically, though not always, the majority)[19] does the eugenic project of excising or otherwise containing the defective minority away from the body politic make sense as within the realm of possibility and practicality.

At first, the above analysis may seem problematic as regards Wagner. Surely, the Nazi ideology he greatly influenced produced a eugenic project of unparalleled horror. However, though the Holocaust—including and alongside the Third Reich's T-4 project to exterminate people with disabilities—may have had no parallel, it was certainly not without recent precedent, including, but by no means limited to, the great colonial empires and the manifold racial and other discriminatory policies and practices of, for example, the United States, including forced institutionalization and sterilization of people with disabilities.[20] Even if anti-Semitic and other racist impulses were already well-established in Wagner's Germany, the German-speaking states were still relatively small players in the business of overseas colonization and overtly racial war as compared to other Western nations.[21] It is not, I think, outrageous to suggest that the cultural and political climate essential for the nineteenth-century empires of Britain, France, and other Western nations required a bourgeois, literate citizenry from whom to recruit colonists, and that the place of the novel in this project is clear, at times even utterly obvious, in, for example, the work of Kipling and Forster.

The culture of the mid-twentieth-century eugenics of the Axis and of Germany in particular differed in numerous ways from that of the nineteenth century, not least of which was its conviction that the Other was seen by the Nazis as utterly incapable of improvement through "civilization"—that harsher measures were required. In this context, the irredeemable villains of both Wagner's music dramas and his polemics provide cultural capital.[22] Further, the antiquarian elements of fascist ideology, such as the notion of a Third Reich and the revival of Gothic script, obviate the attraction of the mythic/legendary character of Wagner's operas which, if subtle in their anti-Semitic imagery, were totally unabashed in their fervent, Teutonic, revivalist nationalism.

I do not find it disingenuous to contemplate different kinds or degrees of eugenics and colonization any more than the application of such taxonomy in jurisprudence to varieties (murder, manslaughter) and degrees of homicide. If, as appears to be the case, different programs of empire are fueled by different psychologies, different intentions (even though there may be similar results), and different inspirations, it is natural (*and* monstrous) that they be fueled by different literary, dramatic, and musical imaginations, as strikingly contrasting as Wagner versus Gilbert and Sullivan.

"IS THAT ALL THERE IS?"[23]

The fat (or otherwise disabled) lady sings.

When participating in a relatively new project such as Disability Studies and an even newer subfield such as Disability Studies in Music, every article serves not only to make its own points but also to demonstrate and promote its methods. If there is a symbiosis between Wagner Studies and Disability Studies, the process of find-ing it has revealed more, perhaps bigger, things to explore.

In organizing the Lingering Dissonances conference that begat this book, it was never our intention to limit the sociocultural dimension of Wagner studies to Jewish issues, only the product of scholars' availability. As Gottfried Wagner has often said, there is much in his great-grandfather's musical and literary output that is sexist, even misogynist, that must be addressed, as he and others have done. Much of what Marc Weiner has observed about Wag-ner's notions of Jewish effeminacy, autoeroticism (which Wagner believed to be the cause of his archcritic Frederick Nietzsche's fail-ing health), and the masculine/feminine binary of poetry and music of which he regarded his own music dramas as the apotheosis, smacks of homophobia and begs for an appropriate critique.[24] And, to paraphrase Douglas Baynton, disability may be everywhere in Musicology, and, aided especially by Weiner's excellent ground-work, I believe I have found a veritable wellspring in Wagner. In any case, cultural and historical Wagner Studies are, and should con-tinue to be, about more than Jewish issues. The next phase of Wag-ner Studies will need to apply cultural and historical perspectives to music analysis, and vice versa, in order to bring us to a deeper understanding of the music, the man, and his milieu.

In doing this research, I marveled at the striking parallels between the analyses of the era in question by Douglas Baynton and Lennard Davis, whose work on disability issues is in matters of methodology and perspective so different. Juxtaposing their work, one sees the exceptional degree to which Davis, as a literary critic, thinks historically. In particular, his revelations about the early novel—and through them, what is revealed about Wagner—are deeply dependent on using as his point of departure definitions of the novel contemporaneous with its emergence. A fresh perspective sometimes requires divesting oneself of the benefit of hindsight.

The study of Wagner confirms, in a way few things can, the need to revise the way we read and write music history in general and the way we teach it to young musicians in particular. Much music his-tory is written only from the perspective of composers, much of it, especially from the nineteenth century on, heavily focused on those works regarded as having significant innovations. As a history of inventions, music history tends to be organized as a chronology of important composers and compositions.

Apart from the obvious deficiency of a music history primarily or exclusively devoted to composition and negligent of, for example, performance, reception, economy, and technology, much of the importance of musical works throughout their lives as repertoire will be missed if they only put in an appearance at the time of their composition, a date that may be unrelated to the eras of their greatest influence. A case can certainly be made for suggesting that, as pivotally important as Wagner was during his own lifetime, the influence of his works on history and culture grew appreciably, if not always in the most desirable ways, long after his death. We make—and teach—mistakes in music history that would never be made in, for example, religion, where faith and dogmas are understood to have influential and mutable lives millennia past their initial epiphanies. If I appear to be making a case for a music history fortified with social and cultural context, as well as a special pitch for the new, disabled kid on the block, perhaps it is largely because those who do not know the full import of the legacy of Wagner—not only the good, but the bad and the ugly—may be doomed to repeat it.

WORKS CITED

Baynton, Douglas. "Disability and the Justification of Inequality in American History." *The New Disability History*. Ed. Paul K. Longmore and Lauri Umansky. New York: New York University Press, 2001. 33–57.

Davis, Lennard. "Who Put the *the* in *the* Novel?" In *Bending over Backwards: Disability, Dismodernism & Other Difficult Positions*. New York: New York University Press, 2002.

Nattiez, Jean-Jacques. *Wagner Androgyne: A Study in Interpretation*. Trans. Stewart Spencer. Princeton, NJ: Princeton University Press, 1993.

Small, Christopher. *Music, Society, Education*. Lebanon, NH: University Press of New England, 1996.

Weiner, Marc. *Richard Wagner and the Anti-Semitic Imagination*. Lincoln: University of Nebraska Press, 1997.

NOTES

1. The same argument could be made for the use of the word "queer" in Queer Studies, though it differs in that disability is literally negative

because of its prefix "dis" and is customarily derogatory, while "queer" is literally derogatory but customarily negative.

2. Weiner, 304.

3. Wagner was an enthusiastic admirer of Darwin. Ibid. 343.

4. I prefer "standard/deviant" precisely because of both its redolence of (pseudo)science and its ability to subsume all other more familiar but also more era- and place-specific binaries such as natural/unnatural or normal/abnormal. Moreover, "standard/deviant" is inherently hierarchical, in contrast to the only customarily and associatively hierarchical "Self/Other."

5. Baynton, 34–35. Baynton is careful to emphasize that "the average [that is, the normal] . . . in actual usage . . . functioned as an ideal and excluded only those defined as *below* average" (Emphasis in original).

6. Small, 102–3.

7. Although a detailed musical analysis of the opening of *Tristan* would be a distraction in the body of an article whose thrust is disability theory, the Small/Debussy position begs at least a mild rebuttal. In the context of tonal practice, what may be most remarkable about these opening bars is less the famous "*Tristan* chord"—whose fascinations are more one of the work's idiosyncrasies than permanent contributions to tonal harmonic language—than the succession of key-defining cadences on V7: of I, III, and V in the key of a minor. By cadencing on V7 instead of V, Wagner has at once elevated the status of tonality's most important dissonance and its most powerful and unique key-defining signifier. V7 is at once a harmony and a dissonance and identifies its tonality with far less ambiguity than a major or minor triad, whose sonorities regularly appear on other, lesser scale degrees. This truly does represent a sort of endgame for tonality—dissonance as consonance.

   Additionally, I offer the following observation—one I have not heard alluded to even remotely elsewhere, in support of the "forward-looking" Wagner: The unprecedented long, unaccompanied, crescendoed appoggiaturas and the gaping rests that follow each cadence dominate (at least in terms of time spent) the opening bars of the Prelude and they are strongly evocative of early Anton Webern, in particular number five of his *Six Bagatelles* for string quartet. Certainly, some features of *Tristan* are "forward-looking," and, given both Small's and Debussy's concern elsewhere with musical matters beyond pitch relations, it is perhaps surprising that this facet of Wagner's work has escaped their notice.

8. In Vienna, the operas of Alban Berg, though not of Arnold Schoenberg, may represent a hyperrealistic, Expressionistic terminus to Wagnerian late Romanticism.)

9. Davis, "Who Put the *the* in *the* Novel?" 81. While Davis's position on the British/French origins of the novel has certainly been contested, Davis's article, to which I refer, is brilliantly argued and persuasive.

10. Ibid. 91.

11. Ibid. 92–93.

12. Ibid.

13. Ibid. 95.

14. Ibid.

15. Ibid.

16. An interesting touchstone between Wagner and Gilbert/Sullivan is the extraordinary attention both lavished on the text; in each of these operatic production units, the librettist received top/equal billing, something rarely seen outside the Broadway musical (With Wagner, this was, of course, unavoidable). Additionally, despite the light, comedic tone of all but one of Gilbert and Sullivan's works, their racism can be utterly forthright, such that its subtleties need not be unearthed by a scholar such as Marc Weiner. This is contemplated most interestingly and curiously in the 1999 film, *Topsy-Turvy*.

17. Davis, 94–95.

18. Ibid. 97.

19. I presume here that in the antebellum southern United States, regions existed with a slave majority. Certainly, apartheid-era South Africa, Namibia, and Rhodesia (now Zimbabwe) possessed citizen minorities.

20. Differing points of view as to whether the term "Holocaust" refers to the entire Nazi eugenics project or only its racial/racist component must be respected.

21. Weiner notes Wagner's prejudice against all peoples of African descent, among whom Jews were popularly included at the time. Dark skin was regarded as part of the Jewish racial phenotype.

22. The one redeemed villain in the late Wagner music dramas in which Weiner reads anti-Semitic stereotypes is Kundry in *Parsifal*, the composer's only "Jewish" woman. While her sex may be linked to her exceptionality in this regard, the nature of her redemption, first in baptism and then in death, is hardly a program of redemption a Jewess or anyone else would elect.

23. Jerry Leiber and Mike Stoller (written for Peggy Lee)

24. See Nattiez for a monograph-length study of Wagner's gendered discourse as it relates to the interaction between poetry and music.

CHAPTER 10

ANTI-SEMITISM IN MUSIC: WAGNER AND THE ORIGINS OF THE HOLOCAUST

Paul Lawrence Rose

In this chapter, I want to look at two blocks, obstacles, lines of defense, that are often encountered when we try to discuss Wagner's own anti-Semitism and the problem of his relationship to Nazism and Hitler. The first block is an aesthetic one. Yes, admittedly Wagner was an anti-Semite (though Daniel Barenboim seems to have difficulty in admitting even that), and he wrote anti-Semitic articles, but that is as far as we can go with the anti-Semitism, we are often told.[1] The music itself, the operas, remain pure—a realm into which anti-Semitism does not enter. How can music be anti-Semitic any more than it can be "Jewish"? Wagner notoriously believed that music could be "Jewish," and indeed he used the title *Jewishness in Music* (*Das Judentum in der Musik*) for the most influential of all his anti-Semitic essays. But he was, we are often assured, simply wrong about that, as he was about many things.

This is a difficult subject that would be rash to pursue, but it is obvious that there are some pieces of music that are by definition "Jewish"—Bloch's *Sacred Service*, for example, or, more interestingly, the non-Jewish Max Bruch's *Kol Nidrei*. At any rate, we may allow that if a composer intentionally wishes a piece of music to be "Jewish," then we may call it "Jewish." And if Wagner intentionally programmed his operas to be "anti-Semitic," then why not grant him his argument? In saying this, I have no wish to argue with those who like to invoke the "intentional fallacy" to prove that the author's intention is irrelevant to the finished work of art, nor with those who dispute that an intention can be ascertained, nor with those who deny the existence of any "intention" at all, and certainly not with those scholars who denounce any quest for "essentialism." I am simply appealing to common sense and to the need to take Wagner on his own terms and at his word.

The second line of defense is historical, or rather "historicist." The argument linking Wagner with Hitler and Nazism, and indeed with the Holocaust, is often stopped in its tracks by lofty declarations of historicist principle: Wagner belonged to a different world, a different historical context, from that of Hitler. Wagner's was the world of the nineteenth-century bourgeois and liberal. It is not legitimate historically to read him with hindsight—that cardinal historical sin—in the appalling light of the unimaginable world that emerged after the First World War—a world of violent social revolution and political murder, a world brutalized and barbarized by the experience of the war and defeat of 1918, a world in which mass industrial death had become conceivable and which opened the way to the Holocaust. Wagner died in 1883, a full six years before Hitler was even born. How could Wagner have possibly imagined that his nationalism could lead to the Third Reich, and his anti-Semitism to the Holocaust?

I am going to try to show in this essay that these two lines of defense are not quite as substantial and impenetrable as they are usually taken to be.

JEWISHNESS IN MUSIC

Before looking at Wagner's anti-Semitism in music, let me put his *Jewishness in Music* into context. As I have argued in my book, *Wagner. Race and Revolution*,[2] Wagner experienced an epiphany in 1847–1850. During these years, he converted to revolutionism; he embraced political, social, and human revolution and liberation; he revolutionized his art; and he adopted a new kind of fanatical revolutionary anti-Semitism. He also left his wife. All these things were in fact connected. Minna Wagner wrote to him in May 1850:

Only during the last *two* years, ever since you turned to miserable politics . . . have I been unwise enough not to avoid violent scenes with you. . . . I used to be close to you while you created all the beautiful things . . . you always sang and played almost every new scene for me. But since *two* years ago, when you wanted to read me that essay in which you slander whole races which have been fundamentally helpful to you, I could not force myself to listen, and ever since that time you have borne a grudge against me, and punished me so severely for it that you never again let me hear anything from your works.[3]

We have, therefore, a date for the first draft of *Jewishness in Music* that places it two years before its publication in 1850—namely 1848. This re-dating has an immense significance for Wagner's biography and his anti-Semitism, for it shows us that *Jewishness in Music*, far from being an aberration, was part of a constellation of revolutionary treatises that Wagner conceived in 1848–1849, and that his anti-Semitism, far from being a crudely right-wing nationalistic sort, was actually a revolutionary and progressive variety. It was only later that Wagner broadened and deepened it by the addition of racial biological concepts that became available in the 1860s and after. *Jewishness in Music*, then, is anything but an isolated, atypical, irrelevant, occasional expression of its author's mind. It is a fully integrated component of the revolutionary "turn," as central to Wagner's art as it is to his life and his politics. Or, as he later put it to Liszt, "this hatred [of Jewishness] is as essential to my nature as gall is to the blood" (April 18, 1851).[4]

MUSICAL ANTI-SEMITISM

"It's not in the music"—isn't it? Let me quote the words of a musician, conductor, and composer who adored and knew intimately Wagner's operas: "With Mime, Wagner intended to ridicule the Jews with all their characteristic traits—petty intelligence and greed—the jargon is textually and musically so cleverly suggested; but for God's sake it must not be exaggerated and overdone as Julius Spielmann does it . . . I know of only one Mime and that is myself . . . you wouldn't believe what there is in that part, nor what I could make of it."[5]

That was Gustav Mahler writing after seeing a production of *Siegfried* at Vienna in the 1890s in which Mime had been caricatured as a Jewish dwarf; for Mahler, this was unacceptable crudeness. Mime was undoubtedly a Jewish figure, but some subtlety and taste were required to realize fully the intricacy of Wagner's anti-Semitic portrait on stage. The anti-Semitism was there in the drama, in the characterization, in the singing, in the music itself—as Mahler says, *textually* and *musically*. At several points in the opera, we do indeed see and hear "Anti-Semitism in Music." There it is in the gigantic forging scene where the ignoble Mime plots the death of the noble Siegfried. While Siegfried brews a "broth of metal," Mime whips up for him a bowl of drugged pottage (the allusion to Jacob's embezzlement of Esau's birthright by a mess of pottage is no coincidence). And while Siegfried fights the dragon, we have Mime and his evil brother Alberich fighting it out between them to see who is the more cunning and greedy and vicious "Jew." And afterward we witness the woodbird teaching Siegfried how to understand what murderous treachery lies beneath Mime's honeyed words of love for him. But it is the opening scene that is the most skillfully woven tapestry of anti-Semitism. It begins with a depiction of utter frustration as Mime tries yet again to make a sword that Siegfried can use to kill the dragon. The Jew cannot create— whether it is art or a heroic sword. Siegfried then enters preceded by a bear who molests the terrified Mime—a scene that always gets a laugh and a nice example of Wagner's typically cruel sense of humor. Mime's complaints at this treatment are hardly taken seriously by Siegfried who calms him down—a rather apt portrait of what Wagner believed to be the unhappy and disgusting codependency of Jews and Germans.[6] Mime then begins a lament, which is unmistakably Yiddish-sounding and wheedling in its musical character. Moreover, the actual wording—lamenting Siegfried's ingratitude to his caring "parent" Mime—refers twice to what Wagner elsewhere wrote off as the great Jewish con game perpetrated on naive non-Jews, the notion of "gratitude" that placed the non-Jew in a position of dependency and indebtedness to the Jew, the child to the parent. We also find here Siegfried ridiculing the sputtering, cackling, misshapen speech and manner of Mime (and later Alberich) in terms very similar to the way Wagner describes the Jewish voice and singing in *Jewishness in Music*: "A croaking, squeaking, buzzing snuffle . . . that sense and sound confounding gurgle, yodel, and cackle." And note too Mime's characteristic wails of anguish and terror—the only words missing are "Oy, veh." There was indeed a surfeit of richness of anti-Semitism in this scene for Mahler to savor. No wonder that when Wagner himself saw that in the 1881 Berlin production, a dwarfish Jewish singer (Julius Lieban) had taken the role of Mime, the composer reacted with delight. "But that's great," he exclaimed.[7]

Wagner was not content with generalized expressions of anti-Semitism in his operas; he liked to target particular Jews who incurred his displeasure. Meyerbeer, of course, whose imagined machinations at Berlin in 1847 and again in Paris in 1848–1850 had provoked the writing of *Jewishness in Music*, was a prime mark. In *Rheingold*, the music relating to Alberich's character is not only generically anti-Semitic as prescribed by the essay (the usual shuffling, spitting noises and grotesque angularity of phrasing), but also specifically a parody of Meyerbeer's own operatic style. Thus, having been cruelly teased by the first two Rhinemaidens, Alberich engages in a duet with the third, only to be rejected again even more roughly. *Formally*, the duet is a clear parody of Meyerbeer's grand opera style, notably the verse beginning in "Deine Anmuth" (Your charms), a derivation of Wagner's Wegalaweia melody. *Dramatically*, the scene is a derisive allegory of the Jews' attempts to enter German, indeed human, society and culture. *Musically*, Wagner mocks Meyerbeer's compositional style by having the cellos imitate (the only time in the opera) Meyerbeer's orchestral doubling of the vocal line. Incidentally, it is one of the curiosities of the *Ring* cycle that Alberich has no specific leitmotiv of his own—yet another indication of how cunningly anti-Semitic concepts are inscribed into the operas. It is natural that a character symbolic of Jewishness should have no fixed quality, just as Meyerbeer as a Jewish composer should have no fixed authentic style. As Wagner later expressed it, "the Jew is the plastic demon of humanity's destruction."[8]

The best known butt of Wagner's wit was famously the critic Eduard Hanslick, who was of partly Jewish descent and who has gone down to posterity in the ignominious character of Beckmesser in *Die Meistersinger*, that elephantine five-hour "comedy" and investigation of "Germanness" and art whose popularity I cannot fathom. It was the hapless Hanslick's own favorite Wagner opera, and (to my mind inexplicably) Toscanini conducted the Prelude more frequently than any other piece during the war years. *Meistersinger* is—among

much else—a recasting of Wagner's rather simple anti-Semitic concept that the Jew is the negation of Germanness—of German art,
feeling, history, culture, et cetera, and that the Jew remains permanently alien to the German *Volk* and its culture, especially its language and its music. Beckmesser is the troublesome pedantic—that
is, sterile Jewish—intellect who is always causing division and disor-
der among the otherwise community-minded citizens of Nuremberg. The finales of Acts I and II testify to his disastrous presence,
while in Act III, he is finally routed and all is harmony again.
Beckmesser is actually a kind of "devil" or goblin or spook or ghost
who in the opera is blamed at several points for subverting and
destroying the stability and happiness of the citizens of Nuremberg—a personification of the alleged subversive role of the Jews in
Germany from the middle ages to the Nazi era. A minor character
in the original 1840s draft, Beckmesser attained great prominence
in the reworked versions of the 1860s and acquired a whole set of
noxious Jewish traits, as well as a central dramatic role. In Act II we
find him soliciting Hans Sachs's approval of his bizarre song for the
contest—his caterwauling indeed leads to the riot finale of the Act.
But what is interesting is the parodic parallel between the forging
scene of *Siegfried* and the hammering interruptions of Beckmesser's
serenade by Sachs; in both cases we have a noble German figure
interacting with a stereotypically Jewish figure. This dramatic parody is supported by the musical imagery—there are close similarities
in the syncopated orchestral figures that accompany the bear's entry
in *Siegfried* and those that underlie Sachs's comic provoking of the
unfortunate Beckmesser. Beckmesser's serenade itself is also curiously Jewish—or what Wagner imagined to be Jewish. The melis-
mata, for instance, recall those of synagogue cantorial chanting, and
the tonality is also peculiarly non-Western; in fact, the tonality is
very unclear, and the melody lacks harmonic structure. The serenade displays incompetence in the fundamentals of European art
music, lacking balance, proportion, and melodic/harmonic direction. The serenade is an alien, otherworldly intrusion, one might
say, into the ordered harmonious tonality of merry Nuremberg—in
a word, a Jewish intrusion. Note also that Wagner lays the vocal line
at an unnaturally high level for a bass, one that even baritones have
difficulty with; the high tessitura forces a certain amount of falsetto,
evoking a castrated Jew (circumcision in the German literature of
the time was often confused with castration). Wagner himself told a

singer that "musically the high tessitura is the result solely of an impassioned, screeching tone of voice intended to bring out as much as possible"—that is, of Jewishness. There is very little question here of actual "singing;" "the whole style of delivery rests upon a highly complicated musical basis which can be intelligible only to an experienced singer"—and audience, one might add.[9] "The extremely high notes (Wagner tells another singer) are of course only vehement or ridiculous speech accents, not singing."[10] On this whole subject, one should read the brilliant pioneering essay by Barry Millington and Marc Weiner's admirable book.[11] Their expositions have met with a great deal of abuse, but so far, the misguided if ingenious apologists have failed to come up with any convincing refutation.

Take for instance the inability of the apologists to provide any serious analysis of the utterly grotesque transmogrification of the song that Beckmesser actually sings in the contest in Act III. Here the words and ideas are chaotically fouled up as a splendidly graphic illustration of the Jewish style of music and poetry defined by Wagner in his essay. The words, of course, Beckmesser had endeavored in true Jewish fashion to steal from Sachs, but even with them written down in front of him, he can't get them right. And then there is the humiliation of Beckmesser—the symbolic Jewish outsider—by the *Volk*. No need for him to be listed as a Jew in the cast list; he has all the recognized attributes of one. As to the words, the nonsense words of the song are not entirely nonsense. They are actually a cunning set of coded references to Jewish characteristics and, in particular, to the Grimm Brothers' tale of *The Jew in the Thornbush*, which Wagner had already alluded to cryptically in Act I. Thus, Beckmesser alludes to elements of the Grimm tale that bear on the mistreatment of the Jew in the tale and include a series of not-so-veiled references to Jewish persecution—"rope," "hang," "pillory," "the scent of blood." Even the term "nasty (*garstig*) and nice" refers to Jews—in this case, Alberich and Mime who are described in the *Ring* as "nasty." And the great deal of *Schadenfreude* (malicious pleasure) that Beckmesser attracts on stage is also featured in any number of descriptions of Jewish persecution in German history. All this has been demonstrated in an excellent and objective article by the Germanist Karl Zaehnker.[12]

There is, too, the wonderful earlier scene in which Beckmesser steals the lyric, a scene that vividly depicts Beckmesser's aches and pains and enervating frustration—rushing chromatic scales that get nowhere and sag down—and that again parallels the musical and dramatic delineation of Mime's sufferings in *Siegfried*. Just as Mime cannot forge the sword, so Beckmesser is in the depths of despair because he cannot frame the song.

In any case, it was Beckmesser's serenade that was the lightning rod for Jewish disgust at Wagner's anti-Semitism. The work was premiered in 1868, and at Mannheim, Berlin, and elsewhere it was hissed—especially during the serenade.[13] Wagner was so incensed by this "Jewish attack" that in March 1869 he insisted against all advice on reissuing *Jewishness in Music*, this time under his own name. It is this version that proved to be the seminal text of modern German anti-Semitism, the document that set the discourse and terms and launched the great public debates on anti-Semitism that raged on for the next century (and after). In the meantime, audiences now could recognize the composer's anti-Semitism not only in his political writings, but also in his operas.

These examples are far from recondite, and I cannot pretend to great originality in citing them. Indeed, anyone with an innocent ear can hear them for him or herself. Adorno hinted at them years ago, as did Robert Gutman in his wonderful biography of Wagner.[14] Since 1976, the anti-Semitism has actually been evoked in stagings by Chereau and Kupfer, among others. In the last decade, moreover, Barry Millington, Marc Weiner, Jean-Jacques Nattiez, Hartmut Zelinsky, Ulrich Druener, and Gottfried Wagner have all in their writings deepened and focused musicological analysis of this kind in precise terms.[15] Yet these new analyses have met with virtually no serious musicological responses by the otherwise wordy experts of the Wagner defense team. There has, in fact, been no recognition by the apologists that there is a problem to be faced here that radically affects our understanding and responses to the operas. Instead, there has been the sneer that the critical camp is absurdly reducing the whole meaning of Wagner's operas to anti-Semitism. Yet none of the above mentioned writers, nor myself, believe this; we simply say that the anti-Semitic element is a crucial and indispensable part of the operas that deserves serious consideration, if only to sharpen the problem of how Wagnerians may respond aesthetically to these works in a post-Holocaust world of consciousness.

Before leaving the operas, you may well ask, "Why then aren't Mime, Alberich, and Beckmesser listed as 'Jews' in the cast lists rather than as Nibelungs and Nuremberger?" The short answer is that they didn't need to be—Wagner endowed them with every Jewish characteristic to convey their essential Jewishness to the audience. On a deeper level, of course, the operas were not political tracts; their message was to be conveyed subliminally and instinctively rather than explicitly and superficially. As Wagner himself said in a letter, "I believe it was a true instinct that led me to guard against an excessive eagerness to make things plain, for I have learned that to make one's intentions too obvious risks impairing a proper understanding of the work in question; in drama—as in any work of art—it is a question of making an impression not by parading one's opinions, but by setting forth what is instinctive."[16]

WAGNER AND HITLER: THE HISTORICIST OBJECTIVE

I now turn to the Wagner-Hitler problem and the historicist objection to making the link.[17] Hitler's worship of Wagner is well known, though it is often reduced, as in Ian Kershaw's recent biography, to a trivial German nationalist interest. But what Hitler looked for in Wagner was the prophecy of a revolutionary redemption of humanity founded on anti-Semitism. This is why Hitler took so much to heart the National Wagner Monument dedicated at Leipzig in March 1934, which he funded from his privy purse over the next ten years—a massive monument and park left unfinished at the end of the war, though pieces of sculpture and blueprints still exist. The short speech of 1934 is notable for its lack of any explicit mention of Wagner's anti-Semitism. But this actually exposes the depth of genuine emotion in Hitler's reverence—the radio commentator described him as "visibly moved."[18] It would be a mistake to think this silence indicates that Hitler felt his own anti-Semitism had nothing to do with Wagner's, as one recent historian has argued. If we bear in mind an earlier 1925 speech by Hitler to his Nazi officials in Bayreuth, we will see that it was precisely because Wagner was so important to him that he declined to make vulgar political capital out of the Master. Thus, in Bayreuth to see the 1925 *Meistersinger*, Hitler declared:

> I cannot find the words to say what an overwhelming work of art Wagner has created here. I ask that the Wagnerian art and its institutions here be held in respect. I have not come here to speak political words in any form. I have complied with the official decrees (to exclude politics from the Festival) and I ask you my followers to do the same. Even if I were prepared or had the intention of speaking about politics, still would it be utterly impossible after the joyousness of such art.

Hitler ended by exhorting his audience to abide by the precept of the *Meistersinger* to hold "this art high and holy" (July 30, 1925).[19]

Hitler was especially inspired by the racial program of Wagner's last opera, and we have some interesting racial assessments of *Parsifal* that connect the mentalities of Wagner and Hitler. After reading out loud the Germanic racial sections of Gobineau's *Essai* in 1881, Wagner felt impelled to play the *Parsifal* Prelude for his French guest. A year later, as he was writing the music for *Parsifal*, Wagner congratulated himself on his earlier recognition of his final music drama's racial theme in *Siegfried*, which he had just heard again. Of *Siegfried's* Act III, Wagner remarked enthusiastically, "That is Gobineau music, that is race." Hitler also grasped this connection between *Parsifal* and race. In a famous conversation in 1934, taken down by Hermann Rauschning, a Nazi official who later fled to America, Hitler avowed, "It is not the Christian religion of compassion that is acclaimed, but pure, noble blood. . . . For myself I have the most intimate familiarity with Wagner's mental processes."[20] And in 1936, Hitler confided, "I have built up my religion out of *Parsifal*." Indeed, my own correspondence with both Winifred Wagner and Albert Speer has confirmed that for Hitler, *Parsifal* was indeed the special opera. But if there is a great deal of evidence that Hitler was inspired by Wagner, it does not prove that this is what Wagner would have wanted.

The problem turns largely on Wagner's prophetic prescriptions to the Jews that they "should die," that they should "self-annihilate" or be annihilated.[21] In the famous ending to *Jewishness in Music*, Wagner tells them, "Remember, the only redemption from the burden of your curse is the redemption of Ahasverus—destruction [*Untergang*]!"[22] And in 1881, Wagner prophesies that "we Germans will be the first nation to achieve the grand solution—no more Jews!"[23] Can Wagner then be seen as a prophet of the Holocaust? Did his anti-Semitic solutions to the Jewish Question prefigure those of the Third Reich? What exactly did Wagner mean by the destruction (*Untergang*) or annihilation (*Vernichtung*) of Judaism? Did it correspond to the Nazi concept of extermination (*Ausrottung, Vernichtung*)?

To answer these questions we have to grasp several contexts: We need to know Wagner's own personality and usage. We need to know the contemporary world of cultural discourse in which the words are used. And we need to know something that goes beyond the purely intellectual meaning of the terms—their affective context, something that historians are loath to study. We need to know what lies behind the lips of the person speaking the word; we need to know the mood and the sensibility that give the words their full meaning. And one of the key pointers here is the joke. A joke's a joke, but whether a joke has an edge, a touch of malice, depends very much on the emotional makeup, the personality of the teller. Sometimes the *tone* of the joke is enough to tell us how it is meant; sometimes, we need to know about the personality of the teller; sometimes we need to know what is left unsaid, what is necessarily implicit, but not spelt out.

Let us then quickly look at these terms, starting with *Untergang*. Is it a metaphorical destruction of the Jew that Wagner has in mind, or is it a physical one? In 1850, it seems to me, Wagner is primarily thinking of a self-destruction of Jewish identity rather than physical destruction by violent means. But, as always in the discourse of German anti-Semitism, there is present, even here, interplay of practicality and metaphor. There is the implied threat that if the mass of Jews cannot redeem themselves and cease to be Jews, then perhaps in the end more practical methods may have to be conceived. But this remains at the back of Wagner's mind in 1850. His personality has not yet coarsened enough to think of it as a desirable or realistic solution. Nevertheless, the wish is still there, inchoate as it may be.

In the 1869 reissue, *Untergang* is amplified by the term *Selbstvernichtung*, which might seem to be enhancing the metaphorical sense, but Wagner now negates this by adding his *Aufklärungen*, in which he speaks physically and politically, though a bit opaquely, about the "violent removal of the foreign [Jewish] element" from German life. Then, in *Siegfried*, we find the hero threatening Mime (jokingly?) with melting him down and later with throwing him into the furnace. And in *Meistersinger*, the crowd clamors,

"Beckmesser will soon hang from the gallows"—but, then, that's a comic opera. Finally, in *Parsifal* and its associated essays on *Kunst* (Art) *und Religion*, there is the prophecy of redemption for the Aryan race by compassion and for the Jews by "Tod" and "sterben"—all very ambiguous.

An earlier book of mine, *German Question/Jewish Question*, illustrated at dispiriting length the ambiguity and ambivalence of a wide spectrum of German writers on the Jewish Question as to whether they meant their solutions to be taken physically or metaphorically. Starting, say, with Fichte, we find this ambiguity transmitted through jokes. Fichte jokes about the only solution being "in one night to cut off all their Jewish heads and replace them with others in which not a Jewish idea exists." Very much a joke, if you were to have asked him, but here we must recall the context of his remark: 1793, the year of the Terror and the guillotine in France. Cutting off heads, then, was to anyone reading Fichte a real physical activity. The joke, therefore, is a nasty, even menacing one, referring to actual political practice and no mere innocent jest.[24]

Other solutions proposed in the early nineteenth century are just as prophetically humorous. Jakob Fries in 1815 calls for the *Ausrottung* (eradication) of the Jewish commercial caste. Interrogated by the police after the Hep-Hep riots, Fries charmingly claims he was speaking only spiritually, metaphorically.[25] Others joke about "exterminating" the Jews or just "hounding the vermin out of Germany." In this discourse, one writer was moved to satire, suggesting ironically but being taken seriously, that the total extermination of the Jews might include melting them down into candles and using the "total massacre of Jewry [*Niedermetzelung*] to improve the soil."[26] Then, later in the century, we have the veiled, obscure Sibylline threats and prophecies of such as Paul de Lagarde, who regarded his contemporaries as being too humane or cowardly to "destroy the usurious vermin. With parasites and bacilli one does not negotiate. They are annihilated as quickly as possible." Karl-Eugen Dühring more explicitly still asserted that the solution could be achieved "only through extermination and killing," though even this was ambiguously camouflaged in a seemingly spiritual passage. In his later writings, only the thinnest disguise was given to Dühring's true solution: "Criminal Jewry has no right to existence and must in all its embodiments be annihilated. . . . It is they who have murdered and exterminated. . . . One draws the final and most extreme consequence that the Jewish fundamental evil must be seized and exterminated."[27]

I have found a great deal more of this kind of talk in late-nineteenth-century Germany and Austria, even though much of the fantasizing was denied on a cognitive level. For instance, when the objective of mass murder was actually, in 1899, preached by Count Pückler, that was an embarrassment even for the most radical anti-Semites, who conveniently wrote him off as a deranged madman. When Pückler was pulled into court, he naturally claimed that he was speaking only metaphorically since his peasant audience enjoyed colorful expressions: "That is . . . a form of rhetoric. I love language rich in imagery." Acquitted at this trial, Pückler found later judges just as indulgent. Said one, "Pückler, in saying that the Jew-boys everywhere must be crushed and annihilated, could not have meant his words literally. . . . He would not wish to harm anyone physically." As Goebbels wrote in 1929, "How wonderful it was that such a fellow should have strayed into the twentieth century!"[28] As I have written elsewhere, there are subtle and emotional continuities between this fantasizing, joking culture of nineteenth-century advocacy of extermination and Nazi mentality. (In passing, I might note that Daniel Goldhagen, despite his reliance on my earlier work, has rather misunderstood the problem of continuity, among other things.)

Like many of the jokey extermination proponents of his time, Wagner too was a keen anti-Semitic joker. In 1881, a theatre fire in Vienna prompted him to propose that "all the Jews should be burned at a performance of *Nathan the Wise*." Cosima realized just how edged and prophetic this joke was; she calls it "a grim joke."[29] If only, if only. . . . The idea was not practicable, but it represents a recurring wish in Wagner that is rooted in the prophetic discourse of *Ausrottung*. The wish occurs again as a grim joke in *Siegfried*, where Siegfried twice threatens Mime with being smelted down in the furnace—an operatic prophecy only?

Was Wagner's anti-Semitism not pro-extermination but rather a redemptionist, spiritual anti-Semitism as Saul Friedlaender has argued?[30] Certainly in 1850, the demand for *Untergang* (extermination) seemed to be far more a spiritual cry, but, as I have said, there is always the ambivalence, the tension between the physical and the metaphorical in the German discourse on Jews. By the time Wagner reissued the text in 1869, the accompanying explanations proved that his thinking was by then moving into a far more physical domain. In both cases, we have to see that Wagner is thinking within the context of the anti-Semitic discourse of destruction and extermination. And let us not pass over the steady deterioration of Wagner's character: his enthusiastic approval of the 1881 pogroms in Russia betrays a brutalized sensibility by any standard. For Wagner, as quoted by Cosima, "that's the only thing one can do with them—throw the bastards out!" (Das ist das Einzige, was sich tun lässt, die Kerle hinauswerfen und durchprügeln).[31] That's fairly physical. Two years before Wagner had shown his true thinking, Cosima noted that "Richard is in favor of expelling the Jews entirely. We laugh to think that it really seems as if his (1869) article on the Jews marked the beginning of this (anti-Semitic) struggle."[32]

But would Wagner have changed his mind once he saw Hitler? Why should we think so? Wagner's disciple Houston Stewart Chamberlain never did; in fact, Chamberlain greeted Hitler rapturously. But assume for a moment that Wagner might have reconsidered. After all, the Jewish conductor Hermann Levi had apologized for Wagner to his father (a rabbi) by saying that his patron was really a wonderful man who espoused what was actually a "noble anti-Semitism." With this testimonial in mind, let us try to provide Wagner with a possible explanation of his prophecies, an alibi, a recantation, that he might have offered in 1945 once he had known the full evil to which his anti-Semitism had led:

> My anti-Semitism was intellectual and idealistic, above all noble, and the policy of removing the Jews from Germany and Europe was a chivalrous solution. I did use very strong words about the Jews and did say something about extermination, but all that propaganda was not to be taken literally. Extermination and extinction were never meant to be taken in a killing sense. A decent and dignified anti-Semitism is one of the noblest ideas which I will not disown because it was abused and perverted by Nazi leaders. Despite my strong opposition to the Jews, I did not want the extermination of Jewry, but advocated the political expatriation of the Jews. . . . As to my advocating the extermination of the Jews: The word *Ausrottung* means to "overcome," not with respect to individuals, but legal entities and certain historical traditions. . . . In any case, there is a distinction between the extermination of the "Jews" themselves and of "Jewry" [*Judentum*]. The thought of the physical extermination of

the Jews never entered my mind. The fact in itself that I preached anti-Semitism justifies my punishment as a murderer of Jews as little as one could hold Rousseau and Mirabeau responsible for the subsequent horrors of the French Revolution.

Or more succinctly: "I wrote of extermination purely in a rhetorical way. I was interested only in enlightenment, not killing. I would not be able to kill anybody or have somebody killed. I had in any case no political influence. I learned to my horror of the KZ deaths only late in the war."

These alibis draw on the psychological strategies, concepts, and categories of what might be termed a *continuum*—a *web*—of German discourse about Jews that extends from Kant and Fichte to 1945. Operating within this discourse, Wagner would not have had any problem in resorting to such alibis or in understanding them receptively. Certainly, other people had no problem in resorting to them in 1945–1946. As a matter of fact, I have been quoting verbatim two separate defenses actually offered at Nuremberg in 1946. The longer apologia was that of Alfred Rosenberg; the other was Julius Streicher's.[33] Both were laughed out of court. It's time we did the same with the current Wagner defenses and apologies.

Works Cited

Adorno, Theodor W. *In Search of Wagner*. Trans. Rodney Livingston. London: New Left Books, 1981.

Barenboim, Daniel, and Edward Said. *Parallels and Paradoxes: Explorations in Music and Society*. New York: Pantheon Books, 2002.

Burk J. N., ed. *Letters of Richard Wagner: The Burrell Collection*. Trans. J. N. Burk. London: MacMillan, 1951.0.

Cosima Wagner's Diaries. Trans. Geoffrey Skelton. Ed. Martin Gregor-Dellin and Dietrich Mack. London: Collins, 1980.

Drüner, Ulrich. *Schöpfer und Verstörer: Richard Wagner als Künstler*. Cologne: Böhlau, 2003.

Dümling, A., and P. Girth, ed., *Entartete Musik: Dokumentation und Kommentar zur Düsseldorfer Ausstellung von 1938*. 3rd ed. Düsseldorf: Dkv. der kleine verlag, 1993.

Ellis, W. A., ed. *Correspondence of Wagner and Liszt*. Vol. 1. London: H. Grevel, 1897. Rpt. New York: Vienna House, 1973.

Ellis, W. A. *Richard Wagner's Prose Works*. London: Kegan Paul, 1892–1899. Rpt. New York: E. P. Dutton, 1964.

Friedländer, Saul. "Hitler und Wagner." *Richard Wagner im dritten Reich*. Ed. Saul Friedländer and Jörn Rüsen. Munich: Beck, 2000. 165–78.

Gutman, Robert W. *Richard Wagner: The Man, His Mind, and His Music*. New York: Harcourt, Brace, Jovanovich, 1990.

Hitler, Adolf. *Reden, Schriften, Anordnungen: Februar 1925 bis Januar 1933*. Ed. Clemens Vollnhals. Munich: K. G. Saur, 1992.

Millington, Barry. "Eyes Right: Wagner and the Jews." *Opera* 46 (1995): 902–8.

———. "Nuremberg Trial: Is there Anti-Semitism in *Die Meistersinger?*" *Cambridge Opera Journal* 3 (1991): 247–60.

———. "Wagner Washes Whiter." *The Musical Times* 137 (1996): 5–8.

Nattiez, Jean-Jacques. *Wagner Androgyne: A Study in Interpretation*. Trans. Stewart Spencer. Princeton, NJ: Princeton University Press, 1993.

Rauschning, Hermann. *The Voice of Destruction*. New York: G. P. Putnam's Sons, 1940.

Rose, Paul Lawrence. *German Question/Jewish Question: Revolutionary Anti-Semitism in Germany from Kant to Wagner*. 2nd ed. Princeton, NJ: Princeton University Press, 1992.

———. "Wagner, Hitler und historische Prophetie: Der geschichtliche Kontext von 'Untergang', 'Vernichtung' und 'Ausrotttung.'" *Richard Wagner im dritten Reich*. Ed. Saul Friedländer and Jörn Rüsen. Munich: Beck, 2000. 283—308. Trans. of "'Extermination/Ausrottung': Meanings, Ambiguities and Intentions in German Anti-Semitism and the Holocaust 1800–1945."*Remembering for the Future 2000*. Ed. Y. Bauer. Vol. 1. London/New York, 2002. 726–50.

———. *Wagner: Race and Revolution*. New Haven, CT: Yale University Press, 1996.

Spencer, Stewart. "'Judaism in Music': An Unpublished Letter." *Wagner* 15 (1994): 99–104.

Spencer, Stewart, and Barry Millington, eds. *Selected Letters of Richard Wagner*. Trans. Stewart Spencer and Barry Millington. London: Dent, 1987.

Wagner, Gottfried. *Twilight of the Wagners: The Unveiling of a Family's Legacy*. Trans. Della Couling. New York: Picadot, 1999.

Wagner, Richard. "What Boots This Knowledge?" A Supplement to "Religion and Art." Trans. William Ashton Ellis. Vol. 6 of *Religion and Art: Vol. 6 of Richard Wagner's Prose Works*. The Wagner Library. Edition 1.0. Available online. Accessed on June 14, 2007.

Weiner, Marc A. *Richard Wagner and the Anti-Semitic Imagination*. 2nd ed. Lincoln: University of Nebraska Press, 1997.

Zähnker, Karl A. "The Bedevilled Beckmesser: Another Look at Anti-Semitic Stereotypes in *Die Meistersinger von Nürnberg.*" *German Studies Review* 12 (1999): 1–20.

Zelinsky, Hartmut. "Verfall, Vernichtung, Weltentrückung. Richard Wagner's antisemitische Werk-Idee als Kunstreligion und Zivilisationskritik und ihre Verbreitung bis 1933." *Richard Wagner im dritten Reich.* Ed. Saul Friedländer and Jörn Rüsen. Munich: Beck, 2000. 309–41.

NOTES

1. See Barenboim and Said, for Barenboim's remarks at a Wagner conference at Columbia University in 1995, resumed in his rather cloying compilation of conversations with Edward Said.

2. Rose, Wagner: Race and Revolution chapters 3–5.

3. May 8, 1850. See Burk, 290f. Wagner had provoked this reaction by his self-righteous and self-pitying letter to Minna of April 16, 1850: "All my views and ideas remained an abomination to you—you detested my writings, in spite of the fact that I tried to make clear to you that they were now more necessary to me than all my useless attempts to write operas" (Spencer and Millington, 194).

4. Ellis, Correspondence I, 145f, 221f.

5. Quoted in Rose, Wagner: Race and Revolution 71.

6. As repeatedly expressed in Wagner's essays from Jewishness in Music to his last series on Religion and Art, his letters, and his comments as noted in Cosima's diary.

7. This author's [that is, Paul Rose's] seems to me a better rendition of the German than the more neutral English version in Cosima Wagner's Diaries II, 662 ("Mime 'A Jewish dwarf', R. says, but excellent").

8. "What Boots This Knowledge?" (1st Supplement to Religion and Art, 1880), quoted and analyzed in Rose, Wagner 153.

9. Letter to Gustav Hoelzel, January 22, 1868, in Spencer and Millington, 723. Millington was the first to understand the significance of this and the following quotation.

10. Letter to Rudolf Freny, October 25, 1872, Ibid. 814.

11. Millington, "Nuremberg Trial" 247–60; and Weiner, chapter 2.

12. Zähnker, 1–20.

13. Cosima Wagner's Diaries April 14, 1869, July 4, 1869, April 15, 1870. See Millington, "Nuremberg Trial" 259ff.

14. Adorno, In Search of Wagner; and Gutman.

15. To list only their more recent works: Millington's further essays include "Eyes Right" 902–08; and "Wagner Washes Whiter" 5–8. Jean-Jacques Nattiez, (see Nattiez), develops the analysis of anti-Semitism in the operas that he began with his Tetralogies reflections on the Chereau Ring. Gottfried Wagner's Twilight of the Wagners, often facilely condemned as a personal quarrel with his father, is in fact a deeply revealing account of how he came to realize that the problem was not just his family's association with Hitler, but rather the anti-Semitic mentality of Wagner himself that was embedded in the operas. Zelinsky's fundamental writings are still available only in German; the most recent of these is his "Verfall, Vernichtung, Weltentrueckung." 309–341. A penetrating treatment of both the musical and political anti-Semitism has recently been published by Druener, Schoepfer.
16. Letter to Roeckel, January 25, 1854, in Spencer and Millington, 308.
17. I have tried to circumvent the usual hackneyed historicist objections to drawing a connection between Wagner and Hitler in Rose, "Wagner, Hitler" 283–308, and more generally in English form in "Extermination/Ausrottung" I, 726–50.
18. The speech may be heard in the 4-CD collection Entartete Musik: Eine Tondokumentation compiled by A. Duemling and issued by POOL Musikproduktion, Berlin, 1988. See Duemling and Girth.
19. Hitler, I, 139ff.
20. Rauschning, 228–233. Saul Friedlaender and other historians have, in recent decades, tended to discredit Rauschning as a source—at least as far as Hitler's Wagnerism is concerned—but the grounds for doing so are specious, and the ring of authenticity in Hitler's statements seem to me to resist any such efforts to refute them.
21. See Rose, "Wagner, Hitler" cited above for a fuller discussion of this problem.
22. For a contextual history of the concluding pages of Jewishness in Music, see Rose, Wagner: Race and Revolution 78–88. For the standard, though often perplexing, translation of the essay, see Ellis, Richard Wagner's Prose Works III, 79–100, to which I refer for convenience. See also Spencer, 99–104.
23. Wagner's Know Thyself (1881), quoted in Ellis, Richard Wagner's VI, 273ff. See Rose, Wagner: Race and Revolution 152ff.
24. Rose, German Question chapter 8.
25. Ibid. 125–31.
26. Ibid. 33.
27. Ibid. 37–39.
28. For these and a plethora of other references see Rose, "Extermination/Ausrottung."

29. Cosima Wagner's Diaries December 18, 1881 (see Rose, Wagner: Race and Revolution 124, 179ff, 228n, where a typographical error has led to it being dated 1880).

30. Friedlaender, 165–78.

31. Cosima Wagner's Diaries August 11, 1881 (see also the entry for August 14).

32. Cosima Wagner's Diaries October 11, 1879.

33. For the sources of these composite defenses, see Rose, "Extermination/Ausrottung" 743–44; and Rose, "Wagner, Hitler" 308.

INDEX